JOHN CAM

THE MYSTICS, ASCETICS AND SAINTS OF INDIA

A STUDY OF SADHUISM, WITH AN ACCOUNT OF THE YOGIS SANYASIS, BAIRAGIS, AND OTHER STRANGE HINDU SECTARIANS

Elibron Classics
www.elibron.com

Elibron Classics series.

ISBN 1-4021-6746-6 (paperback)
ISBN 1-4021-2126-1 (hardcover)

This Elibron Classics Replica Edition is an unabridged facsimile of the edition published in 1905 by T. Fisher Unwin, London.

THE MYSTICS, ASCETICS, AND SAINTS OF INDIA

THE MYSTICS, ASCETICS, AND SAINTS OF INDIA

A Study of Sadhuism, with an Account of the Yogis, Sanyasis, Bairagis, and other strange Hindu Sectarians

BY

JOHN CAMPBELL OMAN

FORMERLY PROFESSOR OF NATURAL SCIENCE IN THE GOVERNMENT COLLEGE, LAHORE

AUTHOR OF
"INDIAN LIFE, RELIGIOUS AND SOCIAL" "THE GREAT INDIAN EPICS"
"WHERE THREE CREEDS MEET" ETC.

WITH ILLUSTRATIONS BY
WILLIAM CAMPBELL OMAN, A.R.I.B.A.

SECOND IMPRESSION

LONDON
T. FISHER UNWIN
PATERNOSTER SQUARE
1905

Biologists teach that the body of every human being is an aggregation of various and innumerable protoplasmic cells which are ever undergoing changes, constructive and destructive. And yet we can plainly see that each man, though perceptibly changing with the passing years, persistently retains to the end a marked individuality, together with corporeal and mental characteristics peculiarly his own. So, too, is it with each race of men and the comparatively short-lived units of which it is made up. Of the latter, some are, at every moment of time, passing away and giving place to newer and slightly modified ones; but the race as a whole, though thus steadily undergoing mutation—perhaps suffering decay—with the fleeting centuries, still holds fast certain physical and psychological traits, its special heritage and possession, which have in the past differentiated it from all other races, and will continue to do so as long as it enjoys a separate existence.

Thus it happens that every distinct ethnic division of the world's population has its own peculiar ideals and aspirations, its own philosophy and religion, and also its own intellectual and moral limitations.

Obviously, then, nothing can be more helpful for the comprehension of the history, condition, and prospects of any people than the discovery and recognition of those salient and persistent habits, mental peculiarities and tendencies, which it has uninterruptedly exhibited through a long period of time.

Now the study of Indian Asceticism and Mysticism affords, I believe, not only an admirable, but the very best means of obtaining such desirable information in regard to the great Hindu race. I hope, therefore, that the present volume, which is concerned with the results of the most deep-seated and abiding ideas and sentiments of the Indian people, may, notwithstanding its necessary imperfections, meet with appreciation in some quarters at least, and help to interpret the people of India to that section of the English public which is, more or less, interested in a little-understood but most fascinating land, with whose fortunes are irrevocably linked, for good or evil, the destinies of Great Britain and the Anglo-Saxon race.

At the threshold I ought to explain that a description of the peculiarities and minor differences of the innumerable Hindu ascetic sects and sub-sects has not entered into my plan, though all the more important sectarian divisions have been noticed, and such details as seemed essential for the comprehension of the whole subject have not been omitted.

A great many curious myths, legends, and stories about ascetics of various sects have been included in this volume; but I make no apology on this account, because such myths and stories reveal, far better than any dissertations could possibly do, the true nature of Indian asceticism, as well as the intellectual level and ethical ideals of the Hindus from times immemorial.

A word as to the plan of the book may perhaps be acceptable. In the first place, I should state that throughout this volume the word *sadhu* stands as a general name for any Hindu ascetic, monk, or religious mendicant, without reference to sect or order; and *faquir* as the corresponding term for ascetics, etc., who profess Islam. The earlier chapters (I. to IV.) are designed to acquaint the reader with the leading or root ideas of Indian asceticism, or *sadhuism* as I call it, and to introduce him to the *sadhus* themselves as they appear at the present day. Old Indian dramas and tales and the accounts of European travellers are drawn upon in Chapters V. and VI., to show that *sadhuism* has been an ancient and persistent feature of Indian life. And as Hindu asceticism is not to be understood without some knowledge of the principles which underlie the philosophico-religious ideas of the Brahmans, these are succinctly explained in Chapter VII., and supplemented with a brief summary of the modifications which Hinduism has undergone in the progress of its development through more than a thousand years.

In Chapter VIII. the principal ascetic sects and their subdivisions are described, the *Yogis*, commonly called *jogis*, and the *yoga* system receiving especial attention. In Chapters IX. to XI. the reader is taken into the company of many *sadhus* I have known, and within the precincts of a few of the monasteries I have visited. Probably these last-named chapters may help to bring European readers into actual touch, as it were, with *sadhuism* as it exists to-day; and, if so, I shall not regret the time and the trouble, by no means inconsiderable, involved in collecting the particulars which I have embodied in them.

PREFACE

The concluding chapter is devoted to general observations upon the past effects, present state, and future prospects of *sadhuism*.

For all the illustrations and for many of the photographs reproduced in this volume I am indebted to my son. Mr. William Campbell Oman.

J. C. O.

LONDON.

CONTENTS

CONTENTS

CHAPTER III

SADHUS BEFORE THE PUBLIC AT FAIRS AND ELSEWHERE

CHAPTER IV

THE WONDERS THAT PRESENT-DAY SADHUS AND FAQUIRS ARE SAID TO PERFORM

CHAPTER V

SOME GLIMPSES OF SADHUS IN INDIAN FICTION

CHAPTER VI

SADHUS AS DESCRIBED BY SOME EUROPEAN VISITORS TO INDIA

CONTENTS

CHAPTER VII

A VIEW OF THE SUCCESSIVE PHASES OF MODERN HINDUISM AND OF THE ORIGIN OF THE MORE IMPORTANT HINDU SECTS, IN RELATION TO THE DEVELOPMENT OF SADHUISM IN INDIA

CHAPTER VII—*continued*

CHAPTER VII—*continued*

CHAPTER VIII

HINDU ASCETIC SECTS AND THEIR SUBDIVISIONS

CHAPTER VIII—*continued*

CONTENTS

CHAPTER VIII—*continued*

CHAPTER VIII—*continued*

CHAPTER VIII—*continued*

CHAPTER IX

PERSONAL EXPERIENCES WITH SADHUS, GOOD AND BAD

CHAPTER X

SOME SADHVIS OR FEMALE DEVOTEES

CONTENTS

LIST OF ILLUSTRATIONS

THE MYSTICS, ASCETICS, AND SAINTS OF INDIA

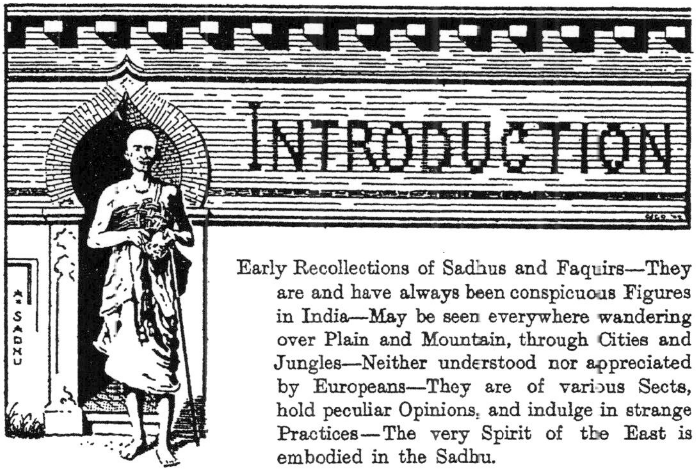

Early Recollections of Sadhus and Faquirs—They are and have always been conspicuous Figures in India—May be seen everywhere wandering over Plain and Mountain, through Cities and Jungles—Neither understood nor appreciated by Europeans—They are of various Sects, hold peculiar Opinions, and indulge in strange Practices—The very Spirit of the East is embodied in the Sadhu.

Lingering in the far background of my memory is a vivid picture of certain *sadhus*, and of a winter evening long years ago on the banks of the sacred Ganges—a picture which the lapse of over half a century has not been able to dim, much less to obliterate.

Clear though the picture is, I almost fail at this distance of time to fully identify myself with it, and yet I certainly took part in the little episode which is enshrined in my recollections. With the mind's eye I see two children, a girl and a boy, rambling hand in hand at some distance from their dear old home hard by the sunny hills of Colgong, and as they wander back together through the fields in the quickly deepening twilight a feeling of trepidation seems to take possession of them, for, infants though they are, they know full well that murderous *thugs* [1]—a fearsome name in those days—infested the countryside. Their eyes strain with anxiety towards the dim outlines of a gigantic banian tree which serves them as a homeward landmark; but it seems very far away, and even receding, as a thin veil of white smoke steals gradually over the landscape in the rapidly failing twilight. Suddenly two gaunt *sadhus* appear not ten yards off before the astonished children. So unexpected is their presence, so unaccountable the apparition, that it was as if the unwelcome intruders had sprung up out of the ground beneath their own feet. Clothed in salmon-coloured robes are these meagre, sharp-featured *sadhus,* with clean-shaven heads and faces. They advance, and with soft words and insinuating smiles endeavour to entice the startled children to approach them, offering, with various alluring promises, to show them the wonderful contents of the ugly wallets which hang from their shoulders. Good Lord! how the little boy and girl did race towards the river when all at once there flashed upon their minds the horrible suspicion that the men before them might possibly be villainous *thugs* disguised as *sadhus*! How rejoiced were the children to find themselves at last safe amongst the wondering and sympathetic boatmen on the river bank, after a breathless run across country, and after what seemed a hot pursuit, though probably it was so only in their own excited imaginations!

Belonging to the same early period of my life I recollect well the highly picturesque rocks of Colgong, standing like bold intruders in the noble river, with the *faquir's* lone hermitage perched amidst their gigantic boulders. Many tales of wonder were told of the recluse who dwelt amongst those crags; and when every year, in due season, the rocks and the hermitage were completely cut off from the river bank by the mighty flood, roaring, fretting, and

[1] The *thugs* are a secret sect, votaries of the goddess Kali, banded together for the purpose of robbery by means of cold-blooded assassinations perpetrated with religious rites and under religious sanctions.

swirling around the unwelcome barrier, the one inhabitant of those desolate islands, the isolated *faquir*, the solitary wonder-worker, would become to us little folks an interesting subject of solicitude and childish speculation.

Out of that old India, so different, so remote in every way from the playground of the present-day winter tourist, I recall to mind a long journey by palanquin *dák*, a halt under some shady trees in a straggling thatched village, an apparently dying infant in my mother's arms, and a white-bearded *faquir* with many strings of beads about his neck, offering some medicine, contained in a mussel-shell, which, with Allah's blessing, would save the child's life. I recall to mind also how some hours later the venerable old man, respectfully but firmly, declined a handful of rupees, and, indeed, any reward whatever, for the help which Allah had graciously enabled him to afford the distressed mother and her sick infant.

Ever since those now far-off days the Indian ascetics have been to me objects of special curiosity and interest, not diminished in maturer years by more extensive knowledge of them and their strange beliefs, practices, and pretensions.

Sadhus are and have always been too conspicuous figures in India to escape the notice of any intelligent European traveller in that country—from Megasthenes to Mark Twain and Pierre Loti—and their accentuated outward peculiarities have proved so attractive to the ubiquitous modern camera-man that his photographs and snapshots reproduced in popular pictorial magazines have made them, at least in their more uncouth forms, familiar to the Western world.

Wherever at the present time the tourist in India may go, he meets *sadhus* and *faquirs* in the guise of one or other of the many existing sects, orders, or fraternities. He comes across them in the busy mart, in the quiet grove by the river, in the gay and crowded fair, on the lonely hill track, and in the dense forests, where many perish miserably, devoured by wild beasts. Indefatigable rovers, they usually do not linger long in any one place, but are ever on the move, like their gipsy kindred in the West.

From about November, when the autumn harvest is gathered and the seed for the spring crop committed to the soil, till March, when the first-fruits of the year are ready for the sickle, the Hindus—men, women, and children—spend much of their time in joyous pilgrimages to their innumerable sacred places, sometimes hundreds of miles away from home. Hardly, indeed, could it be otherwise, for a cloudless sky, a crisp exhilarating atmosphere, and bright genial sunshine call them forth with a summons that is irresistible. During this period every year there is a lively and healthy circulation throughout the land of all ranks and classes, and in these currents of life a large proportion of the *sadhus* fully participate, often moving about from place to place in considerable parties under leaders and teachers of reputation. And far beyond the boundaries of their own vast country do the Hindu ascetics wander, as indeed they have done since remote antiquity, carrying to distant lands their subtle speculations about the origin, nature, and destiny of man and the universe to which he belongs.

As a rule *sadhus* are cautiously reticent, but they may occasionally be induced to tell of long wanderings and strange experiences. I have met some of them in Kashmir on their way from Puri by the Bay of Bengal to the lone ice-caves of Amarnath, and it need not be doubted that men who range the whole Indian Peninsula, as these do, and wander over the eternal snows of Himalaya, find food for lofty thought and deep emotion in the mystery and grandeur of the scenes which often meet their gaze. Indian poets early appreciated the æsthetic charms of nature and the soothing calm of solitude; and we may be sure that even the unsocial *sadhu* in his journeyings amongst the giant mountains looks with wondering admiration upon the vagueness and inscrutability of their wayward moods, their vast silent snowfields, their whispering rills, and furious torrents. It is impossible for any man not to experience an indefinable feeling of elation, of buoyancy, as he breathes the pure, light, pine-scented air of the higher mountain ranges, and watches the rising sun paint with rosy flush the icy pinnacles around him; nor can he avoid a weird sense of complete isolation and utter helplessness when the cloud-wreaths, surging up from the valleys, blur and blot out the fair world from view and wrap surrounding nature in a pall impenetrable to human vision. But not only do the far-ranging *sadhus* commune with Nature in all her various humours and aspects, their peregrinations bring them also into touch, in crowded cities, with their fellow-men, and, by winning the confidence of people of all ranks, they become a potent agency for the circulation of news, true or false, and the dissemination of ideas, religious, political, or other, which might be fermenting in the world with which they come in contact.

Yet though the *sadhus* as they may be seen have come to be familiar to European eyes, they are rarely understood by the foreigner, be he temporary visitor or permanent resident. Of the beliefs and subtle philosophical ideas of these men the stranger, as a rule, knows nothing, while their ill-clad forms, and too often grotesque appearance, only excite his aversion and unreasoning contempt.

How much, and how deeply, the Indian people have suffered, for habilitory reasons, in the estimation of Europeans it would be hard to say; but of this I have no doubt, that the style of their national dress, and particularly the extreme scantiness of their garments, which in most cases hardly pretend to cover the persons of the wearers, reduce the intellectual and civilised Indians to the level of *naked savages* in the eyes of the majority of the people of the West. And the Indian *sadhus*, frequently all but nude, and rubbed over with ashes, undoubtedly incur the amused disdain of Europeans, who commonly look upon these ascetics as droll fellows or sorry simpletons.

The *sadhu*, such as he is, is no recent importation, no modern excrescence, but has been flourishing in India, a veritable indigenous growth, from a time which dates many centuries before the advent of Christ, or even the preaching by Buddha of the eightfold path leading to enlightenment and deliverance. Alexander of Macedon, in his wonderful march across the plains of the Punjab in the fourth century B.C., saw, and took an interest in, the Indian *sadhu*; but *sadhuism* in his day was already hoary with antiquity.

Sadhus as we find them are of various sects, hold peculiar opinions, indulge in strange practices, and subject themselves in many cases to cruel hardships and fantastic disciplines. They come from all ranks of life and from all the hereditary castes into which Hindu society is divided. Amongst them we find all shades of religious opinion and philosophical speculation, and dietary habits ranging from the most fastidious vegetarianism to revolting cannibalism in the case of the egregious *aghoris* described later on.

Though exceedingly numerous, the Indian *sadhus* command the respect and even the superstitious veneration of the vast multitude of their countrymen, who believe that they are often, if not always, possessed of almost unlimited supernatural power for good or evil.

The common proverb, *Gervi Kapron se jogi nahīn hota*, attests the fact that the Indians, quite as much as Europeans, are well aware that the habit does not make the monk, and stories to the discredit of the religious ascetics are current all over India; but they have not shaken the faith of the people in the *sadhus*, at any rate not more than the tales about the gaily immoral behaviour of the mediæval monks have injuriously affected the position of the Romish clergy.

In the ancient legislation of India the *sadhu* bulks largely, and he has a unique place in the romantic tales of more recent date. The very spirit of the East is embodied in the *sadhu*, and it is perhaps not too much to assert that he is so important a feature in the life and civilisation of India that a study of his characteristics and his relations to the general population will not only afford considerable light for the comprehension of the Indian people as they are, and have been since the earliest historic times, but will also, perhaps, be found to have attractions of an even wider and more general nature.

CHAPTER I

ASCETICISM: ITS ORIGIN AND DEVELOPMENT

Asceticism a common Feature in all Religions—Ideas underlying Asceticism—Sinfulness—The Doctrine that Matter is inherently bad—The Belief that the Human Body is the great Hindrance to the Attainment by the Soul of its proper Destiny—Ascetic Practices, and the Conditions, geographical, political, and social, which are most favourable to their Adoption by a large Proportion of any Community—The Existence of such Conditions in India from the earliest up to recent Times.

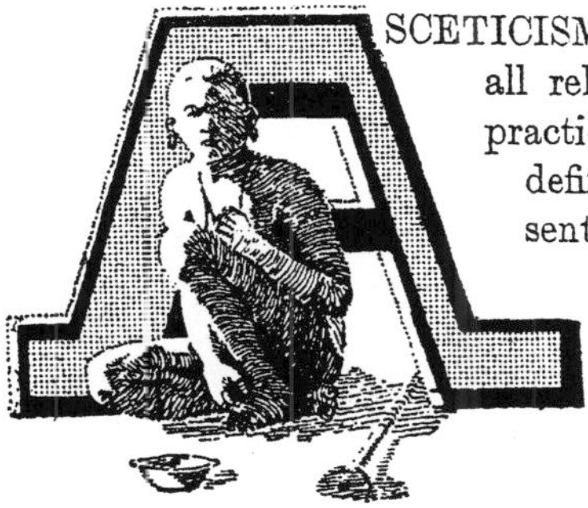

ASCETICISM is a common feature in all religious systems, and is the practical expression of certain definite phases of religious sentiment and philosophical speculation. Probably the earliest promptings towards ascetic practices came from a desire of self-humiliation before the Unseen Powers, in order to propitiate them, and to make atonement for neglected duties,[1] and, consequently, in times of great national troubles, when the protecting gods seem to have turned away in wrath, ascetic practices become more common, widespread, and intense, till sometimes whole communities seem to be smitten by a mania for self-abasement, self-imposed hardships, and severe austerities.[2]

[1] The same feeling is manifest in "the Christian idea of self-sacrifice and the Christian doctrine that it is through such sacrifice that God reveals Himself in man."—Caird's *Evolution of Religion*, vol. ii. p. 258.

[2] The causes which favoured the development of asceticism amongst the Christians of the primitive Church are well stated in Pressensé's *Histoire des Trois Premiers Siècles*, Quatrième Série, pp. 523–39.

Similar results are also sometimes produced when intense religious excitement has awakened thrilling expectations, as in the early Church, when entire congregations, believing the end of all earthly things to be imminent, gave up their possessions and retired to the desert to await the second Advent of the Lord; and as, indeed, that peculiar sect, the Russian Doukhobors, have done in the broad daylight of our own time, to the amusement of an unbelieving generation.

An ardent desire on the part of religious enthusiasts to imitate the life of the founder of their own religion or sect, *such founder being almost invariably an ascetic and a contemner of the things of this world,* has also been a potent influence in originating and perpetuating schemes of life, or particular practices which savour of self-denial more or less rigid.

It would appear that all religions hold that in the thoughts, desires, and actions of every individual there are present elements which, unless conquered, modified, or neutralised in some way or other, disqualify him from attaining that unending *rest* or that most desirable beatitude in a future state of existence which the world-prophets have so freely promised mankind. The disqualifying elements above referred to as hindering the religious in the realisation of their aspirations, although differing remarkably in the various cults, may for convenience be included in the one term *sinfulness.*

Now, what is the cause of this sinfulness so disastrous to the highest interests of humanity? That is a question which has perplexed the ages; but of all the doctrines which men have propounded in their endeavours to solve this permanent enigma of existence, probably none has had more subtle and potent influence than that which holds that spirit is eternally pure and matter inherently bad.

These ideas, of immemorial antiquity and far-reaching influence in the East, found their way to Europe in the early centuries of our era in connection with Manichæism and Gnosticism, and though condemned and suppressed by the Papacy, aided by the strong arm of the secular power, did not fail to make a deep impression on Western thought.

If the doctrine in question be accepted, it is plain that man's corporeal frame comes directly under condemnation, and it also follows that spirit being pure, the flesh and its lusts are responsible for the sins which man commits. Hence, for the preservation of the soul and the furtherance of its aspirations, it is necessary that the body, with its senses, appetites, and desires, should be kept under restraint, should be mortified and suppressed; the logical outcome of this train of reasoning being the ascetic practices so highly honoured in all the great religious systems.[1]

By the Hindu speculative theologians, asceticism with a view to the repression of the animal passions is regarded, in accordance with their dualistic theories, as a means to the purification of the mind, such purgation being, as they say, an essential condition for the attainment of a complete knowledge of Brahman, with its attendant freedom from *samsara*, that is, embodied existence,[2] which freedom, we shall find, is the great aim and object of Hindu religious life. And the *purification of the body by ascetic practices* is also held by Hindu theologians as a necessary condition for even that temporary communion, in this life, of the human soul with the Divine Spirit, which is the object of the ecstatic hope of many a religious man in India.

In the East generally, and in India particularly, man's corporeal frame has been for ages considered the great hindrance to the attainment by spirit of its proper destiny, whether that destiny be, as the Buddhists teach, a release from the evils of successive rebirths with ultimate *nirvana*, or, as the Hindus hold, direct union with and absorption into the Universal Spirit. And whatever other views may have been held, the human body has, under religious zeal, been sacrificed in almost all countries to the supposed advantage of the soul; and this suppression of natural desires, often combined with positive ill-treatment of the body, for

[1] True, the Christian Church prescribed penances on other grounds also, holding that even for sin duly repented of a temporal penalty was still due, and, in order to afford a means for the satisfaction of this obligation, the penitential discipline of the Church made provision in the form of fastings, flagellations, pilgrimages, and fines.

[2] The Upanishads and Sri Sankara's Commentary, translated by S. Sitarama Sastri, B.A., vol. i. especially p. 85.

spiritual ends, is what we now usually call asceticism,[1] though, curiously enough, amongst the Greeks it meant that abstinence from sensual indulgences which was necessary for the *preservation of the body* in a fit state for athletics.

Of those who undergo mortifications, the majority, whatever their creed may be, probably confine their austerities to an occasional fast or a periodical abstinence from particular kinds of food; but everywhere a minority can be found of sensitive natures, who, more deeply affected by world-weariness, and spurred on by the uncontrollable excitement of intense religious enthusiasm, willingly exhaust ingenuity in afflicting themselves with cruel pains and penalties. Early Christian history provides abundant examples of this latter type; but they are not peculiar to Christendom, as we shall presently see. Such heroic contempt of pain and pleasure as these extreme ascetics display commands the wondering attention and respectful homage of the multitude. The voluntary sufferers become objects of veneration; fame makes itself busy with their doings; wonders are attributed to them, and, by a curious irony, spiritual pride and vanity play no unimportant part in encouraging religious asceticism. The reason is obvious. The reputation for sanctity which accompanies self-repression and detachment from the world brings with it not only popular admiration, but often so much substantial power also, that many ambitious men and seekers after publicity are attracted into the ranks of the ascetics in order to enjoy these congenial and by no means inconsiderable advantages.

It happens not infrequently that the spectacle is presented of the contemporaneous existence of unbounded luxury and the most austere asceticism; one being the result of the success of the few, the other of the failure of the many. In such times the ascetic, the renunciant,

[1] Strange as it may seem, suffering in itself comes, in the case of some highly emotional natures, to be regarded as desirable. St. Theresa, for example, says, "Suffering alone can make life tolerable to me. My greatest desire is to suffer. Often and often I cry out to God from the depths of my soul, 'Either to suffer or to die is all I ask of Thee.'"—Joly's *Psychology of the Saints*, p. 168.

becomes the popular ideal of a great man, the guide and leader of the people, the friend of the poor, and the scornful contemner of the exalted. In such times the spirit of asceticism may penetrate into the very highest grades of society, where it could least be expected to find admission, though the reasons for this would not be difficult of comprehension in most cases, could one but get a glimpse behind the curtains of private life. For it is not only discomfiture in the open world-strife that brings men to despondency; domestic disappointments and the ordinary disillusionments of life may drive even the rich and highly placed to seek peace in the retirement of the cloister or in philosophical resignation coupled with contemptuous indifference to worldly advantages.[1]

Even when dominated by ascetic zeal and the spirit of self-sacrifice, the majority of men are gregarious in their instincts. So it happens that many brethren in misfortune, renouncing the world and what they call its hollow sinful pleasures, gather together, for mutual improvement and encouragement, in religious communities, which later on develop into conventual establishments or monasteries governed by fixed rules. Hither gravitate the disappointed, the world-weary. Here in troubled times many seek peace and protection, and here too a few, attracted by the tranquillity of the cenobitic life, come from a sheer love of God and a desire for silent and constant communion with Him.

Like other ideas and other sentiments which have for a time obtained general currency or acceptance, those connected with practical asceticism have a tendency to languish when the causes which stimulated them into special activity have died out. But though the spirit of asceticism may seem at certain flourishing periods of history to be extinct, it can never be quite so while the tedium of existence presses upon weary souls, and while sorrow, want, and

[1] An interesting Indian instance of this is the poet and Prime Minister Mānaka-Vasagur, who in the eighth century A.D. gave up his high position to devote himself in seclusion and penury to the worship of Siva, as the supreme ruler of the universe. His poems preserved in Southern India are said to breathe a true emotional piety.—*Journal, Royal Asiatic Society,* April 1901, pp. 346–48.

misery exist in this world. It slumbers, perhaps, but is ready to quicken whenever circumstances happen which make the burden of life for the majority too heavy for patient endurance. In prosperous times the attractions of the far-off heavens lose something of their force in the presence of the nearer and more tangible allurements of the day, but, as soon as the fierce struggle for existence becomes calamitous to the major portion of any community, the discomfiture of the many once more revives from its still warm embers the dormant spirit of asceticism; and then, new religions, or at least new religious leaders, arise amongst the wretched and downtrodden, to teach again the expediency and beauty of the renunciation of all worldly desires, and to point the way, perhaps a new way, to a delectable existence beyond the grave. Even the rushing stream of modern European life has its quiet backwaters into which the world-weary drift silently and unobserved, resigning themselves, in dismal monasteries and religious establishments, to such austerities as they believe will enhance the heavenly reward to which they look forward with childlike confidence or timid hope.

Nothing is more certain than that, when individuals or communities are suffering from widespread calamities and great national troubles of whatever nature, their thoughts turn imploringly towards their gods and longingly towards heaven, as surely as the magnetic needle seeks the Pole. For the prosperous this earth has its attractions and its rewards, but for the unfortunate and downtrodden there is only the promised hereafter. Hence it is obvious that religion flourishes best where the conditions of life have been most unfavourable for the majority. Now, India has for decades of centuries suffered in no slight degree from certain depressing circumstances most conducive to the production of individual and national despondency. Religion of the gloomy type has consequently always flourished there, and with it asceticism also, exaggerated and intensified by the fact that India is the head-centre of the doctrine of the eternal antagonism between spirit and matter.

The most cursory consideration of facts will bear

out the above statement. Too often, for example, have the invasion and conquest of the wide open plains of Northern India proved a comparatively easy operation, harmful to the dwellers there and baneful even to the conquerors; for, enervated by an indolent life in those warm productive valleys, each successful race of invaders has had to give way before new and more energetic conquerors, destined in their turn to a similar fate. Again, vast stretches of level country like those which lie beneath the mighty Himalayan mountain range are undoubtedly suited for, are indeed the natural homes of, despotisms, under which individualism and many of the finer qualities of men and races get gradually smothered. And despotic governments, whether native or foreign, have for many centuries ruled over these lands. From very early times, too, a rigid system of hereditary castes was adopted in India, by which the spheres and occupations of all classes of the community were strictly defined and enforced, thereby limiting the ambitions and cramping the energies of the entire Hindu people.

Geographical and climatic conditions have also favoured the occurrence, at longer or shorter intervals, of appalling pestilences and famines of stupendous proportions, while, as the Sanskrit epics clearly show, for ages dense forests and malarial swamps covered a considerable portion of the land. Under such circumstances it necessarily came to pass that in the warmth of the steamy plains of India successive generations of men and women were stimulated into early maturity and doomed to early decay, afflicted perpetually with a morbid fatigue both physical and mental.

It is true we cannot recall *details* of the prolonged night of trouble through which the Indian people have passed, for they have written no history of themselves, left behind them no chronicles. But this fact itself is the most impressive, convincing, and pathetic proof of their state of depression and hopelessness through long ages, since flourishing nations endued with energy, buoyed up with hope, and enjoying reasonable liberty, never fail to hand down to admiring posterity the record of their doings ; while, on the other hand, in gloomy periods of stagnation and oppression, not only is the healthy stimulus to the production of historical writings absent, but there is also ever present a powerful deterrent in the dread of offending the oppressors which paralyses the hand of the would-be historian.

Besides the already noted causes predisposing the Indians to habits of despondency and religious quietism, there are others which have also contributed towards the same end. One of these is the strictly vegetarian diet of a majority of the people, which diet, even if always sufficiently nutritious, would certainly have, in the course of successive generations, a cumulative tendency to induce a patient, inaggressive, and probably despondent habit of mind, with physical indolence and apathy in its train. Then, again, the Indian people have always had amongst them in profusion the soporific poppy and the hemp plant, whose narcotic products were discovered early, and their drowsy fascinations extensively appreciated.[1]

Finally, the study of the psychology of the Indian people reveals to us that, combined with intellectual qualities of the highest order, their most striking characteristics are imaginativeness, emotionalism, mysticism, credulity, religious fervour and impressionability,[2] all in a very exaggerated degree.

[1] There is a popular belief that the habit of *smoking* originated with the use of tobacco after the discovery of America at the end of the fifteenth century ; but, whatever may be the fact as regards tobacco, there is ample evidence to show that the barks and leaves of certain plants, also sawdust and mushrooms of sorts, as well as opium and hemp, have since remote antiquity been smoked in the East and Africa, and in Europe too. Sometimes, as in the case of the Scythians described by Herodotus, the smoke was used simply as a fumigant in a closed tent for producing exhilarating effects, but more commonly the *pipe*, with a bowl as we know it, was used, and, as might have been expected, archæologists have not failed to obtain an ample supply of these articles from ancient tumuli and deposits which date back many centuries.—*Revue Encyclopédique*, 3rd April 1897.

[2] Dr. James Esdaile, so well known in India some fifty or sixty years ago as a most successful surgical operator under mesmeric influence, came to the conclusion, after certain experiments in Scotland, that only " the depressing influence of disease will be found to reduce Europeans to the impressible condition of the nervous system so common among the Eastern nations."—*Dictionary of National Biography.*

To sum up, then, it would appear that, under the combined influence of the physical, political, and social conditions referred to, aided powerfully by the intellectual and moral peculiarities of the people, a dull stagnation has been for ages the unenviable lot of the *masses* of the Indian people—a state very conducive to mental depression and gloomy religious speculations, leading naturally to abnegation and ascetic living. Hence it came to pass that the ancient lawgiver was able, with a reasonable hope of success, to model the ordinary life of the Hindu upon a wide basis of poverty, renunciation, and retirement from the world. As prescribed in the sacred *Shastras* of the Hindus, the ideal life for the three superior castes begins with mendicancy and ends with asceticism, according to the following scheme, which divides the ordinary span of a man's existence into four well-marked periods.

1. *Early youth*, which should be passed as a *Brahmachari* or religious student living on alms.

2. *Manhood*, during which period the "twice-born" man should, as a *Grihasta*, devote himself to household duties and the rearing of a family.

3. *Middle age*, which should be spent as a *Banaprastha* or forest recluse, with or without one's wife. In regard to food, the hermit should restrict himself to the spontaneous products of the earth obtained by himself, and should abstain, under all circumstances, from partaking of anything grown in towns or the produce of any man's *labour*.

4. *The closing period of life*, during which final stage the good Hindu should become a *Sanyasi*, abandoning all sensual desires and *living by mendicancy on the charity of others*.

This is not the place to discuss what baneful effects such a scheme for the conduct of individual life, if acted upon generally, would inevitably produce upon national character and national resources, and such considerations would, in all probability, have been of quite insignificant importance in the eyes of the Hindu lawgiver. Nor need we pause to estimate the extent to which this ideal scheme of life has brought about the accepted low standard of comfort and the extreme simplicity of living in India. But it is necessary to draw attention to the encouragement and sanction which the divinely appointed Hindu ideal of life gives to *mendicancy* as well as retirement from the world, because the inevitable result of this has been that no Hindu feels *ashamed* to beg or to abandon the duties of citizenship at an age when he might be a productive worker for the general good.[1]

It has been argued that the ideal scheme of life with its fourfold division was instituted really in opposition to *sadhuism*, as it postpones the adoption of the ascetic life to a time when a man would, in ordinary course, be too feeble to endure all its hardships. But, while it is doubtful whether there is any truth whatever in this contention, no unprejudiced person will deny that the scheme itself countenances and enjoins a system of asceticism of unparalleled scope, for it embraces every superior individual within the pale of Hinduism.

It may be added that the strong restraint which natural solicitude for the comfortable maintenance of one's family would ordinarily exercise upon the decision of a parent, husband, son, or brother disposed to abandon his home, is considerably weakened amongst Hindus by the co-operative system which prevails amongst them, under which, in ordinary circumstances, the burden of supporting the family—this term being understood in a wide sense—would fall upon and be shared alike by all the male members thereof. Indeed, this joint system, although not without its advantages, does undoubtedly encourage unprofitable idleness, leading in many cases to the adoption of a life of respectable vagrancy under the convenient mask of religion.

Without any pretence of an exhaustive analysis of the various and complex motives which underlie religious asceticism, I may before concluding this chapter draw attention to what appear to me to be the more general reasons which prompt men to ascetic practices: (1) A desire, which is intensified by all personal or national

[1] "The Power and Beauty of Beggary" is the subject of an article by an Indian journalist in *East and West* for December 1901 (Bombay).

troubles, to propitiate the Unseen Powers. (2) A longing on the part of the intensely religious to follow in the footsteps of their *master*, almost invariably an ascetic. (3) A wish to work out one's own *future* salvation, or emancipation, by conquering the evil inherent in human nature, *i.e.* the flesh. (4) A yearning to prepare oneself by purification of mind and body for entering into *present* communion with the Divine Being. (5) Despair arising from disillusionment and from defeat in the battle of life. And lastly, mere vanity, stimulated by the admiration which the multitude bestow upon the ascetic.

I have, I hope, made it sufficiently clear that the political and other causes which induce the frame of mind wherein the above-stated reasons are most operative, have for ages existed in India in a more than ordinary degree.

What other powerful, and peculiarly Indian, motives stimulate the ascetic practices of the *sadhus* will be mentioned in the next chapter.

CHAPTER II

SOME PECULIAR AND DISTINCTIVE CHARACTERISTICS OF HINDU ASCETICISM

Hindu Idea of the unbounded Power over Nature attainable through Ascetic Practices—The Rationale of this Notion—Examples of Power acquired by Asceticism cited from the Mahabharata, the Ramayana, the Siva Purana, and the Vishnu Purana—The Supreme Being Himself practises Austerities—Rivalry of Sects gives rise to Legends of Conflicts, based on successful Ascetic Practices, between rival Leaders—Titanic Conflict between Vasishta and Visvamitra, also between Nanak and the Siddhas—Hindu Asceticism has usually no relation to Ethics.

I ENDEAVOURED to show in the last chapter that asceticism was fostered in India by causes which have given birth to similar developments elsewhere, and that owing to special circumstances, referred to in some detail, it has assumed a chronic form in the country to the south of the Himalayas. But there are striking peculiarities about Hindu asceticism which differentiate it from that associated with Buddhism, Christianity, or Islam; and to these peculiarities, and the motives underlying them, I now invite attention.

All the most esteemed sages of India are believed to have practised austerities. The great poets, too, even the more modern ones, such as Tulasi Das, author of the Hindi Ramayana, and Jayadeva, author of the Gītā-Govinda, were religious devotees and thaumaturgists of the highest order.[1] Martial heroes, and demigods

[1] *Sketch of the Religious Sects of the Hindus*, by Professor H. H. Wilson, pp. 41–43.

like Arjuna and Rama, are credited with ascetic practices; but it is decidedly startling to learn that the gods themselves have undergone self-inflicted tortures for the attainment of the objects of their desires. Referring to this point, the late Professor Sir Monier Williams wrote as follows:[1] "According to Hindu theory, the performance of penances was like making deposits in the bank of heaven. By degrees an enormous credit was accumulated which enabled the depositor to draw to the amount of his savings, without fear of his drafts being refused payment. The power gained in this way by weak mortals was so enormous, that gods as well as men were equally at the mercy of these all but omnipotent ascetics, and it is remarkable that even the gods are described as engaging in penances and austerities, in order, it may be presumed, not to be outdone by human beings. Siva was so engaged when the god of love shot an arrow at him!"[2]

The genesis of these notions, so extravagant and far-fetched in appearance, is, I think, susceptible of explanation. From the accepted doctrine that ascetic practices, by conquering the evil tendencies of *matter*—that is, the flesh,—purify the imprisoned *spirit*, and render it fit for re-union with the Absolute Being, the Hindu thinker might reasonably argue that as the austerities were increased and intensified the probability of the wished-for reunion of the ascetic's soul with the Absolute Being would become greater and greater, and that by virtue of such approaching reunion the power of the soul over matter and natural phenomena generally would also grow more and more effective. This being conceded, the next step would be to gauge a man's unknown supernatural powers by his self-inflicted tortures; and conversely, if one desired superhuman

[1] *Indian Epic Poetry*, note to p. 4.

[2] To the Indian notion of merits hoarded up for future use, a curious resemblance may be traced in the idea that "the Church possessed a 'treasure' in the merits of Christ and of the saints and martyrs, from which 'treasure' could be drawn upon, from time to time, satisfaction for the penalties of sin;" an idea which underlay the Romish practice of granting indulgences. See Canon Knox Little's *St. Francis of Assisi*, chap. viii. Going a step further, "the friars took upon themselves to distribute the surplus merit of their order."—*Social England*, by Traill and Mann, vol. ii. p. 372.

power for the accomplishment of any definite object, he would resort to austerities to gain his end. What a plentiful crop of extravagant myths and legends could, and did, spring out of such ideas, is clearly shown in Hindu literature, which may now be drawn upon for a few typical examples requisite for the exposition of the subject.

In the Mahabharata it is related of two brothers, *daityas* of the race of the great Asura, that they undertook a course of severe austerities with the momentous object "of subjugating the three worlds." They clothed themselves in the bark of trees, wore matted hair, besmeared themselves with dirt from head to foot, and in solitude, upon the lone mountains, endured the greatest privations of hunger and thirst. They stood for years on their toes, with their arms uplifted and their eyelids wide open. Not content with these sore penances, they, in their zeal, cut off pieces of their own flesh and threw them into the fire. The Vindhya mountains, on which these determined ascetics had placed themselves, became heated by the fervour of their austerities, and the gods beholding their doings, and alarmed for the consequences that might ensue, did everything in their power to divert them from the strict observance of their vows. The gods "tempted the brothers by means of every precious possession and the most beautiful girls,"[1] but without success. Then the celestials tried "their powers of illusion," making it seem to the ascetics that "their sisters, mothers, wives, and other relatives, with dishevelled hair and ornaments and robes, were running towards them in terror, pursued and struck down by a Rakshasa with a lance in hand. And it seemed that the women implored the help of the brothers, crying, 'O, save us!'"[2]

Even this harrowing scene of domestic affliction failed to shake the constancy of the ascetics to their vows, and

[1] Mahabharata—Adi Parva, section ccxi. Babu Protap Chandra Roy's translation.

[2] This temptation of the earnest ascetic, especially when engaged in severe austerities, is not confined to Hinduism, instances being easily found in the history of all the religions of Asiatic origin, not excluding Christianity, and is an unmistakable indication of the general and widespread belief in the potency of self-mortifications.

Brahma was at last obliged to grant them very extensive powers and privileges, including complete immunity from danger except at each other's hands. When these successful ascetics returned home they arrayed themselves in costly robes, wore precious ornaments, "caused the moon to rise over their city every night," and from year's end to year's end indulged in continual feasting and every kind of amusement. Evidently, no thought of sin or expiation nor any regard for virtue entered into the consideration of the objects kept in view by these resolute *daitya* brothers. The above story shows clearly the existence of an underlying idea that the practisers of austerities, whoever they might be, appropriate energy, as it were, from some universal store, and that they are thus strengthened at the expense of the rest. Consequently, when their voluntary penances exceed certain limits they become a terror to all other beings. Hence we learn, without surprise, that, when one of these dangerous ascetics eventually met his death, all nature was exceedingly relieved and rejoiced accordingly.

Another story in the same sacred epic tells of a king who underwent ascetic penances to obtain a child.[1] It is also recorded of a certain monarch that he did the same to secure the assistance of the god Rudra in the performance of a great sacrifice.[2]

One *rishi*, the *muni* Aurva of the Brighu race, influenced by a fierce craving for vengeance on account of some wrongs suffered by his ancestors, subjected himself to the direst penances for "the destruction of every creature in the world," and was only persuaded to desist from his terrible purpose by the intercession of the *Pitris* or souls of his forefathers.[3]

We have also the case of Princess Amvā of Benares, who practised the most terrible austerities for many years for the destruction of Bhishma, and was gratified by the god Mahādeva, who promised that in her next life she should be "a fierce warrior who would destroy the hated Bhishma. Upon this, that faultless maiden of the

[1] Mahabharata—Adi Parva, section ccxvii.
[2] *Ibid.* section ccxxv. [3] *Ibid.* section clxxxi.

fairest complexion, the eldest daughter of the King of Kaçi, procured wood from that forest in the very sight of those great *rishis*, made a large funeral pyre on the banks of the Yamuna, and having set fire to it, herself entered that blazing fire with a heart burning with wrath, uttering the words, 'I do so for Bhishma's destruction!'"[1] The princess was reborn in due course, and, needless to say, was the instrument of Bhishma's death.

The Ramayana affords us many instances of exceptional powers and privileges acquired by ascetic practices. For example, the ten-headed Rakshasa, Ravana, had, by long and painful austerities, obtained from Brahma the boon that neither god nor demon should be able to deprive him of his life. Protected by this decree of the Creator, the ten-headed Rakshasa became a terror to the world, but he had, in his pride, omitted to ask for protection against *men*. Taking advantage of this oversight, the god Vishnu became incarnate as Rama, and, after wonderful adventures, eventually destroyed the troublesome demon-king.

A somewhat similar story is told in the same epic about the Rakshasa Viradha, who had by his asceticisms obtained the privilege of being proof against every kind of weapon. However, he met his fate at the hands of Rama, who overcame him, *not with weapons*, but with his *fists*, and flung him into a deep pit.

In the Siva Purana there is a story of a *daitya* (demon) named Tarika, who, by voluntarily undergoing eleven distinct forms or methods of self-mortification, each extending over a period of one hundred years, so alarmed Indra and the lesser gods that they went to Brahma to beseech him to frustrate the ambitious designs of this terrible ascetic. The Supreme Being had to admit that he could not resist such austerities, and was constrained to reward them; but he told his petitioners that, after granting the boon for which Tarika had inflicted so much suffering upon himself, he (Brahma) would devise a plan of ultimately neutralising the demon's long labours. What Tarika sought was, "that he should be unrivalled in strength, and that no hand should slay him, but that of a son of Mahādeva

[1] Babu Protap Chandra Roy's translation.

(the god Siva)." This boon having been conceded, as indeed it had to be, the demon, in his pride of power, tyrannised over the lesser gods, and kept the entire universe in terror, himself feeling perfectly safe, as he reckoned confidently that the austere Mahādeva would never be the father of a son. In this, however, he miscalculated, and in the fulness of time his destruction was accomplished.[1]

The above three legends of Ravana, Viradha, and Tarika, besides being good examples of privileges wrung by ascetic practices from the reluctant gods, illustrate the appreciation which the Eastern has always felt for the crafty overreaching of a dangerous foe.

It is related in the Vishnu Purana[2] that a certain King Uttánapáda had two wives, each of whom bore him a son. One day the king, seated on his throne, was fondling on his knee the son of his favourite wife, while his other son, Dhruva, a child of only five years of age, who happened to be present, attempted, quite naturally, to share the same privilege. The favourite queen, Suruchi, who was at hand, lectured the little one rather haughtily on his unbecoming presumptuousness, telling him that the throne was a fit seat for *her* son, but certainly not for him. Abashed and indignant, little Dhruva withdrew to his own mother's apartments, and there unburdened his bursting heart of its feelings of anger and mortification. His distressed mother tried to console the sulky child, and recommended, with true Indian feeling, the exercise of patience and the cultivation of a spirit of contentment; but Dhruva was too deeply hurt to accept his mother's well-meant advice, and, infant though he was, said, "Mother, the words that you have addressed to me for my consolation find no place in a heart that contumely has broken. I will exert myself to obtain such elevated rank that it shall be revered by the whole world. Though I be not born of Suruchi, the beloved of the king, you shall behold my glory, who am your son. Let Uttama, my brother, possess the throne given to him by my father; I

[1] Moor's *Hindu Pantheon*, London, 1810, pp. 51–53.

[2] Professor H. H. Wilson's translation, bk. i. ch. xi. and xii.

wish for no other honours than such as my own actions shall acquire, such as even my father has not enjoyed." Cherishing these aspirations, the very precocious infant prince, in quest of the highest honour and glory, followed a course which no European child or man, with a similar object in view, could dream of entering upon. Dhruva, who, it will be remembered, was only five years of age, left the city "and entered an adjoining thicket, where he saw seven *munis*[1] sitting upon hides of the black antelope." Explaining to these holy sages the circumstances which had drawn him forth from his royal home, and his ardent wishes for the attainment of a lofty position, he respectfully asked for their advice. The saints were good enough to listen to the child, to recommend the worship of Vishnu and to instruct him in the path he should pursue. "Prince," said the *rishis*, "thou deservest to hear how the adoration of Vishnu has been performed by those who have been devoted to his service. His mind must first be made to forsake all external impressions, and a man must then fix it steadily on that being in whom the world is. By him whose thoughts are thus concentrated on one only object and wholly filled by it, whose spirit is firmly under control, the prayer that we shall repeat to thee is to be invariably recited: 'Om! glory to Vasudeva, whose essence is divine wisdom, whose form is inscrutable, or is manifest as Brahma, Vishnu, and Siva.'"

To work out his great project, the little prince repaired to a holy place on the banks of the Jumna, and there followed very carefully the instructions he had received from the *rishis*, with the gratifying result that *Vishnu became manifest in his mind.* When this occurred, the earth itself was unable to bear the weight of the diminutive ascetic. The celestials took alarm, and tried every art to disturb and distract his meditations, but all their efforts were ineffectual. Still more alarmed by their want of

[1] "*Muni*—a holy sage, a pious and learned person, endowed with more or less of a divine nature, or having attained to it by rigid abstraction and mortification. The title is applied to the *rishis*, and to a great number of persons distinguished for their writings considered as inspired, as Panani, Vyasa, etc."—Dawson's *Dictionary of Hindu Mythology*.

success, the lesser gods appealed to Vishnu, addressing him thus: "God of gods, sovereign of the world, god supreme and infinite spirit, distressed by the austerities of Dhruva, we have come to thee for protection. As the moon increases in his orb day by day, so this youth advances incessantly towards superhuman power by his devotions. Terrified by the ascetic practices of the son of Uttánapáda, we have come to thee for succour. Do thou allay the fervour of his meditations. We know not to what station he aspires, to the throne of Indra, the regency of the solar or lunar sphere, or to the sovereignty of riches or of the deep. Have compassion on us, lord; remove the affliction from our breasts, divert the son of Uttánapáda from persevering in his penance."

To allay the fears of the gods, and for the general good, Vishnu at last came down to earth in person and granted the boy-ascetic's wish to obtain "an exalted station, superior to all others, and one that shall endure for ever." This ambitious desire was gratified by Dhruva's exaltation to the skies, *as the pole-star of the visible universe.*

This legend differs somewhat from the previous ones, inasmuch as it brings out very clearly the idea of the almost unimaginable efficacy of mental abstraction from human affairs when coupled with profound concentration of attention upon the Supreme Being alone. This is a decided modification of the *original* doctrine, and will be referred to again.

Myths and legends similar to those already given in the preceding pages of this chapter may be indefinitely multiplied, showing that, according to the beliefs of the Hindus, if one ardently coveted anything, the most effectual course to follow was to practise rigid austerities, self-denial, and suffering, till, in spite of the lesser gods, the Supreme Being would be constrained, by immutable and primordial laws, to grant the desired boon. But, more than that, we also learn that even the Supreme Being, "the cause of the creation and its course," endured, in the form of a *muni*, the greatest self-inflicted penances for thousands of years on the Gandhamādana mountains by the lake Pushkara and on the banks of the Saraswati, apparently to obtain sovereignty over all created things.[1] Fantastical as these statements and notions, no doubt, appear to European apprehension, we may profitably pause to note that if the Hindu were to point out that a kindred idea seems to be at the root of the story of the Crucifixion, as well as of the motive assigned for that astounding voluntary humiliation on the part of the Deity, it would be impossible for the unbiassed seeker after truth to deny the validity of the contention, since in the "cross and passion" of the Redemption we distinctly find the notion of the efficacy of voluntary hardships, poverty, physical suffering, and death, for the attainment of a great object *otherwise unachievable even by the Deity Himself*.[2]

I have no wish to labour this point, but I may in passing emphasise the fact that it is upon faith in the efficacy of self-inflicted hardships that Hindu asceticism, with its strange and cruel practices and its marvellous legends of superhuman feats, really rests, and that, according to Christian doctrine, mankind could not have been rescued from the Powers of Evil by any other means than the bitter sufferings and the supreme self-sacrifice of the second person of the Triune-God.

No doubt, the Hindu has arrived at ideas of asceticism and its fruits other than those embodied in the legends cited in the foregoing pages: as, for example, when Sanatsujata said to Dritarashtra, "The words esteem and asceticism (practices of *munis*) can never exist together. Know that this world is for those that are candidates for esteem, while the other world is for those that are devoted to asceticism,"[3] the object of the asceticism contemplated in this passage being spiritual emancipation, not worldly advancement or the gratification of desires of any kind. But the value of austerities for the attainment of practical ends, commendable or the reverse, and the power for good

[1] Mahabharata—Vana Parva, section xii. A zinc statuette in the India Museum, South Kensington, figured in Moor's *Hindu Pantheon*, plate 3, represents the four-headed Brahma as an ascetic with a rosary in one hand, a mendicant's water-pot in another, a sacrificial spoon in a third, and so on.

[2] The usual accompaniment of *temptations* is also not wanting.

[3] Mahabharata—Udyoga Parva, section xli.

or evil possessed by the ascetic, are the considerations connected with asceticism which are most deeply graven on the Indian mind; and this fact enables us to appreciate the standpoint from which the Hindu looks up to the *sadhu* who has practised, or may pretend to have practised, austerities, as one who might help him to gain his ends, or, on the other hand, might hurl a curse at him with the most direful consequences.

Although I should hesitate to aver that the possibility of attaining power for good or evil has at any time been, for the majority of *sadhus*, the sole inducement for embracing the ascetic life, yet there can be little doubt that this possibility has always had a considerable fascination for Hindus of all classes. But there are, and always will be, amongst good Hindus, many timid ones, weaker vessels, who shrink from pain or physical hardships of a severe kind, and yet long to attain and enjoy the substantial fruits of asceticism; and others also, mystics and dreamers, whose fervent emotionalism would discover a ready method for the reunion of the soul with the Infinite Spirit, without necessarily disdaining the possession of the much-coveted power over man and nature which such mystic union with the All-Spirit might involve. A case in point is the Dhruva myth narrated above. But the aspirations of the less resolute or more emotional spirits find most complete expression in the *yoga* system, described in a later chapter, its more salient features being posturings, abstraction, and concentration of mind.

Where all believe in the efficacy of ascetic practices for the attainment of extraordinary powers, it is inevitable that the rivalry of classes and of sects should be productive of competing claims for their respective leaders in regard to superiority in supernatural potency. A characteristic example of this is the more than titanic old-world conflict of which Vasishta and Visvamitra are the heroes, between whom, says the Mahabharata,[1] "there existed a great enmity, *arising from rivalry in austerities*." At the same time, since the two men named belonged to the sacerdotal and warrior castes respectively, their antagonism illustrates

[1] Cust's *Original Sanskrit Texts*, vol. i. p. 420.

the early and vigorous struggle for supremacy between the castes they represented.

The marvellous legend of their enmity and warfare is to be found variously related in both the great Indian epics, as well as in the Puranas; but only the main outlines of the story need be reproduced here. According to the chroniclers, King Visvamitra had in one of his ordinary hunting expeditions been entertained very sumptuously by the Brahman sage Vasishta in his forest hermitage. Discovering that the hermit was enabled to thus provide a magnificent feast, and costly presents too, in the midst of the wilderness, because he was the fortunate possessor of a wondrous "cow of plenty," the king became covetous, and expressed a wish to purchase the animal, offering no less than a hundred million cows, or even his entire kingdom, for her.

Vasishta, however, declined to part with his "cow of plenty" on any terms whatever.

At this unexpected rebuff, Visvamitra was so offended that he haughtily resolved to exercise his kingly prerogative and forcibly appropriate the object of his cupidity. But he had miscalculated. The marvellous cow, after a *wonderful* colloquy with her master, refused to move, and, when assailed by the king's attendants, created out of her own sweat, urine, excrement, etc., such hosts of strange warriors armed to the teeth that the royal army could not stand before them. In the battle which took place one hundred of the king's sons rushed upon Vasishta, but were at once reduced to ashes by a blast from the sage's mouth. Defeated and humiliated by the Brahman, the king turned to the only resource open to him, and resolved to acquire superhuman power by ascetic practices, solely with a view to an eventual triumph over the Brahman Vasishta. For this purpose he abandoned his kingdom, proceeded to the Himalaya mountains, and there for a long period subjected himself to the severest austerities. As a consequence, the great god Mahādeva appeared to him, presented him with celestial weapons, and instructed him in the use of these terrible instruments of destruction. Elated with pride, confident in his newly acquired powers, and thirsting for vengeance, Visvamitra hurried off to punish his victorious foe. He burnt down Vasishta's hermitage, and drove away, in headlong flight, all the dwellers in that quiet retreat. But the Brahman sage was not to be overcome even by the wondrous weapons of the gods. A battle ensued, and once more was demonstrated the unapproachable superiority of the sacerdotal caste, even in the use of the deadly weapons of war. Visvamitra might now have been destroyed; but, at the earnest intercession of the *munis*, the victorious Brahman stayed his hand and spared his vanquished enemy. Taught by bitter experience, Visvamitra now fully realised that only the acquisition of Brahmanhood could place him on an equality with Vasishta, and so once more he resorts to that infallible source of power, *austerities*. By self-inflicted hardships for a thousand years he earned a place in the heaven of royal sages, but was intensely dissatisfied with this reward; yet, seeing no other way of attaining his object, he renewed and intensified his mortifications, which were, however, interrupted by various episodes, one of them being an exploit on the part of the royal ascetic in translating to the celestial regions in his human body one Trisanku, who, banned by the priesthood, had appealed to Visvamitra for help. It was a terrific affair this introduction of Trisanku into heaven, for it was actively opposed by the celestials themselves, and it was not accomplished until Visvamitra had terrified the astonished gods by creating new stars and constellations of stars, and had even threatened, in his rage, that he would create another god Indra, or leave the world without any Indra at all. Indeed, the masterful ascetic actually began to call new gods into being, when the celestials yielded the point in dispute, and came to terms with him. After this incidental war against heaven, the royal ascetic renewed his austerities for a thousand years, when Brahma announced to him that he had attained the rank of a *rishi*. By no means contented with this reward, the king continued his self-inflicted penances, but for a short time fell into the snares of a lovely nymph of heaven, Menaka by name, who had been sent down to earth by the celestials expressly to attract Visvamitra's attention and spoil his labours. After recovering his self-command and dismissing the fascinating nymph kindly, the king went through another course of penances for a thousand years, and at the end of that period received from Brahma the dignity of *māhārishi* (great *rishi*). He learned from the Supreme Being that he had not yet acquired that perfect control over his senses which would entitle him to the exalted distinction of *Brahman-rishi* which he coveted and had striven for. So the indomitable king, and *māhārishi* now, put himself through a *more* rigorous course of austerities, involving the most painful bodily tortures, the maintaining of absolute silence, and the suspension of breathing for hundreds of years.

"As he continued to suspend his breath, smoke issued from his head, to the great consternation of the three worlds. The gods, *rishis*, etc., then addressed Brahma. 'The great *muni* Visvamitra has been allured and provoked in various ways, but still advances in his sanctity. If his wish is not conceded, he will destroy the three worlds by the force of his austerity. All the regions of the universe are confounded, no light anywhere shines; all the oceans are tossed and the mountains crumble, the earth quakes and the wind blows confusedly. We cannot, O Brahma, guarantee that mankind shall not become atheistic. Before the great and glorious sage of fiery form resolves to destroy (everything), let him be propitiated.'" [1]

Accordingly, the gods, headed by Brahma, approached the mighty ascetic, hailed him as "*Brahman-rishi*," and pronounced a blessing upon him. The *Kshatriya* king had thus, by thousands of years of intense mortification and stern self-discipline, attained the exalted rank of Brahmanhood. Yet, curiously enough, his special and final hope of triumphing over Vasishta, for which in fact he had voluntarily suffered and endured torments of body and mind through successive millenniums, was never gratified; for, through the mediation of the gods, he was eventually reconciled to his still unvanquished foe.

For us, the noteworthy points of this madly extravagant legend are: (1) the excellent illustration it affords of the

[1] Muir's *Sanskrit Texts*, vol. i. p. 409.

firm faith of the Hindus in asceticism as a means of obtaining superhuman power of the most astonishing kind; (2) the all but unapproachable dignity of Brahmanhood, which was the lesson the Brahman inventors of the story expressly desired to impress upon their grossly credulous countrymen.

As the above fantastic story relates to mythical events of an extremely remote past, it might well be thought that the old world of marvels therein depicted has long ceased to exist for the Hindu; but, to show that this is not the case, I shall now outline another legend which purports to record wonders of quite recent date, arising out of the pretensions of the modern *Sikh* sect, in the person of its original founder, Baba Nanak (1469–1539 A.D.), as against the far older sect of the *Yogis*.[1]

During a halt in one of those extensive wanderings which Baba Nanak loved to take in quest of wisdom, his faithful attendant Mardanah went about collecting fuel for their *dhoonee* or smoky fire. Not far from their temporary camping-ground there apparently lived some of those perfect *Yogis* known as *Siddhas*,[2] and, as soon as Mardanah had got together a small quantity of fuel, one of these *Siddhas* came up and wantonly snatched it all away. Mardanah, deprived of the fruits of his labour, went back to his august master and related what had occurred. Nanak, without any exhibition of temper, immediately produced some fuel out of the folds of his flowing garments, and with these miraculously acquired combustibles Mardanah kindled the vesper fires. Baffled and vexed, the *Siddhas* raised a violent storm in order to extinguish Nanak's *dhoonee*; but its only effect was to scatter their own fuel and quench their own hearths. Notwithstanding their superhuman powers, the *Siddhas* were now reduced to wandering about to get wood and fire for themselves; but as Baba Nanak had commanded the

[1] Chap. VIII.

[2] *Siddhas*—a class of semi-divine beings of great purity and holiness, who dwell in the regions of the sky between the earth and the sun. They are said to be 88,000 in number.—Dawson's *Classical Dictionary of Hindu Mythology, etc.*

The *Siddhas* referred to in the text are *some of the eighty-four perfect Yogis* specially venerated by the *Yogi* sect described in Chap. VIII.

spirit or genius of fire to abstain from helping them, in the end the *Siddhas* were obliged to come to the Baba himself, and humbly entreat him to ignite their fuel for them. However, Nanak would consent to their request only on condition that Goraknāth, their much-venerated chief, should send him one of his own ear-rings and one of his wooden shoes, as, presumably, tokens of acknowledgment of defeat. In order to test Nanak further, the *Siddhas*, smarting under their discomfiture, asked him to give them milk there and then. He did so immediately by merely commanding the water in a well close by to be converted into milk. The transmutation took place in obedience to the saint's behest, the milk thus produced welling up to the surface.

Nanak's next miracle in this contest was bringing water from the Ganges, as the *Siddhas* had challenged him to provide them with fresh river-water for their morning bath. Mardanah was sent with a spade to trace a continuous line from the distant river, and was instructed not on any account to look back. As he drew the spade along behind him a stream of water followed it, but, when he neared the spot where his master was seated, his curiosity prevailed over his habit of obedience, and, like Lot's wife, he turned his head round to look over his shoulder. The stream which had flowed so far ceased to advance any farther.

"Now," said the *Siddhas* boastfully, "we shall, by our own power, cause it to come along," but their efforts were all in vain.

Chagrined by these displays of Nanak's superiority, his opponents resolved to perform certain marvels of their own. Some of the *Siddhas* began to fly about, or make their deerskins skim through the firmament, like ordinary denizens of the air. One boastful *Siddha* would ride on flames of fire, and another on a bit of a stone wall as if it were a horse. Nanak's stolid indifference to their displays of extraordinary power exasperated these thaumaturgists greatly, and they openly challenged him to do *something* similar to the wonders they had shown him, if only for his own credit's sake; but the Baba protested that he was a humble man, and had nothing startling to show them, adding, however, that if they would hide themselves, he would find them wherever they might be.

The *Siddhas* accepted the *guru's* challenge to the proposed game of hide-and-seek. One of them flew up into the heavens and hid there, another sought concealment in the recesses of the far Himalayas, a third secreted himself in the bowels of the earth; but Nanak soon found them, one and all, and dragged them forth from their hiding-places by the scalp-locks which adorned the crowns of their heads. Then it was Nanak's turn to hide himself, and that of the others to seek for him. What he did was to resolve his corporeal frame into its pristine elements—fire, air, earth, and water—while his soul was reunited with God. The *Siddhas,* of course, could not find the disintegrated *guru*; but he had told them before his disappearance how they might get him to come back if they were unable, as he foresaw they would be, to discover him. They were to place a small offering at the foot of the tree where he usually sat, and to pray to God for the return of Nanak, when he would reappear. Utterly discomfited, they did so, and the Baba graciously came back.[1]

There are, in both Hindu and Buddhist story, no end of similar marvellous contests, which, strange and whimsical as they may appear to the modern European, are, after all, only the deliriously extravagant Indian equivalents of the biblical contests between Moses and the Egyptian magicians (Ex. vii. 8–12), and between Elijah and the priests of Baal (1 Kings xviii. 21–40), or of the traditional struggle between St. Peter and St. Paul on the one side and Simon Magus on the other.[2] Muslim

[1] Janam Sakhee. *Guru* Angad Sahib received the account from Bala (another of Nanak's devoted attendants), and had Pirāmookha to write it down.

[2] In this trial of strength, carried out in the presence of the Roman Emperor Nero, the test consisted in raising a dead man to life and in putting to practical proof the claim of the magician that he could fly. In the first case Simon Magus failed utterly, while the apostles, of course, succeeded. Then the magician, to prove his power of sustaining himself in the air, leaped from a high tower, and seemed, for a time, to float in the atmosphere, no doubt supported by invisible demons; but, eventually overcome by the superhuman power of the apostles, he fell to the earth, and, being mortally

hagiography also abounds in trials of strength between rival leaders of the people, attended with striking displays of miraculous power on the part of the opponents.[1] It is not too much to say that religious literature everywhere affords examples of appeals to striking *works* in attestation of the truth of the mission of the prophet or the holiness of the saint.[2]

From the myths and legends cited above, a fair idea can be formed of the *motives* which the Hindu mind has deemed sufficient and proper for the most protracted and terrible self-mortifications imaginable, and it is also as clear as day that these motives have no conscious or unconscious relation to ethics.

Moreover, there is no denying the fact that, regarded from the ordinary standpoint of morals, the celebrated Hindu sages do not generally command especial admiration outside the charmed circle of their own countrymen. This, naturally enough, the Christian missionary was not slow to discover. On this subject the Rev. Mr. Ward of Serampore says—

"These tupushivēēs (ascetics) are supposed to have been the authors of the most ancient of the Hindoo writings, in some of which, it is admitted, sentiments are to be found which do honour to human nature. But it is equally certain that these sages were very little affected

injured, died a few days later. This story is told by St. Justin (second century) and several others amongst the early Christian writers.

It may be added that we learn from tradition that St. Matthew defeated certain redoubtable magicians in Ethiopia, and that his brother evangelist, St. John, came out triumphant from a contest with the high priest of Diana at Ephesus.—*Lives and Legends of the Evangelists, Apostles, and other Early Saints*, by Mrs. Arthur Bell (George Bell & Sons, 1901).

[1] A good example of this is the very wonderful story of Sidi Ikhlef given in chap. x. of Colonel Trumelet's *Les Saints de l'Islam.*

[2] A recent writer says, "The monkish historians pit their heroes against each other. What Moschus tells us of orthodox monks is balanced by the tales of John of Ephesus about the Monophosytes, and Thomas of Marga is not outdone by either when he recounts the performances of his Nestorians. The monks competed against each other individually, and their achievements were boasted of by the adherents of the various parties into which the later Christological controversies rent the Church."—*The Spirit and Origin of Christian Monasticism*, by James O. Hannay, M.A., pp. 172, 173 (Methuen, 1903).

by these sentiments; and perhaps the same might be said of almost all the heathen philosophers. Vushishthu inflicted on himself incredible acts of severity; but in the midst of his devotions he became attached to a heavenly courtesan, and cohabited with her five thousand years. Purashuru, an ascetic, violated the daughter of a fisherman who was ferrying him over a river, from which intercourse sprang the famous Vyasu and the author of the Muhabharutu. Kupilu, an ascetic, reduced King Sagurus' sixty thousand sons to ashes, because they mistook him for a horse-stealer. Brigoo, in a fit of passion, kicked the god Vishnoo in the breast. Richeeku, for the sake of subsistence, sold his son for a human sacrifice. Doorvasa, a sage, was so addicted to anger that he was a terror both to gods and men. Ourvvu, another sage, in a fit of anger destroyed the whole race of Hoihuyu with fire from his mouth, and Doovasa did the same to the whole posterity of Krishnu. Javalee, an ascetic, stands charged with stealing cow's flesh at a sacrifice: when the beef was sought for, the saint, to avoid detection, turned it into onions; and hence onions are forbidden to the Hindoos. The Pooranus, indeed, abound with accounts of the crimes of these saints, so famous for their religious austerities: anger and lust seem to have been their predominant vices."[1]

Ward's indictment of the *rishis* partakes of the obvious, yet the Christian missionary, while right as to his facts, has entirely failed to understand the mental constitution of the pantheistic Hindu, and has consequently been unable to appreciate the exalted position of the successful ascetic as compared both with his fellow-men and celestial beings, or to perceive his complete enfranchisement from ethical laws which might be binding upon ordinary humanity.

These points will become clear as we proceed.

[1] *A View of the History, Literature, and Religion of the Hindus*, pp. 286, 287. Mr. Ward's spelling of the Sanskrit names has been retained, although it differs much from the modern style.

CHAPTER III

SADHUS BEFORE THE PUBLIC AT FAIRS AND ELSEWHERE

Sadhus as seen at Fairs—Their Dress—Sect Marks and their Explanation—Hairdressing—Rosaries—Various Ornaments and their Significance—Sadhus' Alms-bowls, Tongs, Arm-rests, Charas-pipes, Bhang-mortars, etc.—Hermitages—Ascetic Practices of various Kinds and Degrees—Minor Asceticisms—Posturings—Strange Purificatory Rites.

F the vast army of *sadhus* who roam about India, either alone or with companions, not many have any settled home. There are, it is true, scattered all over the country, substantial monasteries, but these afford only temporary abodes, and, so far as I know, are available as residences only to a privileged few, who have some hereditary claim or pecuniary interest in the establishment.

As a rule, the *sadhus* adopt a life of easy, irresponsible indolence and mendicancy. Their calendar of fairs and festivals is comprehensive and accurate. They know well how to time their devious wanderings so as to make them fit in with the festal events of each locality within their usual annual round of pilgrimages to sacred places, where, on all important occasions, they congregate in hosts, and where they may be studied to advantage as regards the peculiarities of their costume and external appearance generally.

Leaving out of account, for the present, the thoughts, motives, beliefs, hopes, and aspirations of the *sadhus*, let us take a superficial survey of these interesting representatives of Indian mysticism, as they appear at, say, a great religious gathering on the Ganges.

Amidst the bustle of the fair, amongst the moving crowd of ordinary pilgrims and cheerful holiday-makers, in the flying dust and round about the booths and tents, may be seen quaint figures robed in peculiar salmon-coloured garments. These are usually *sadhus*, salmon-colour being the prevailing though not universal tint of the raiment worn by such Hindu ascetics as care at all about clothing themselves, even in the somewhat scanty fashion of Brahmanic India. It is not, however, always on foot that the *sadhus* are to be seen. Sometimes they appear in more lordly fashion, borne aloft on the backs of tall elephants in company with, or in attendance upon, the abbot of some considerable monastery or the high priest of some important temple.

A great number of *sadhus* discard all attire but the scantiest of rags; and amidst so much nudity one is not surprised to find that in their case the skin, for its mere protection from the sun's rays and insect pests, is usually rubbed over with ashes, prepared by some ascetics with the greatest care, being sifted repeatedly through folds of cotton cloth till quite as impalpable as any toilet powder. The application of this greyish-white powder to a dark skin gives a peculiar effect, which, I believe, is not without attractiveness in Indian eyes.[1]

Wherever many *sadhus* congregate, close inspection will soon reveal the fact that on their foreheads and noses most of them have white or coloured marks, neatly painted. Some have symbols also depicted on the breast and arms.

[1] Some folk-lorists suggest that Indian ascetics rub their bodies over with dust and ashes because these substances are potent scarers of demons. —W. Crookes, *Popular Religion and Folk-lore of Northern India*, pp. 29, 30.

The *tilaks*, or *tikas*, as the forehead marks are called, may not be beauty spots, but they are worth looking at, for they serve as insignia of different sects. For example, one *sadhu* bears on his forehead the *trifala*, three lines drawn upwards from near the meeting of the eyebrows, the central line red, and the outer ones white, this being the sect mark of the *Ramats*. The red line is painted with *roli*, a preparation of turmeric and lime, the white lines with *gopichandana*, a calcareous clay procured from Dwarka out of a pool in which, according to the Krishna legend, the frail *gopis* (milkmaids) drowned themselves in despair upon hearing of the death of their lover, the divine Krishna. The triple lines of the *trifala* are not without significance, being emblematic of the three gods of the Hindu triad, the central line representing Vishnu, and those on the right and left respectively Siva and Brahma.[1] Thus the *trifala* suggests and recalls to mind not only the Creator, the Preserver, and the Destroyer, but also, at the same time, the amours of the gay god Krishna on the banks of the Yamuna.

If for the red line in the *trifala* a black one (painted with charcoal from incense offered to Narayana) appears on a *sadhu's* forehead, he is one of the peculiar sect of the *Madhavacharis*.

Again the *tripundra*, three lines along the forehead from side to side, painted with *vibuti* or sacred ashes, distinguishes the Sivaite followers of Sankaracharya. "The *Kowls* (extreme *saktas*) usually betray their cult by painting their foreheads with vermilion dissolved in oil. The *Dakhinacharis* have generally an *urdhapundra*, or perpendicular streak, in the central part of the forehead, the colouring material being either a paste of sandalwood or a solution in *ghi* of charcoal obtained from a *hom* fire."[2]

More examples of sect marks need not be given now; but it is necessary to state that such marks are not

[1] That other interpretations of the *trifala* are also offered, and accepted, need not surprise us. *Vide* Mr. C. W. King's *The Gnostics and their Remains*, p. 301.

[2] Dr. J. N. Bhattacharjee, *Hindu Castes and Sects*, pp. 411, 412.

peculiar to professed *sadhus*, and appear also on the foreheads of Hindus who have not abandoned secular life.

One has only to look in the most casual way at an assemblage of *sadhus* to find out that amongst them some have their hair braided and coiled upon the anterior part of the crown of the head, and that others have their matted locks loose and shaggy. Men who wear their hair coiled up carefully upon the head are, irrespective of sect, called *jhuttadarees*; those who wear their hair falling in disorder about the face, *bhoureeahs*. This latter style is adopted by a great number of monks, who, if we may judge by appearances, evidently desire to give themselves a forbidding and formidable look.[1]

Shaven pates may also be seen wherever Hindu ascetics, particularly of the more advanced orders, congregate.

Most *sadhus* wear strings of beads about their necks or carry rosaries in their hands, reminding one that it was from the East, probably during the time of the Crusades, that Christendom borrowed these aids to devotion. From the nature of the prayer-beads worn by them it is usually easy to distinguish between the followers of the gods Vishnu and Siva respectively, according as they favour beads of the holy basil wood (*ocymum sanctum*) or the rough berries of the rudraksha tree (*elæocarpus ganitrus*). If they wear two necklaces made of the wood of the basil plant (the *tulsi* or *tulasi* of the Indians), they are probably of the sect of the *Swami Narayanis*, who worship Krishna (Vishnu) and also his mistress Radha.

It has been stated by the late Sir Monier Williams[2] and others, that the rosary (*japa-mālā* or *muttering chaplet*) of the votary of Siva consists of 32 or 64 rudraksha berries,

[1] "Magistrates in Northern India are often troubled by people who announce their intention of 'letting their hair grow' at someone whom they desire to injure. This, if one can judge by the manifest terror exhibited by the person against whom this rite is directed, must be a very stringent form of coercion. For the same reason ascetics wear their hair loose and keep it uncut, as Samson did; and the same idea probably accounts for the rites of ceremonial shaving of youths, and of the mourners after death."—W. Crookes, *Popular Religion and Folk-lore of Northern India*, i. 239.

[2] *Modern India*—Art: Indian Rosaries.

and that the follower of Vishnu affects one of 108 beads of basil wood. But, as I have seen rudraksha rosaries of 108 berries, I presume the rule referred to is not very closely observed.[1]

The *sadhus*' self-adornment is not restricted to necklaces and rosaries. Some of them wear phallic emblems depending from the neck by woollen threads, or fastened on the arms. A few have small bells attached to their arms. Others wear great ear-rings. Armlets of iron, brass, or copper may also be seen adorning these ascetics. Necklaces of little stones glitter on the throats of a small number. Occasionally one may be met having his hair embellished with a metallic substance called *swarma maksh* (golden fly). Again one has a conch shell tied on to his wrist, and another various quaint figures and devices, painted, or even branded, on his arms.[2]

"What very queer, eccentric, and barbarous attempts at beautification!" says the European, with a contemptuous smile, as he takes stock of these strange-looking philosophers. Yet, quaint and simple as their adornments undoubtedly are, the *sadhus* have evident pride in them; and with good reason too, for to them and to their fellows they are, like the palm-leaf in the hand of the Christian friar returned from Palestine, and like the different pewter medals with

[1] In the discussion which followed the reading of a paper by the Rev. Herbert Thurston, S.J., before the Society of Arts on "The History of the Rosary in all Countries," Sir George Birdwood said, "Nothing can be simpler than the art of the Hindu rosary, the Saiva rosary of 84 beads and the Vaishnava of 108; but when you learn that the sacred number 84 (*chaurasi*) is made up of the number of the 12 signs of the zodiac, multiplied by the number of the 7 planets; and that the sacred number 108 is similarly made up, the moon being counted as three—the rising, full, and waning moon—instead of one, then you understand that every Hindu rosary symbolises the whole circuit of the hosts of heaven; and this knowledge henceforth transfigures them in your eyes. He was satisfied from the numbers of the beads strung on them, and their mode of division, in 12 groups of 7, that the earliest Christian rosaries, like the Baudha and Islamitic rosaries, were originally derived from the rosaries of the Hindus." —*Journal of the Society of Arts*, 21st February 1902, p. 275.

[2] "It appears, however, that stamping the mark with a hot iron is commonly in use in the Dekhin. A similar practice seems to have been known to the early Christians, and baptizing with fire was stamping the cross on the forehead with a hot iron."—Professor Wilson's *Religious Sects of the Hindus*, footnote, p. 28.

which the mediæval visitors to celebrated shrines adorned their hats and dresses,[1] precious souvenirs and legible signs of holy pilgrimages accomplished by plain and mountain. Those rude armlets of iron, brass, and copper recall to mind and are well-known badges of visits to the lofty Himalayan monasteries of Pasupatinath, Kedarnath, and Badrinath. The necklace of little gleaming stones and the "golden flies" tell of far wanderings to the shrine of Kali at Hingalaj in distant Beluchistan; the white conch shell on the wrist indicates a pilgrimage to Rameshwar in the far south; and the symbolical marks branded conspicuously upon the arm may be the evidence of the favour of Krishna obtained by a visit to Dwarka by the sea, where the incarnated god ruled in the olden days.[2]

Having renounced the world, the Hindu ascetics have reduced their belongings to a minimum; yet being human, they have not been able to cast *everything* aside. As wandering mendicants depending for their daily food upon the charity of their fellow-countrymen, and often traversing long distances in the course of their annual tourings, most of them, though not all, have in practice recognised the necessity of possessing an alms-bowl and a water-pot. These consist of, perhaps, a mere cocoanut-shell or a calabash, but in many instances the shell, if examined, will be found provided with a lid, a handle, and a spout; the gourd will also present evidences of improvement, being cut into a convenient shape for easy carriage, while brass imitations of the gourd will not be uncommon. Some taste, too, is often displayed in adorning these very homely vessels.

Amongst many races iron is believed to have the virtue of scaring away demons and evil spirits; it is certainly both friend and foe to evil-doers. As a protection against more substantial enemies than wicked spirits—wild beasts, for example—the iron fire-tongs to be found in the

[1] *Social England*, edited by H. D. Traill and J. S. Mann, vol. ii. pp. 374, 375.

[2] Marking or branding the body with the Vishnu symbols is known as *bhajana*. Amongst the early Christians, many branded the name of Christ upon their foreheads.

possession of a majority of these ascetics ought to be effective, since in many cases they are so exaggerated in both size and weight as to become formidable weapons in strong hands,[1] especially when they happen to have been sharpened along the edges.

Amongst the *sadhu's impedimenta* will be noticed tau-staves used as chin-rests and arm-rests, known as *bairaguns*,[2] of different sorts, adapted to the various positions favoured by the contemplator when silently engaged in his profound and pious meditations. I understand that occasionally one of these *bairaguns* may conceal a sharp dagger. I have not myself come across any of this dangerous kind, but have no reason whatever to doubt their existence, especially when I call to mind that even the crucifix itself (the crucifix of Crema) has been sacrilegiously used as a receptacle for a cruel and treacherous poniard.[3]

As narcotic drugs are in favour with Hindu ascetics, charas-smokers amongst them will naturally have their *chillums* (pipes) stowed away somewhere about their persons ; and confirmed bhang-drinkers will not find a stone mortar and wooden pestle too burdensome, even when wayfaring. It would be an interesting philosophical study to endeavour to trace the influence of these powerful narcotics on the minds and bodies of the itinerant monks who habitually use them. We may be sure that these hemp drugs, known since very early times in the East, are not irresponsible for some of its wild dreamings,[4] whilst there is good reason to believe that they have often given the user protection from malarial and other diseases.

Diminutive idols in stone and metal or pictorial representations of the deities will be found in the miniature chapels which some *sadhus* set up when they halt for a while at any convenient spot; and, along with the idols

[1] *Vide* initial letter, Chap. VII. Section II.

[2] An arm-rest is used as the initial letter of Chap. VIII. Section II.

[3] *Sketches and Studies in Italy and Greece,* by John Addington Symonds, vol. i. pp. 219–21.

[4] The Christian missionary sarcastically remarks, " A great number of Hindu modern saints live in a state of perpetual intoxication, and call this stupefaction, which arises from smoking intoxicating herbs, *fixing the mind* on God."—Ward's *Hindus*, p. 283.

A BAIRAGI AND HIS HERMITAGE.

FIG. 1.

To face page 42.

and pictures, various objects specially associated with the divinities in the holy legends of Hinduism. Of course the gods and the sacred objects present will, in each case, depend upon the particular *sadhu's* sect, his beliefs and preferences. In this connection it may be mentioned that amongst *Saivas* the following are likely to be found: a *lingam*, a human skull, a tiger's skin, a *trisula* or trident, and a *dameru* or drum. Among *Vaishnavas* may be looked for the *saligram* stone (a kind of ammonite), the *tulasi* plant, the conch shell (*sankha*), and the discus (*chakra*), emblematic of the sun.

Sadhus vary their extensive peregrinations by halts, often very long ones, especially when old age is creeping insidiously upon them and long journeys become fatiguing and distasteful. A hermitage of some sort by the riverside, or a cool place in the shade of a spreading peepul or banian tree near a temple, may be the *sadhu's* quiet home for months or even years. Here, on the selected spot, he maintains in the open air the wood fire, whose soft smoke, most useful in keeping off mosquitoes and other troublesome insects, seems an indispensable accompaniment, as well as an outward and visible sign, of the *sadhu's* abode. Here he usually sets up a tiny altar to his favourite or tutelar deity, and is himself visited regularly by the religious who wish to earn merit by charity to holy men. Persons desirous of securing his good offices for the attainment of more definite worldly ends also find their way to his hermitage, and here he lives on the alms of the neighbourhood till his own caprice, or inexorable death, puts a period to the sojourn. Whether resting or on the march, *sadhus* who are strict observers of the rules of the order or sect they belong to would have their time well occupied from sunrise to sunset in the performance of the many detailed ritualistic duties and exercises prescribed for them ; and as most of the present-day ascetics are ignorant men, rarely under the direct control of any superior, they usually neglect or curtail their ceremonial obligations, or, at any rate, discharge them quite perfunctorily.

The illustrations (Figs. 1 and 2) will give a fair idea of the hermitages of Indian *sadhus*, which, picturesque though they may be, are certainly not comfortable, and could be habitable only in a warm climate.

To account for his long rest at the foot of the peepul tree (*Ficus religiosa*) where he had established himself, the man depicted in Fig. 1, a *sadhu* of the Bairagi order, informed me that he had come there in obedience to a gracious summons from the goddess Devi, whose temple was alongside, and that he would move on when the divinity, of her good pleasure, should direct him in a vision, as before, to leave the place. Within his shed he had installed an image of Rama Chandra, before which he was enabled, through the kindness of friends and admirers, to heap up every day a small pile of rose petals. Outside, as the illustration shows, there lies a rather suspicious-looking bottle, while the hermit himself is seen busy grinding, in a stone mortar, some dried leaves of the hemp plant (*cannabis Indica*) preparatory to infusion in cold water, in order to enjoy his favourite appetiser and intoxicant bhang.

Of the men in the group, Fig. 2, the one with averted face was not actuated by any feeling of modesty or self-depreciation from facing the camera. He joined the others casually while the instrument was being adjusted, and, when asked to assume a suitable attitude, pompously replied that he obeyed no man's behests, recognising no master save Rama Chandra. It required some little persuasion on the part of his brother *sadhus* to induce him even to take up the ungracious and ungraceful pose in which he was photographed. He might, perhaps, have been a *shady* character wanted by the police, and might have acted as he did for prudential reasons, or, which is quite as probable, his rudeness may have been due merely to an objection to be photographed, on the ground that any likeness taken carries away with it some virtue from the original—possibly a portion of the living soul—this being by no means an uncommon superstition.

Lay Hindus are often subjected by the Brahmans to penances for offences such as the ill-treatment or killing of a cow, or for some other equally serious breach of the ethical or ceremonial law. And occasionally *sadhus,* for reasons of their own already indicated, voluntarily

SADHUS AT HOME.

FIG. 2.

To face page 44.

undergo inconveniences, pains, and even terrible tortures. In doing so they follow the traditional path, and do not exercise any special ingenuity in the invention of methods of self-torment.

One favourite mode of mortifying the flesh is to sit under the open canopy of heaven girt about with five small fires.[1] Sometimes only four fires are lighted, the sun overhead being regarded as the fifth one; and an intolerable fire he is, too, on a cloudless summer day in the plains of India. As a rule this arrangement is devoid of sincerity, and is indeed a mere performance or show. Yet the fires, insignificant though they be, serve the very practical object of advertising the *sadhu* and attracting admirers and clients. *Sadhus* who follow this practice are known as *panchadhunis*.

Another way of afflicting and subduing the body is to sit and sleep on a bed of spikes. I have even seen a *sadhu's* wooden shoes bristling inside with a close crop of pointed nails. That the discomfort in such cases due to the constant contact of acute spikes with some portion or other of the almost naked body is real, there can be little doubt, but it need not be very injurious to health. Referring, in connection with this practice, to Bhishma, one of the heroes of the Mahabharata, Mr. W. Crookes writes: "To the Hindu nowadays he is chiefly known by the tragic circumstances of his death. He was covered all over by the innumerable arrows discharged at him by Arjuna, and when he fell from his chariot he was upheld from the ground by the arrows and lay on a couch of darts. This sara-sayya or 'arrow-bed' of Bhishma is probably the origin of the *kantaka-sayya* or 'thorn-couch' of some modern Bairagis, who lie and sleep on a couch studded with nails."[2] To the discredit of human nature it must be admitted that deceptions and impostures even in asceticism are unfortunately inevitable. An Indian gentleman, not, however, too favourably disposed towards the ascetics, assured me that he once found out that a *sadhu* whose practice it was to sit in public on spikes

[1] For illustrations of this and other forms of asceticism *vide* Frontispiece.

[2] *The Popular Religion and Folk-lore of Northern India*, vol. i. p. 92.

had cunningly taken the precaution to protect his buttocks with thin iron plates so artfully made with irregular surface as to deceive almost any onlooker into the belief that his flesh was being pitted by the cruel points.

There are *sadhus*—*tharasri* they are called—who will stand leaning on some kind of rest for days or weeks together, with what painful fatigue and hardship it is easy to imagine. Occasionally in this form of self-torture only one leg is used, the other being drawn up.

A prominent feature in the ascetic practices of some *sadhus* is hanging head downwards suspended from the bough of a tree or a suitable framework, for perhaps half an hour at a time. Such *sadhus* are known as *urdhamukhi*, Fig. 3, but must be exceedingly rare, as I have come across only a single example of this class, described later on in Chap. IX.

Severer forms of voluntary torture are also known, as when a man ties his arm to a support such as a light bamboo, so as to keep it erect overheard, till, at last, the disused limb, reduced to a shrunken and rigid condition, refuses to be lowered again to its natural position. When both arms are so dealt with, the subject becomes a helpless cripple entirely dependent for everything upon the kindness of others. *Sadhus* who practise this form of austerity are known as *urdhabahus*. A modification of the last-mentioned practice is the closing of the hand till it becomes useless and the long nails grow like curving talons from the cramped and atrophied fingers, or even find their way through the flesh between the metacarpal bones of the hand.

Burying alive, or performing *samadh* as it is called, is a very rare yet well-known practice amongst Hindu religious devotees. The period of inhumation may be from a few days to five or six weeks, and, if the buried man lives out the fixed time, he emerges from his temporary grave an undoubted saint and an object of popular veneration ever afterwards. The advantages in view are great enough to tempt the more ambitious *sadhu*; but *samadh* is attended with the gravest risks, even when undertaken by cunning and designing impostors for their own

Photo] [A. J. Combridge & Co., Bombay.

AN URDHAMUKHI SADHU.

FIG. 3. To face page 46.

glorification and profit. Two recent instances, both ending fatally, are described by Sir Monier Williams in his *Modern India* (pp. 50–53).

A well-known and well-authenticated instance of a *samadh* lasting forty days and ending satisfactorily is the case of the *yogi* Haridas in the time of Ranjit Singh of the Punjab [1] (A.D. 1792–1839).

Great hardship attends what is known as the *ashtanga danddwat*, or prostration of the body, involving the performance of a pilgrimage by a slow and most laborious mode of progression,—in fact, the application of *eight* parts of the body—the forehead, breast, hands, knees, and insteps —to the ground. The vower determines to traverse the distance to his destination, a shrine or some noted place of pilgrimage, by prostrating himself full length on the road, then crawling along till his heels touch the spot where his forehead last rested, then prostrating himself again, and so on, with repetitions on repetitions, till his goal is reached. The performance savours of great humility, and is not confined to short distances. I once met a youthful *sadhu* at Burdwan in Bengal, on the Grand Trunk Road of Northern India, moving in this leech-like fashion from Juggernaut to Benares, a distance of about six hundred miles, and I have heard of pilgrims thus measuring, as it were, their toilsome way towards the sacred source of the Ganges, amongst the eternal snows of the Himalayas, pursuing for months, and even years, with patient courage a journey almost impossible of accomplishment in such inhospitable regions under the imposed conditions.[2]

There are others also who climb the mighty Himalayas, not to visit the source of the Ganges, but to reach the far-off heavens beyond. In the olden time, so the story goes, King Yudhisthera, weary of life and its disappointments, journeyed towards Mount Meru, and, after many painful vicissitudes on the way, arrived at the celestial mountain,

[1] Described after Dr. Honigberger in my *Indian Life, Religious and Social* (T. Fisher Unwin), pp. 28–30.

[2] It is a curious fact that *ashtanga* is sometimes undertaken simply with the object of collecting money for a daughter's dowry. I came across an instance of this kind in December 1898.

and was finally admitted into *swarga*, the abode of bliss;[1] and ever since then many a *sadhu* has resolutely directed his footsteps towards the same goal, has gone alone upon the same great journey across the rugged mountains, *and has not turned back.*

Fasting is too obvious a penance to have been overlooked by *sadhus* as a means of macerating the body; and abstinence, combined with vigils and meditations, carried to excess, must in many cases have led amongst them to those hallucinations and ecstasies of an enfeebled constitution which are as familiar in the history of the saints of Christendom as in that of other Asiatic religions.

Vows of silence are not uncommon, and, however trying in the observance, may be very convenient under easily conceivable circumstances.

Once only I made the acquaintance of an ascetic who had afflicted himself by loading his person with massive iron chains, weighing in the aggregate about five hundred pounds, and he was a Muhammadan. On the opposite page is a photograph (Fig. 4) of this man, to whom I shall refer again in a later chapter.

Sadhus sometimes mutilate themselves cruelly, as one did, to my knowledge, in an ungovernable fit of temper. His deserted wife had followed him to a great gathering of ascetics, and, in the hearing of many, entreated him to return home with her. A few of the ascetics within earshot made jeering observations in regard to the new *sadhu* and his predicament, which stung him into a fever of rage, to be cooled only by the sharp edge of a knife and a dangerous hæmorrhage. I learned subsequently that the case was by no means an unusual one.[2]

[1] The story is retold from the Mahabharata in my *Great Indian Epics* (1899), pp. 194, 195.

[2] Self-mutilation prompted by religious fanaticism is not even now a thing of the past in Christian Europe. As an example, I may cite the following instance recorded in the *Daily Mail* of 7th May 1901.

FANATICAL SELF-MUTILATION
(From our own Correspondent).

St. Petersburg, *Friday, 3rd May.*

Ivan Plotnikoff, a peasant, twenty-eight years of age, residing at Bielovodsk, in the government of Kharkoff, called at the public library there

A FAQUIR WEIGHTED WITH HEAVY CHAINS.

FIG. 4.

To face page. 48.

At certain periods of the year, particularly in the month of April, many men of the lower castes observe temporarily the discipline of the ascetic sects, and may then be seen to cheerfully undergo self-inflicted tortures of a cruel kind, as, for example, passing *thick* metal skewers through the tongue, the cheeks, or the skin of the arms, the neck, and the sides,[1] walking upon live charcoal, and rolling upon thorns. Amongst the motives most commonly ascribed to these temporary low-caste ascetics are the gratification of vanity and the desire for the pecuniary gain which their *performances* usually bring them; but there can be no doubt that many of them hope, and look for, other and less obvious rewards for their self-inflicted sufferings.

Not to all men is it given to submit voluntarily to the more trying austerities, and therefore, as might have been expected, we find a number of minor asceticisms indulged in for the sake of attracting attention and perhaps gaining some pecuniary advantage. For example, a *sadhu* whom I saw at a religious festival, a big and powerful fellow, had a strong wooden framework erected to support a huge earthenware jar provided with a perforation at the bottom, from which a stream of water could flow out. Round about there were at least twenty-five large pots of water, to replenish the great jar when in use. Under the jar the

and asked for a book which would teach him "to live in truth," as he expressed himself. He was given the Holy Gospel. A few days afterwards a rumour spread about the place that Plotnikoff had cut off his hand.

When Plotnikoff had read in the Gospel that popular text, "And if thy right eye offend thee, pluck it out" (Matt. v. 29), he took it in a literal sense, and, being in a state of exaltation, decided then and there to proceed with the operation of removing his own eye. Not finding, however, an awl with which he could do it, he got hold of an axe, and with remarkable coolness began to chop the wrist of his hand, which he cut off after the fourth blow.

Plotnikoff is now lying in the Starobielsky Hospital, whither he went on foot. It is amazing that he could manage to walk a distance of about fifteen or twenty miles after having lost so much blood.

[1] These piercings, although very real, and seemingly cruel, do not, I must admit, appear to be attended with serious inconvenience. I have always seen them carried out by a *master* upon his *chelas* or disciples, and on every occasion the impression I received at the time was that the *chelas* were under hypnotic influence—an idea strengthened by my knowledge of the fact that practical hypnotism is not a new thing in India.

sadhu was in the habit of sitting during the night, particularly in the small hours, from about three o'clock till daybreak, with a stream of water falling on his head and flowing down over his person to the ground. It was winter time, and very cold work no doubt, but the *sadhu* had his reward in gratified vanity; for in the eyes of his numerous admirers he was Siva himself with the Ganges falling from heaven upon his head and flowing thence to bless and fertilise the earth.[1] This man, on account of his peculiar ascetic practice, would be known as a *jaladhara tapashi*. *Sadhus* who sit all night immersed in water are called *jalashayi*, but, as my night wanderings have not been very extensive, I have not seen any of these peculiar nocturnal soakers.

I once came across a *sadhu*, or pseudo-*sadhu*, who would put pieces of live charcoal into his mouth and chew them, pretending that they were savoury morsels and his usual food. He was an agriculturist and an ignorant fellow, whose only claim to notice was this stupid practice. There are some ascetics who pretend to live only on wheat bran, others who give out that the water they drink is invariably mixed with wood ashes. Some of these cases are merely instances of *depraved appetite* of a kind not unknown in the West. Some *sadhus* there are (known as *farari*) who eat fruits and nothing else, others (*dudhahari*) who subsist on milk alone, while those known as *aluna* never eat salt with their food.

Amongst the devices for attracting attention which take the form of self-inflicted penances, all are not so innocuous or unobjectionable as the ones just referred to. For example, lusty fellows often go about affecting to keep a restraint upon their sexual desires by mechanical arrangements which they do not conceal. A sect given to this practice is noticed by Professor H. H. Wilson under the name of *kara lingis*.[2] On the other hand, certain *sadhus* (Bairagis) are credited with effectually keeping their desires under control by subjecting themselves to a cruel

[1] The story of the descent of the Ganges, reproduced from the Ramayana, is given in my *Great Indian Epics* (1899), pp. 87–90.

[2] *Religious Sects of the Hindus*, p. 151.

SADHUS IN VARIOUS PRESCRIBED POSTURES.

FIG. 5.

To face page 50.

discipline entirely destructive of particular nerves and muscles of the body.[1]

As aids to meditation, possibly also in some cases as means for the mortification of the flesh, a great number of *âsans*, or postures, with such fantastic names as, for instance, the *padma âsan* or lotus posture, have been devised.[2] Some of them are really very difficult contortions, only to be acquired by a long and painful apprenticeship to the art, as will be readily understood from a consideration of the attitudes of the *sadhus* in Fig. 5.

This chapter cannot be closed without a reference to certain purificatory rites, which are practised by some *sadhus* : for example—

1. Drawing a thread through the mouth and one of the nostrils, with the object of cleansing the nasal fossæ : this process is called *neti karm.*

2. Swallowing a long strip of cloth, and after it has reached the stomach drawing it out again : this process of cleaning out the stomach is *dhoti karm.*

3. Cleaning the throat with a long brush called *Brahma datan.*

Two purificatory processes known as *brajoli karm* and *ganesh kriya* are, to say the least, so *peculiar* that I will not particularise them beyond stating that the latter is a process of flushing the colon without instrumental aids. I only allude to these practices, in order to lay stress on the fact that the cleansing of all the reachable interior portions of the body seems to have been nothing short of a mania with some sectarians in India.

[1] *Hindu Manners, Customs, and Ceremonies*, by the Abbé J. N. Dubois, part ii. chap. xxxiii.

[2] There are *âsans* and *âsans* known to the Indian people, and they are not all connected with *sadhuism* nor with religious practices; many of them quite the reverse. A book descriptive of these latter exists, but it is, I believe, on the Index *librorum prohibitorum* of the Indian police.

CHAPTER IV

THE WONDERS THAT PRESENT-DAY SADHUS AND FAQUIRS ARE SAID TO PERFORM

Visionists like the Sanyasi Ramakrishna—Sadhus to some extent what the Magicians and Necromancers have elsewhere been—Tales and Anecdotes of the Wonders performed by Sadhus and of Calamities brought on or averted by them—Transmutation of Metals by Sadhus—Story of Muslim Thaumaturgist who was the Disciple of a Sadhu—Claims of Superiority over Sadhus made by Faquirs—Strange Treatment of a Faquir by a co-Religionist—Sadhus as Physicians, Palmists, Fortune-tellers, and Acrobats.

AMONGST the Indian ascetics of our day there are some — like the highly emotional and tearful Bengali *Sanyasi* Ramakrishna,[1] subject to hysteria, trances, and catalepsy — who see visions, are believed to have been favoured with personal visits from the very gods and goddesses themselves, and are reputed to be

[1] Of this *sadhu,* who died in 1886, a good deal has recently been heard both in Europe and America. *Ramakrishna : His Life and Sayings,* by Professor Max Müller.

able to work miracles, though indisposed to do so, thinking that such performances are hindrances in the way to perfection. But apart from such neurotic saints, who always excite attention and sometimes found new sects, every Hindu knows that, though not nearly so powerful as the ancient *rishis*, whose fame has grown with the centuries, many *sadhus* do, even in our degenerate days, work wonders, and these not always of a beneficent kind. What the magician is, or has been, in other countries, that, to some extent, is the *sadhu* in India. Elsewhere the necromancer and the witch have been in antagonism with, and under the ban of, the hierarchy, but in India the ecclesiastical mantle has proved elastic enough to cover even some sorcerers, though certainly not all.

The Christian Church has always admitted, on biblical authority, the existence of wizards and witches. It has abhorred their dread power, and, when the vengeance of Heaven did not directly overtake them for their deeds,[1] persecuted them to the death, in obedience to the divine command, "Thou shalt not suffer a witch to live" (Ex. xxii. 18; Lev. xx. 27).

Mediæval history is painfully blurred with the smoke of the penal fires which attest the zeal of the Church in the suppression of witchcraft, whose successes were attributed to diabolical agency; but in India, since the earliest times, magic and sorcery, however much dreaded, have not been without a certain acknowledged respectability.

Of course there has been in India the inevitable rivalry between the hereditary priesthood and the lay professors of witchcraft, but the Brahmans, with their wonderful faculty of adaptation to circumstances, themselves adopted, at a very early date, the rôle of sorcerers (as the Atharva Veda amply proves), and by so doing have inevitably, though

[1] The wicked, if we may believe the chroniclers, were sometimes visited with the vengeance of God in a startling manner. For example: "Matilda was a great and potent witch, whose summons the devil was bound to obey. One day she aspired, alone of all her sex, to say mass; but when the moment came for sacring the elements, a thunderbolt fell from the clear sky and reduced her to ashes."—*Sketches and Studies in Italy and Greece*, by J. A. Symonds, ii. 179.

unintentionally, dignified the calling of the lay magician; since spells for the attainment of much which is elsewhere stigmatised as base, immoral, and impious have not been excluded from the sacred canon of the Hindus.

"Even witchcraft," says Mr. Bloomfield, "is part of the Hindu's religion; it has penetrated and become intimately blended with the holiest Vedic rites; the broad current of popular religion and superstition has infiltrated itself through numberless channels into the higher religion that is presented by the Brahman priests, and it may be presumed that the priests were neither able to cleanse their own religious beliefs from the mass of folk-belief with which it was surrounded, nor is it at all likely that they found it in their interest to do so." [1]

What the *sadhu* is credited with doing or being able to do, what the people think of him as a wonder-worker and a person capable of signally and very unpleasantly resenting any disrespect from worldlings, will be apparent from the following characteristic little stories picked up in my wanderings in India.

In the Deccan a certain sardar, or chief, who openly expressed disbelief in the existence of *bhuts* (goblins) was assured by a *sadhu* that they really *did* exist. The sardar wanted some tangible evidence in proof of this assertion, so the *sadhu* offered to give the sceptic ocular demonstration of the truth of his statement, on condition of his receiving one hundred rupees for his trouble. The offer was accepted. A lonely spot in the jungle was selected for the exhibition. Here, at midnight, the sardar and two or three of his friends, together with the *sadhu*, assembled within a space ringed in with a conspicuous line traced on the ground. Outside this boundary or magic circle no one was to move on pain of death or the most serious trouble. When all were seated and were peering anxiously into the darkness which surrounded them, the *sadhu* kept repeating his *muntras* (spells), till, lo! in the mirk, at the distance of a musket-shot, there appeared a lot of fantastic bald-headed urchins, jumping about with lighted pieces of wood

[1] Introduction (pp. xlv, xlvi.) to Bloomfield's translation of the Atharva Veda.—*Sacred Books of the East*, vol. xlii.

in their hands. In a little while, however, the capering *bhuts* all disappeared. Even after this demonstration the sardar was sceptical, and challenged the *sadhu* to reproduce his uncanny sprites again. The wise man excused himself; but, in consideration of the present of a valuable gold *kurra* (bracelet), repeated the performance the following night. On this second occasion the imps of darkness who appeared were girl-*bhuts*, and instead of lighted sticks carried lighted *charaghs* (terra-cotta lamps) in their hands. These they waved about in the darkness, but no inducements could make them approach the spectators within the enchanted enclosure nearer than the distance of a musket-shot. Needless to add that, as my informant, a learned pundit, assured me, the sardar's scepticism on the important subject of the existence of goblins was entirely dispelled by this second demonstration.

The following extract from an Anglo-Indian newspaper will serve as another example of what is currently reported about *sadhus* in our time.

"EXTRAORDINARY TALE OF A JOGI.

"The orthodox Hindus of Trevandrum, a correspondent writes to a Southern contemporary, have lately been much excited about a *jogi* or *sanyasi* who for some time past has been literally worshipped and reverenced as a god come down to men. No one appears to know where this man came from, or to what particular race or caste he belongs; but he was supposed to be a Hindu. On his arrival he sat under a banyan tree, on the northern bank of the Padmatheertham tank, and there he remained for three years. For the first week or so after he had taken up his arboreal residence, he partook of some milk or a plantain or two twice or three times a week. Then he gradually extended the intervals, till after three or four months he took no food at all, spoke to no one, and passed his time huddled up before a fire night and day for three long years. He looked no one in the face; he heeded no sounds, no question, nothing. The Maharajah of Travancore on one occasion stopped near the *sanyasi* and addressed him, without, however, obtaining the slightest recognition. Exposed to the cold and wet, to the heat and dust, the *sanyasi*, without partaking a morsel of food, passed his three years' existence in divine contemplation, and, although every morning and evening numbers of people paid him homage, he appeared oblivious of all external circumstances. A few days ago he died."—*Civil and Military Gazette*, Lahore, 23rd April 1895.

Calamities are often due to *sadhus*. For example, a serious and extensive fire broke out one night in June 1899 in a bazaar at Amritsar, causing great loss of property and of a few lives too. It appears a *sadhu* had been asking for alms from one shop to another in this bazaar. The *khatri* merchants, puffed up with the pride of wealth, repelled him with sharp words, one of them saying to him, "You are dressed grandly enough! why do you pester me for *pice*?"

Now the *sadhu* was robed in a new sheet which some liberal person, most likely a woman, had kindly presented to him. Irritated by the *mahajun's* (merchant's) taunts, he removed the cloth from his shoulders, and, having procured a bit of fire, deliberately burnt the offending sheet to ashes in the open street, and then went his way. Hardly had the mendicant *sadhu* disappeared from the scene of his operations when flames broke out in the shop of the merchant who had affronted him. Realising at once that the calamity was the result of the *sadhu's* displeasure, the *khatri* merchant hurriedly despatched messengers in all directions to find the offended man, in order that he might propitiate him if possible; but the saint was not to be discovered anywhere, so the shop of the niggardly *bunneeah* and those of his immediate neighbours were all burnt down to the ground.

The person who kindly put me in possession of these interesting facts narrated to me also another story of a past generation, one likewise connected with Amritsar and well known to his own father, who, at the time to which it relates, was himself a dweller in that city.

A *sadhu*, as is not unusual with these gentlemen, entreated a *pansări* (druggist or herbalist) to give him the wherewithal to have a good smoke of his favourite charas. "I am on fire," pleaded the *sadhu*, "do give me a little charas to cool my tortured body." "Go and burn," was the shopkeeper's churlish reply. "No," responded the enraged *sadhu*, "let the fire seize *you*!" and he left the spot in anger. Within a minute of his departure the druggist found his store on fire, and, realising that this calamity was due to the holy *sadhu's* curse, made no vain attempt to combat the flames, but ran hurriedly after the saint in order to appease his wrath. He found the object of his search in a crowded thoroughfare, and, falling prone at his feet, entreated him to extinguish the flames he had caused. Promising never to refuse a *sadhu's* request again, the distressed *pansári* humbly begged the offended mendicant's pardon, adding, "Come, maharaj, let me give you the charas now." Mollified by the attentions of the druggist, the *sadhu* said to him, "Your shop will be burnt down—that is inevitable now; but as you have humbled yourself before me, and are sorry for your unkind treatment of a poor *sadhu*, you may go your way with the comforting assurance that the fire will redound to your advantage." Relieved of all anxiety by those gracious words, in which he placed the most implicit confidence, the druggist went back to his store and watched with a contented heart the fire doing its work of destruction—though, as the shop with its contents disappeared in the flames, he was sorely puzzled to imagine where his promised luck was to come from. However, the mystery was soon cleared up. On inspecting what little remained of the gutted premises, a mass of hot and almost molten silver was discovered, to the great joy of the *pansári*. How it came there was not difficult of explanation. It seems the druggist had a considerable quantity of solder in his store. This, during the intense heat of the conflagration, had been acted upon by some drug or combination of drugs also present there, with the happy result that the cheap solder had been transmuted into fine silver.

Not only trifling and temporary but even widespread and permanent troubles may be caused by the curse of an offended *sadhu*. To believers in these things it is a matter of common knowledge that the scanty water-supply in one of the cities of Upper India—Umballah, if I remember rightly—is the result of the curse of a wandering *faquir*. He had gone from house to house asking for a drop of water. No one had attended to his modest request. One, indeed, had said, by way of excuse, "I have only a little water for my own use." The *faquir*, knowing the statement to be quite untrue, became incensed and immediately uttered this malediction, "Little water shall you henceforth have in the wells of your city!" and the curse was duly fulfilled.

How very advantageous such stories must be to the wandering *sadhus* in their peregrinations, does not need to be pointed out.

Beneficent actions are also, though rarely, connected with *sadhus*. One case came under my own observation.

When in 1898 the bubonic plague made its appearance in the Jullundar district of the Punjab, and the precautionary measures of the sanitary authorities, much more than the fell disease itself, created a great excitement and anxiety amongst the people, a *sadhu* of the sect of the *yogis* came to Amritsar and established himself near a great tank outside the city. He let it be known, through his followers, that the object of his visit was to avert the dreaded pestilence, and to this end he called upon the religious and charitable to afford him the means of carrying out that most meritorious of actions, feasting the poor. An account of my visit to this worthy *yogi* will be found in a later chapter, but I may mention here that, so far as I know, the plague did not appear in Amritsar that year, though one doubtful and subsequently discredited case was reported to the officials.

The transmutation of metals, alluded to in the story about the herbalist on a previous page, is one of those mysterious subjects which still fascinate the Oriental mind. A learned Hindu related to me, in all good faith, the following experiences of one of his intimate friends and a *sadhu*-alchemist.

This friend, when a young man, was most anxious to become a *sadhu*, and attached himself to a Bairagi who had come from the solitudes of the Himalayas beyond Hurdwar and Rikhikesh. The *sadhu* seemed a very holy man, and the youth waited assiduously upon him. At last the *sadhu* noticed him so far as to hand him a piece of silver, giving him at the same time instructions to sell the bullion and buy what was necessary for their food. From time to time he intrusted the boy with bits of uncoined silver in this way, only requiring him to bring back, with the purchased food-stuffs, some copper coins. The regular supply of silver never failed, and at last the boy's curiosity was aroused to such a degree that he ventured to ask the *guru* where the treasure came from. The *sadhu* thus questioned smiled and said, "There is only one man in Hindustan who is my superior. I am a Rajah, but he, indeed, is a Maharajah. I can manufacture silver out of copper; but he can convert silver into gold."

The boy was all eagerness to learn this valuable art, with its glittering possibilities of future pleasures, but his ardour was rebuked by the *guru*, who told him he was not yet morally fit to be admitted to so great a secret—one indeed so fraught with mischief if intrusted to an unworthy man, that it had better be lost entirely than revealed to such a one.

The youth's humble and assiduous attentions to the *sadhu* did not flag, but never having been allowed to sleep in or near the master's abode, probably because it was in the hours of darkness that the transmutations were effected, he had to shift for himself in the town: and one unfortunate night, tempted by the meretricious charms of a loose woman, he committed a very grave indiscretion. When he presented himself next morning before the *sadhu*, he was promptly and peremptorily ordered to go away. It was useless to attempt any concealment from the omniscient *sadhu*, so the youth begged earnestly for forgiveness; but the *sadhu* spurned his unworthy disciple, and with his own hand set fire to the little hut which had afforded him temporary shelter and contained all his worldly possessions. Carrying his huge *chimpta* (tongs) in his hand, which had been sharpened along the edges so that it might make a very formidable weapon, the alchemist strode away towards the abode of the eternal snows. The *chela* ventured to follow him for a while, but the Bairagi, looking back, threatened him with his keen-edged tongs, and the fallen youth thought it prudent to retrace his steps, haunted more than ever with an unsatisfied craving to know the *great secret* of making silver out of baser metal.

A *granthi* [1] told me of an equally unfruitful experience he had with a gold-making Nirmali *sadhu*. This man made friends with the *granthi*, and insinuated himself into his confidence. He first cautiously hinted, and afterwards revealed, under the seal of secrecy, that he was acquainted with the occult art of transmuting metals. The *granthi*, notwithstanding his scriptural knowledge and semi-sacerdotal functions, was much excited at finding that his new friend was a potent alchemist, and he felt the bonds between them strengthen; for, after all, this sort of man is not to be picked up in a day's journey. The transmuter of metals seemed to live very well, yet occasionally borrowed money, showing special favour to the *granthi* in this matter; for he had no hesitation in placing himself under temporary obligations to his most confidential friend. And, of course, it was all right; he was a gold-maker, and, when his arrangements were matured, would resume his profitable business, and, better still, teach the *granthi* the secrets of his mysterious art. One day the *sadhu* showed the *granthi* a common bronze double *pice*, or half-anna coin, and then in his presence put it into a small furnace along with various leaves and roots he had collected. After an hour or so he produced from his crucible a golden fac-simile of the double *pice*. The *granthi*, not to be taken in even by his dear friend, asked to be allowed to have it tested by a goldsmith. Permission was given and acted upon, with the result that the experts in the bazaar pronounced it gold of the purest quality. The *granthi* was now agog to learn the important secret of gold-making, and many were the rupees he willingly lent the *sadhu*, in the hope that he would accept him as a pupil. But the saintly man of science suddenly and unexpectedly decamped.

"Alas!" said the *granthi* after he had narrated these

[1] One learned in the Scriptures of the *Sikh* sect.

circumstances to me, "I lost more than sixty rupees through that impostor. I have since learnt how he fooled me, but never a Nirmali *sadhu* has, since those days, had so much as a drop of water from my hand!"

Some thirty years ago, or thereabouts, Calcutta knew and took much interest in one Hassan Khan, who had the reputation of being a great wonder-worker, though I believe only in one particular line, and his story may be fitly recorded here, as it was through the favour and initiation of a Hindu *sadhu* that this Muhammadan acquired the peculiar and very remarkable powers attributed to him.

Several European friends of mine had been personally acquainted with Hassan Khan, and witnessed his performances in their own homes. It is directly from these gentlemen, and not from Indian sources, that I derived the details which I now reproduce.

Hassan Khan was not a professional wizard, nor even a performer, but he could be persuaded on occasion to display to a small circle his peculiar powers, and this without any pecuniary reward. For example, he would call upon any person present at such a meeting to ask for some ordinary wine, and on the particular one being named would request him to put his hand under the table, or maybe behind a door, and, lo! a bottle of the wished-for wine, with the label of some well-known Calcutta firm, would be thrust into the extended hand.

Similarly he would produce articles of food, such as biscuits or cakes, and cigars too, enough for the assembled company. On a certain occasion, so I was informed by one who was present, the supply of comestibles seemed to be exhausted. Several members seated round the table raised a laugh against Hassan Khan, and jeeringly challenged him to produce a bottle of champagne. Much agitated and stammering badly—he always had an impediment in his speech—Hassan Khan went into the verandah, and in angry tones commanded some unseen agent to bring the champagne at once. He had to repeat his orders two or three times, when, hurtling through the air, came the required bottle. It struck the magician on the chest with force, and, falling to the floor, broke into a thousand pieces.

"There," said Hassan Khan, much excited, "I have shown my power, but I have enraged my *djinn* by my importunities."

A European friend of mine happened to travel, quite casually, in a railway carriage with Hassan Khan, and, having some acquaintance with him, asked him to produce something to drink.

"Put your hand out of the window," said the Muslim, while the train was travelling along.

His request was complied with, and a bottle of excellent wine thrust into the outstretched hand rewarded this slight exertion.

Another of my friends, exceedingly anxious to learn the *modus operandi* of these strange performances, took a special interest in Hassan Khan, and with this important object in view cultivated his society. Driving on one occasion along with him in the bazaar, the wizard expressed a wish to alight at the shop of a money-changer. The carriage was stopped, and Hassan Khan, attended by his companion, asked the money-changer if he had any sovereigns. An affirmative answer being given, he requested that they should be produced, and, when they were brought out of the money-changer's strong box, Hassan Khan, after asking the price at which they might be purchased (for in those days their value had not been fixed by law), thoughtfully passed the gold coins through his fingers, saying he would call for them on the morrow, if he could not make a better bargain elsewhere. The following morning he went to the shop, attended as before by my friend—but only to learn that the sovereigns which he had seen and handled the day before had all mysteriously disappeared after being placed in the strong box. Hassan Khan affected to disbelieve the story, but, as he did so, slyly cast so significant a glance at his companion, that the latter prudently resolved never to be seen in such suspicious company again.

Yet this incident only put a keener edge upon Mr. ——'s curiosity, and he assiduously plied Hassan Khan with questions till he obtained from him the following story, for the sake of which, more than anything else, I have set forth in this narrative particulars which, if correctly reported, are seemingly quite incredible, and possibly not explicable by even the cleverest legerdemainists. However, not having witnessed the Muslim's strange performances myself, and not being a wizard, I leave the matter without further comment, to pass on to the *story* of how Hassan Khan acquired the wondrous powers with which he was credited.

"When I was a mere lad," said this remarkable man, "there came one day to my native village a gaunt *sadhu* with matted locks and altogether repulsive aspect. The boys crowded round him and mocked him, but I reproved their rudeness, telling them that they should respect a holy man, even though a Hindu. The *sadhu* observed me closely, and later on we met frequently, for he took up his abode in the village for some little time. On my part I seemed to be drawn towards the strange man, and visited him as often as I could. One day he offered to confer on me an important secret power, if I would follow his instructions faithfully and implicitly. I promised to do whatever might be required of me, and under the *sadhu's* directions commenced a system of discipline with fasting which lasted many, perhaps forty, days. My instructor taught me to repeat many mystic spells and incantations, and, after imposing a very strict fast, commanded me to enter a dark cavern in the hillside and tell him what I saw there. With much trepidation I obeyed his behests, and returned with the information that the only thing visible to me in the gloom was a huge flaming eye. 'That is well — success has been achieved,' was the *sadhu's* remark, and I began wondering what power I had acquired. Pointing to some stones lying about, the *sadhu* made me make a particular mystical sign upon each one. I did so. 'Now go home,' said my mentor, 'shut the door of your room, and command your *familiar* to bring these stones to you.' Away I went, in a state of nervous excitement, and, locking myself in my chamber, commanded the unseen *djinn* to bring those stones to me at once. Hardly had my mandate been uttered, when, to my amazement and secret terror, the stones lay at my feet. I went back and told the *sadhu* of my success. 'Now,' he said, 'you have a power which you can exercise over everything upon which you can make the mystical sign I have taught you, but use your power with discretion, for my gift is qualified by the fact that, do what you will, the things, whatever they may be, acquired through your *familiar* spirit, cannot be accumulated by you, but must soon pass out of your hands.' And the *sadhu's* words have been verified in my life, and his gift has not been an unmixed blessing, for my *djinn* resents my power, and has often tried to harm me; but happily his time is not yet come."

This explanation brings out very clearly the high esteem in which the occult powers of the *sadhus* are still held even by Muslims, since a follower of Islam could be found to acknowledge, voluntarily, that his own remarkable thaumaturgic abilities were conferred upon him by a Hindu religious mendicant.

But the Indian Muhammadan, as becomes a member of a once dominant race, usually loves to claim superiority even on this ground.

A Mussulman, speaking to me on the subject, admitted that the Hindu *sadhus*, by their austerities and peculiar practices, acquire a strange mastery over the forces of nature. "But," said he, "they are never able to enter *the Divine Presence*, unless by the favour of a *faquir*." Persons well acquainted with such matters had told him that on one occasion a *sadhu* flying through the air recognised, by the aroma which filled the atmosphere, the proximity of some great *faquir*. He stayed his flight, alighted on the ground, but was unable to approach the Muslim saint, about whom was diffused, although invisible, the glory of the Almighty. The *sadhu* sent word to the *faquir* that he would like to meet him, but that he could not pass beyond the threshold of the *baithak*, or saloon where visitors were received, for he perceived that God Himself was there.

"Come!" said the *faquir* confidently, and under his protection the *sadhu* was able to approach. When the two ascetics met, the Muslim recognised in his visitor a worthy kindred spirit, and imparted to him freely the grace of God which he (the *sadhu*) had not been able to acquire by all his penances and ceremonies.

There is a widespread belief that when the *faquir* is *mast* (mad, or in an ecstatic condition) he is under the influence of the Divine Spirit, and that what he then gives utterance to is of the greatest significance. Very strange, indeed, are some of the practices of which this belief has been the parent. When, as is usual, the *mast faquir* is reticent and will not speak the word that is wanted of him, one inquirer will strive to gain his favour by patient service and constant attendance, while another, more impulsive and imperious, will try to *bully* the good man to answer his questions. It came to my knowledge that a native police constable went to a well-known *faquir* to browbeat him into promising something which he wanted; but the *faquir* would not be hectored, so the enraged constable, accustomed to take the law into his own hands, struck the holy man a blow with a stout stick. The *faquir*, thus assaulted, only said, "You are a *zalim* !" (a tyrant, an oppressor), and not another word. On the next day the constable, to his great joy, was promoted to the grade of Deputy Inspector of Police. He came without delay to pay his respects to the *faquir*, and, on reaching the saint, fell at his feet and placed his turban on the ground—a mark of the greatest deference and humility.

"What have you come for ?" asked the *faquir*.

"To thank you, sir, for what you have done for me. By your favour I have been appointed Deputy Inspector of Police."

"Oh," said the laughing *faquir*, not without a suspicion of irony, "I see ! I called you a *zalim*, and you have got that position conferred on you officially."

"Even so," responded the happy officer.

This story and the one preceding it, far-fetched and trivial though they be, throw a sidelight on the ideas of Indian Muslims, and may therefore have some interest for students of Indian life.

Between the marvels wrought by the ancient Hindu

sages, as recorded in the old books, and those attributed to their modern representatives, there is, as the reader will doubtless have noticed, an immeasurable difference, with a sad falling off. But, as in mediæval Europe, the air in India is full of marvels and mysteries, and, if we may believe Hindu apologists, there still live, even in this sinful age, very potent wonder-working *sadhus*, only they are not to be met with in bazaars and the ordinary haunts of men, but where Madame Blavatsky discovered her elusive Koot Hoomi and other *mahatmas*,[1] in the lone solitudes of mysterious Tibet, or the grim snow-fastnesses of the unexplored Himalayas. However, since exhibitions of miraculous powers are necessarily of rare occurrence in these degenerate times, the abilities of many *sadhus* are displayed in less striking ways: for example, as physicians administering, to the sick, drugs and simples of which they have acquired a knowledge in their wanderings, or had solemnly communicated to them by perhaps a dying *guru*. Many remarkable cures are justly attributed to *sadhus*, but they make a mystery of their knowledge, and jealously guard their therapeutic secrets from the common herd. Sometimes their practice is connected with ailments and weaknesses which call for the exhibition of love-philtres and a resort to spells calculated to influence a cold, impassive heart. In such cases, no doubt, the *sadhu's* skill can easily command a considerable pecuniary reward.

Many religious mendicants earn a meal or a penny by disclosing, as fortune-tellers, palmists, and interpreters of dreams, the hidden things of the future. Others astonish the world by acrobatic feats—as the following extract from the Allahabad *Pioneer* will show:—

"A wonderful *faquir* was in view in the main street, who all the time he says his prayers goes through acrobatic performances that would earn him a fortune in England.

[1] "*Mahatman* means literally great-souled, then high-minded, noble, and all the rest. It is often used simply as a complimentary term, much as we use reverend or honourable, but it has also been accepted as a technical term, applied to a class of men who in the ancient language of India are well known to us by their name of *Samnyâsin*."—Professor Max Müller, *Life and Sayings of Ramakrishna*, pp. 2, 3.

As we approached he was standing on one leg with the other curled round his waist; in another second he was on his hands, head downwards, and his legs round his neck; when we left him he was tied up in something resembling a reef knot and clove hitch combined."[1]

One of these religious posturists, named Bava Lachman Das, was induced a few years ago to come across the ocean to exhibit himself at the Westminster Aquarium to admiring thousands. The man and the very strange attitudes he could assume form the subject of a well-illustrated article in the *Strand Magazine* for February 1897.

[1] From "A March through the Cow-rioting Districts," *Pioneer* (Allahabad), 7th February 1894.

CHAPTER V

SOME GLIMPSES OF SADHUS IN INDIAN FICTION

Eight Stories from famous Sanskrit Dramas and other Sources: (1) Sakoontala; (2) Malati and Madhava; (3) Disillusionment; (4) The horned Rishi; (5) The Lost Son restored; (6) A Kind-hearted Lady; (7) The Father duped; (8) Woman's Cunning.

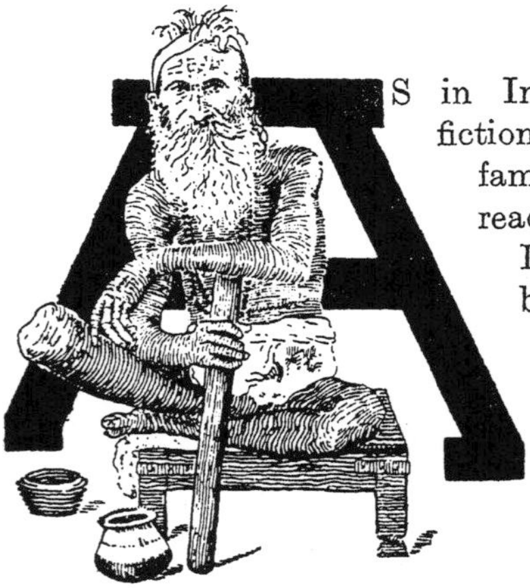

AS in Indian life, so in Indian fiction, *sadhus* and *faquirs* are familiar forms. It has already been shown (Chap. II.) how largely *sadhus* bulk in the sacred literature of the Hindus,—epics, Puranas, etc.,—but I shall now draw upon secular, or I should perhaps say less sacred, sources for pictures of the saints of the Indian world. The following eight stories, in which *sadhus* and pseudo-*sadhus* figure prominently, will serve my purpose, while at the same time affording some interesting glimpses of the inner world of Hindu ideas and sentiments.

The celebrated story entitled Sakoontala, or the Lost Ring, may come first on account of its intrinsic charm and its being chronologically the earliest of those selected, together with the fact that its very atmosphere is surcharged with sentiments of peaceful retirement and mild asceticism.

GLIMPSES OF SADHUS IN INDIAN FICTION

I. The Story of Sakoontala, or the Lost Ring, by Kalidasa.[1]

From the Ramayana we learn, as already stated in Chap. II., that there was once a Kshatriya king named Visvamitra, who, for the purpose of overcoming a famous Brahman sage, Vasishta, with whom he had come into unequal conflict, underwent, for thousands of years, the most terrible austerities, which eventually led to the unprecedented honour of his advancement to the Brahmanical caste. While the king was engaged in the rigours of his self-imposed tortures, the god Indra became jealous of his increasing power, and sent a lovely nymph of heaven named Menaka to distract his meditations and to seduce him from his vows. Visvamitra, unable to resist her allurements, had the beautiful temptress to share his hermitage for many years.

According to the great Hindu dramatist Kalidasa,[2] the result of this union was a daughter, Sakoontala, the heroine of his now world-famous play. The girl was reared in a picturesque and delightful hermitage, or colony of hermits, under the guardianship of Kanwa, the chief of the anchorites. In this retired spot Dushyanta, of the lineage of the renowned Purus, king of India, when out on one of his frequent hunting expeditions, discovered Sakoontala, now grown into a lovely graceful maiden in her early prime. Although the king had many royal consorts, he was large-hearted enough to fall desperately in love with the fair recluse when he met her with two girl-companions, Priyamvada and Anasuya, under the most charming and opportune circumstances; for Sakoontala at the moment was in trouble from the too aggressive and persistent attentions of an angry bee whom she had disturbed amongst the flowers she was gathering. With the maiden too it was a case of love at first sight.

[1] *Sakoontala, or the Lost Ring*, an Indian drama, translated into English prose and verse from the Sanskrit of Kalidasa by Monier Williams, M.A. (Hertford, 1855).

[2] Kalidasa was one of the "Nine Gems" of the court of Vikramaditya, a famous king, who, according to the most recent reckonings or guesses of European chronologists, lived in the sixth century of the Christian era.

Both victims to Kama's darts suffered badly from love-fever, as their emaciated forms only too clearly and too quickly evinced. Through the affectionate, if officious, interference of Priyamvada and Anasuya, a pair of delightful little schemers, it came about quite casually that the lovers were by mutual confessions of affection relieved from all the haunting doubts that had till then disturbed their susceptible hearts.

It would seem that, while the hermit colony was under the control of a chief or abbot, there was also a holy matron there, named Gautami, who had especial charge of the women and girls of this rural settlement. But, perhaps because of her reverence for royalty, her watchfulness seems to have been at fault in the present case, for very soon, by mutual consent, quite secretly and without ceremonies or formalities of any sort, the king and Sakoontala were united in wedlock "by the form of marriage prevalent among Indra's celestial musicians." The king, after a brief honeymoon, returned to his capital (Hastinapur), leaving his new wife with her friends in the hermitage.

Naturally, Sakoontala was much depressed at this early separation from her lord, and, while lost in absent-minded reverie near her cottage, no less a person than the great sage Durvasas arrived to claim the usual hospitality. Apparently, Sakoontala did not notice his coming, an omission which so incensed the affronted and irascible sage that he vented his angry feelings in this terrible curse—

"Woe to thee, maiden, for daring to slight a guest like me!
Shall I stand here unwelcomed; even I,
A very mine of penitential merit,
Worthy of all respect? Shalt thou, rash maid,
Thus set at nought the ever sacred ties
Of hospitality? and fix thy thoughts
Upon the cherished object of thy love,
While I am present? Thus I curse thee, then—
He, even he of whom thou thinkest, he
Shall think no more of thee, nor in his heart
Retain thy image. Vainly shalt thou strive
To waken his remembrance of the past;
He shall disown thee, even as the sot,
Roused from his midnight drunkenness, denies
The words he uttered in his revellings."

Sakoontala, too deeply absorbed in her own thoughts, did not even hear the sage's malediction; but her shrewd and ever-watchful girl-friends did, and, fearful of the consequences, pleaded with the terrible Durvasas to pardon the young and inexperienced offender. Their entreaties so far mollified him that he condescended to say—

"My word must not be falsified, but at the sight of the ring of recognition the spell shall cease."

Having said this, he disappeared. The girls were reassured by his words, recalling to mind the fact that when taking his departure from the hermitage the king had placed on Sakoontala's finger a ring with his own name engraved upon it.

"She has therefore," as Anasuya sagely said, "a remedy for her misfortune at her own command."

However, with wonderful reticence the two girls kept from their dear friend all knowledge both of Durvasas' curse and the extent to which he had been prevailed upon to modify it.

While these incidents were taking place, Kanwa, Sakoontala's foster-father, and chief of the hermits, was away from home, having "gone to Soma-tirtha to propitiate Destiny, which threatened his daughter with some calamity."

When Kanwa returned and learned what had happened during his absence he fully approved of the marriage which had been consummated, and, deeming it the proper course, sent Sakoontala, escorted by some hermits, to join her royal husband. As became a saint, Kanwa gave his foster-child much good advice, including such rules of life as the following—

> "Honour thy betters, ever be respectful
> To those above thee; and should others share
> Thy husband's love, ne'er yield thyself a prey
> To jealousy; but ever be a friend,
> A loving friend, to those who rival thee
> In his affections."

As Sakoontala took a most touching farewell of the hermitage where she had passed the springtime of her days, those dear companions of her girlhood, Priyamvada and Anasuya, mindful of Durvasas' curse, whispered to her that should the king, by any chance, have forgotten her, she should on no account fail to produce the ring, his parting present to her.

Attended by a few hermits, Sakoontala proceeded to her husband's capital and was admitted to his presence; but, in fulfilment of Durvasas' malison, the king had lost all recollection of her, and, conscientious man that he was, declined to receive her, though he was not insensible to the personal charms of the beautiful woman who stood before him claiming to be his wife. Indignant at his conduct, one of the hermits thus addressed the king in lofty strain—

"Beware!
Beware how thou insult the holy sage!
Remember how he generously allowed
Thy secret union with his foster-child:
And how, when thou did'st rob him of his treasure,
He sought to furnish the excuse, when rather
He should have cursed thee for a ravisher."

But Dushyanta's memory was really clouded, and he would neither acknowledge nor receive Sakoontala. In her great sorrow and deep humiliation the poor girl referred to the signet ring her royal lover had given her; but, on being asked to produce it, discovered, to her inexpressible dismay and the king's ill-concealed amusement, that it was lost.

The hermits who had accompanied Sakoontala to the king's presence now refused to conduct her back to the hermitage; while, on the other hand, the virtuous king, who had noticed her condition, would not be guilty of receiving into his house one who was evidently the wife of another man.

In this most painful dilemma the king's domestic priest generously offered to give the lady an asylum in his own house until the birth of her child. Sakoontala while being led away bewailed her cruel fate,

"When suddenly a shining apparition
In female shape descended from the skies,
Near the nymph's pool, and bore her up to heaven."

It was the girl's mother, the celestial nymph Menaka, who had come to the rescue of her child.

Of course the ring was found in due course, and on beholding it the king at once recovered his memory of the events connected with his happy courtship of Sakoontala in the flowery glades of her foster-father's hermitage. Between the feelings of passionate love now reawakened in his heart and the bitterest remorse for his cruel treatment of his now lost darling he was beside himself with grief. His mental torment lasted for years, till at length, in their own good time, the gods kindly interposed. On the pretext of requiring Dushyanta's help against a troublesome race of giants, Indra's charioteer waited on him and took him away through the air in a celestial car. After being received by the ruler of heaven, he was carried to "Golden Peak," the abode of the attendants of the God of Wealth, where

> "Kasyapa,
> With Aditi his wife, in calm seclusion,
> Does holy penance for the good of mortals."

The king asks his guide—

> "In which direction, Matali, is Kasyapa's sacred retreat?"

To which the charioteer, pointing with his hand, replies—

> "Where stands yon anchorite towards the orb
> Of the meridian sun, immovable
> As a tree's stem, his body half concealed
> By a huge ant-hill. Round about his breast
> No sacred cord is twined, but in its stead
> A hideous serpent's skin. In place of necklace,
> The tendrils of a withered creeper chafe
> His wasted neck. His matted hair depends
> In thick entanglement about his shoulders,
> And birds construct their nests within its folds."

In this sacred region of quiet hermitages, "where the holiest sages devote themselves to penitential rites," and where mortals, unless favoured by the higher powers, could never obtain admission, King Dushyanta was designedly brought into contact with his own son, a daring wayward infant, who, as becomes a scion of Purus' famous race, loves to play, not with timid pets, but with lusty young lions. The king feels himself strangely drawn towards the fearless handsome child, and after a little while, in accordance with the will of the gods, meets Sakoontala herself arrayed in the garb of a widow. To her he now explains his strange repudiation of her on that memorable day when she sought his protection at Hastinapur. He obtains her forgiveness, and with the permission and blessing of Kasyapa reascends the car of Indra, taking his wife and son also, to return to his own capital. The pious king leaves "Golden Peak," breathing the characteristically Hindu prayer—

> "And may the purple self-existent god,
> Whose vital energy pervades all space,
> From future transmigrations save my soul."

How saturated with the feeling of peaceful asceticism this charming drama is, does not need to be pointed out; yet I may recall to the reader's memory that it was the terror of the gods at Visvamitra's dreadful austerities that led to the temptation of the ascetic and the birth of the heroine, whose early years were passed blamelessly amidst a quiet restful group of well-ordered hermitages, a sort of pastoral monastery under an easy tolerant rule. The heroine's misfortunes were the result of the curse pronounced by an affronted ascetic, and, when she is rejected by the king, it is to the haven of a celestial hermitage that she is translated from Dushyanta's capital.

Throughout the poem the undoubted power of the ascetic and the unquestioned dignity and importance of his calling are amply recognised.

II. Malati and Madhava.[1]

In Bhavabhuti's famous drama, *Malati and Madhava*, written probably in the eighth century A.D., we have a glimpse of one aspect of Indian asceticism which still has a great and permanent fascination for the Hindus, viz. the

[1] *Select Specimens of the Theatre of the Hindus*, translated from the original Sanskrit by Horace Hayman Wilson, vol. ii. (Calcutta, 1827).

exercise of superhuman power acquired by ascetic practices. If only to illustrate this important point, the plot of Bhavabhuti's charming drama may be briefly sketched in this place.

The curtain rises upon Kamandaki revealing to her disciple Avalokita her desire to bring about a union between Madhava and Malati. These two, as mere infants, were, by a solemn but secret compact, destined for one another by their parents. The projected arrangement was never revealed to the parties most interested; and now a difficulty arose, for the king's favourite, an old and ugly fellow named Nandana, had applied to his royal master for the hand of Malati, and the sovereign had demanded her of her father. To frustrate this project, without giving offence to his majesty the king, Madhava's father enlisted the services of Kamandaki, priestess of Buddha, nurse of Malati and preceptress of Madhava. The plan was to bring about a purely love affair between the young people, and effect a clandestine marriage without the direct interposition of the parents, and to all appearance without their knowledge. To this end it was artfully contrived to make opportunities for the young people to see each other; and, to help in carrying out the plot, Kamandaki bethinks her of a former pupil of hers, one Sandamini, residing on Mount Sri Parvata,

> "——where, won by desperate penances,
> Power more than earthly waits upon her will."

The priestess and her disciples, though themselves vowed to celibacy, take an ardent and truly feminine interest in bringing about the desired result. The action of the play extends over only a few days, but they are brimful of incident.

In pursuance of the plot, it is contrived that Malati should see Madhava from her window. Of course she falls desperately in love with him, and solaces herself by drawing a likeness of him. This her foster-sister, who is in the plot, cleverly makes over to Mandarika, the servant of the convent (*vehara dasi*), who naturally transfers it to the hands of her own lover Kalahansa, Madhava's servant.

Thus one step is gained. Now, by the advice of one of the female disciples of the priestess, Madhava goes to Kamadeva's temple, where he sees Malati in all her virgin beauty, and straightway falls in love with her. Her appearance shows unmistakably that she is herself in love with some fortunate youth or other; but her female attendants, when they cast eyes on Madhava, laughing and whispering amongst themselves, seemed to say—

> "The Fates have favoured us,
> Lady—behold him there!"

The lady on her part did not fail to reveal her admiration and her feelings towards the young man by expressive glances, mute yet eloquent. As she moved away with her train of attendants, one of them, her foster-sister Lavangika, on pretence of admiring the garland of flowers Madhava was wearing, let him know the name and rank of the lady he had been admiring so passionately. At the maid's request, he presented the garland to Lavangika for the acceptance of her fair mistress.

Madhava relates these events to his friend Makaranda, and, while he is doing so, Kalahansa approaches and shows them the portrait of Madhava painted by Malati.

At Makaranda's suggestion, Madhava now draws a portrait of his inamorata. Mandarika, the *vehara dasi*, appears opportunely on the scene, pretending to be in search of the picture which Kalahansa had carried off, and is given, instead of it, the portrait of Malati just drawn by her ardent lover. Thus, through the instrumentality of Lavangika and the others, the hero and heroine fall in love with one another, and also have their mutual passion revealed each to the other.

Thus far all goes well; but the proverbial lovers' troubles have infallibly to come, the king having duly arranged, with the formal consent of her father, to give Malati in marriage to Nandana without delay.

To frustrate the accomplishment of this undesired union, Kamandaki and her disciples insidiously instil into Malati's mind feelings of revolt against her father, and artfully suggest that Sakoontala and other ladies in the past had selected their own husbands. The conspirators also bring about a meeting, at which Madhava makes a personal declaration, offering his lady-love his heart and life, an offering which Lavangika accepts for her bashful friend, saying—

> "I answer for my friend—she deems the gifts
> Deserving her acceptance."

Besides the king's desire to confer the hand of Malati upon his own favourite, there were other and even more serious dangers threatening the accomplishment of the union of the two lovers. There was

> "——a skull-bearing seer, Aghora Ghanta,
> A wandering mendicant, but dwelling now
> Amidst the neighbouring forest,"

who, for the fulfilment of a powerful rite which would terminate all his toils, had decided, in accordance with a solemn vow, to sacrifice to the goddess Chaumandra "the gem of womankind."

To fulfil this dreadful object, he had enlisted the services of his disciple Kapala Kundala, herself a priestess of Chaumandra. This priestess of the dread goddess is described as "freed from all perishable bonds," and she obviously possessed wonderful powers, for she first appears upon the scene riding through the air in a heavenly car, dressed in a hideous garb and girdled with human skulls. The temple of Chaumandra stood alongside a cremation ground, into which Madhava had gone in the dead of night with a lump of human flesh in his hand to win the favour, or compel the assistance, of the goblins who infested that gruesome spot. While pursuing his object a cry of distress comes to him from within the temple, and, recognising with horror the voice of Malati, he hurries thither.

Inside the temple, dressed in scarlet and adorned with a garland, stands Malati, the destined sacrifice, and round about her circles Aghora Ghanta with quick steps, addressing the dread goddess in such prescribed terms of praise as would be acceptable to her. Kapala Kundala was in attendance, and at the proper moment, facing the trembling victim, said—

> "Fair maid,
> Think upon him whom thou in life hast loved,
> For pitiless death is near thee."

But, before Aghora Ghanta's sword could fall upon the unhappy girl, her lover had sprung to her side and forcibly prevented the bloody rite. Meanwhile, by the command of Kamandaki, the aged priestess of Buddha, and quite unconnected with Madhava's interposition, the fane was surrounded, and the exciting temple scene comes to a close with an unfinished fight between Aghora Ghanta and Madhava. However, we learn incidentally, in the next act, that the result of this conflict was fatal to the wandering mendicant, and we find Kapala Kundala vowing vengeance against Madhava for the death of her *venerable guru*.[1]

The artful resources of Kamandaki are not exhausted. Malati, dressed for her marriage with Nandana, the king's favourite, is conducted in state to a temple, where, unknown to her, Madhava and his friend Makaranda are concealed. The girl is in despair, and, wishing to take her own life, reveals her purpose to Lavangika and asks her to consent. As the fair and distracted lady kneels to her, Lavangika moves away, and Madhava takes her place. The deception is presently detected, and a pretty love scene results. The priestess Kamandaki now steps up, and, interposing as the instrument of Fate and Love, confers Malati upon her enamoured swain. Makaranda dresses up in the bride's attire and personates Malati. The lovers are then bid to proceed quickly to the garden of the sanctuary, where, in anticipation of events, the necessary provision had already been made for the performance of their bridal ceremonies.

Makaranda plays his part as a woman so well that he quite deceives Nandana, but, when installed as his *bride*, handles the astonished bridegroom so severely that he leaves the house in a rage. Nandana's sister Madayantika comes to remonstrate with her dear friend upon her unseemly conduct, but to her astonishment, and secret delight, finds in the supposed Malati the youth who had,

[1] That Aghora Ghanta and his disciple should have failed in their object, after propitiating the goddess as they did, is attributed by the Hindu commentator either to their wickedness or their inaccurate pronunciation of some part of the ritual.—Note to p. 60 of Professor Wilson's translation.

at the risk of his life, gallantly rescued her from a ferocious tiger. They were mutually in love these two, and their strange meeting in Nandana's palace ends in an elopement—the lovers making for the place to which Madhava and Malati had already gone. Fate, however, had yet more adventures in store for them. On the way they were stopped by the town guard. Makaranda singly keeps the guard in check while his bride and attendants get away. On learning the state of affairs, Madhava hurries off to help his friend. Malati thoughtfully despatches a couple of attendants to apprise Kamandaki of the course of events, and directs Lavangika to overtake her lord and implore him to shun all needless danger. Lavangika does not return as quickly as Malati could wish, and after a while the bride, unable to bear the absence of her lord, follows him. She is met, alone and unprotected, by her arch-enemy Kapala Kundala. Malati, terrified, instinctively cries in an undertone, "Ah! husband!" To which the cruel priestess of Chaumandra replies tauntingly—

> "Yes, call upon him.
> Where is your love—the murderer of the pious,
> The youthful paramour of wanton girls?
> Let him—your husband—save you, if he can.
> Bird of the wild, that tremblest to behold
> The hovering hawk—what canst thou hope, long marked
> My prey? I bear thee with me to Sri Parvata,
> There to consign thee to a painful death,
> Torn piecemeal—victim of my just revenge."

With these taunting and menacing words the ruthless priestess carried Malati off.

While this abduction was taking place, the two heroes who had routed the town guard were nevertheless taken before the king, charged with having borne away the Minister's daughter.

The king, however, being rather pleased at the prowess displayed by the two young men, treated the matter lightly, and the offenders were set at liberty, to find on their return that Malati had disappeared mysteriously.

Overwhelmed by his loss, Madhava wanders away to the mountains in a fit of despair which knows no consolation, accompanied by his ever-faithful friend Makaranda.

On the breezy mountains he indulges his grief till both reason and life are threatened. Makaranda is so deeply moved by his companion's sad fate and desperate condition that he distractedly contemplates suicide, and is in the very act of precipitating himself from the rocks when he is arrested by Sandamini. In reply to his inquiry who she might be, Sandamini tells him that she is a *yogini*, "the mistress of supernal power," and she shows him the garland which Malati had been wearing when she disappeared. A few minutes later Madhava learns from her that Malati had been carried off by Kapala Kundala, that she still lived, and that for her protection Sandamini would exert

> "The powerful knowledge which mystic rites and prayers,
> Devout observance, and a sainted teacher
> Had armed her with."

As a matter of fact, she had actually rescued the girl from the vengeful hands of her inveterate enemy.

Calling upon Madhava to accompany her, they both instantly disappeared. A little later, at a most critical moment, when Malati's father was about to commit suicide on a funeral pyre on account of her supposed death, Sandamini, the wonder-working *yogini*, conveyed the lovers to their friends, and, by securing the consent of the king and their respective parents to the union of Madhava and Malati, brings about a happy denouement.

Many are the reflections which this charming drama awakens. We find all the usual devices of the modern European romancers resorted to in the plots and counter-plots of this old Hindu play. We have the hero and heroine driven by untoward circumstances and fiendish conspiracies to the very brink of despair, and then opportunely rescued just in time to obviate the most serious consequences. Scarcely do we rejoice with them in their safety and happiness, when they are involved in new and even more serious troubles than before; yet we feel confident that all will end well, and our expectations are not disappointed. So far we are on familiar ground. But as we watch the drama unfolded we are always conscious that the framework of society and the conditions and modes of social intercourse depicted in the play, as well as the religious sentiments pervading it, are alien to the West. The weird scenes in the cemetery at night and in the temple hard by are essentially and characteristically Indian, and so also are the thaumaturgies of the wandering mendicant, the priestesses, and the *yogini*, who have acquired their superhuman power only through the practice of severe austerities.

III. Disillusionment.

In a certain village, within the dominions of a famous Rajah, there lived a poor Brahman woman with her only child, a little boy of tender years. By the labour of her hands, particularly by grinding corn for her neighbours, the widow earned a bare subsistence for herself and her son. Of course their fare was of the simplest and coarsest kind.

One day a prosperous villager who was celebrating a happy domestic event gave the Brahman boy a hearty meal of rice cooked in milk and sweetened with sugar, luxuries to which, till that time, the child had been a stranger. Next day, when his usual cake of coarse brown bread was offered to him, the boy, mindful of the dainties of the previous day, refused to eat it. He wanted milk and rice and sugar!

"That," said his mother, "is more than I can give you. Devi alone can gratify your wishes."

Now, not far from where these indigent people lived there stood a temple of Devi, but in so ruined and neglected a condition that no one visited it. Its walls were rent from top to bottom, and even Devi's image was cracked and mutilated.

To this dilapidated shrine repaired the Brahman boy, and prayed the presiding goddess to grant him rice and milk for his meals. For four days he lay in the temple, refusing to partake of the food offered him by his mother. At last, taking compassion on the infant suppliant, the eight-armed goddess appeared before him in person and asked what favour he sought.

"Only rice and milk every day," replied the child.

"You shall have it," responded the benign goddess, "but ask for something more important than that."

The little Brahman, the horizon of whose ideas was extremely limited, had no other request to prefer, so Devi graciously handed him an *amritphal* or fruit conferring immortality.

The widow, deeming this gift much too good for one in their humble circumstances, advised her boy to present it to the Rajah, who would doubtless make such a pecuniary return for it as would enable them to live the remainder of their lives in peace and comfort. Ushered into the king's presence, the child handed him the wonderful fruit and told the story concerning it.

After accepting the offering and rewarding the little donor in a suitable manner, the Rajah put the wonderful fruit aside, thinking in his heart that the cares of his position were too great to make it worth while to prolong his life indefinitely, but he decided mentally that his beloved Rani should be presented with the *amritphal*, and having eaten it enjoy perpetual youth. To her, therefore, he gave the fruit that same day; but she, consumed with love for a certain *darogah*, secretly made it over to that officer. Though he was the paramour of the Rani, this *darogah* really loved a courtesan in the town, and that same night she was made the possessor of the Devi's gift.

To prolong her sinful life did not seem a very inviting prospect to this Rahab, and thinking over the matter she arrived at the conclusion that the Rajah, who was a kind and just ruler, and the father of his people, would be the most worthy recipient of such an important gift as a fruit of immortality; so, in the morning, she carried it to his majesty and laid it respectfully at his feet.

"Where did you get this?" inquired the astonished Rajah, recognising the strange fruit which was raised in no terrestrial orchard.

"From the *darogah* of the horses," was the courtesan's reluctant reply.

In an instant the whole painful truth flashed upon the disillusioned king.

"What," mused he, "is human happiness or kingly dignity, when my Rani can thus betray my honour, and when her plebeian paramour can prefer the favours of a courtesan to those of a queen!"

Overwhelmed by these bitter reflections upon that well-worn theme "all is vanity," the good king abandoned his throne, and, turning his back upon the world, became a *sadhu*;[1] and this step of his is the reason why the present story appears here, affording as it does a characteristically Hindu illustration of a sentiment—cruel disillusionment—which probably more than any other has driven men in all countries to join the ranks of the discontented contemners of the world's hollow pleasures.

IV. The Horned Rishi.[2]

There was once a *sadhu* named Shringhi Rikh (having horns). He lived in a dense forest, worshipping God and knowing nothing of the life of towns and villages, or of the ways of men. In this manner the solitary hermit passed many years, till at length a dire famine visited the land. When this calamity came, the king naturally asked his *vazir* (prime minister) what was to be done to alleviate the sufferings of his people, and that high officer prudently advised that the Brahmans should be formally consulted with a view to the adoption of some suitable course of action.

They were accordingly sent for by the king, and requested to say how the famine was to be stayed, and how the much-needed rain was to be obtained to fertilise the thirsty fields.

The wise Brahmans, having considered the matter, replied that the famine was not a judgment from Heaven due to any sins committed by the king himself, and that the earth would certainly be blessed with rain if the "horned *rishi*" who dwelt in the forest could by any means

[1] Substantially the same story, but in a somewhat different form, is told in the Baital Pachisi.

[2] This and the four following stories are from the Granth of Guru Govind Singh, which contains no less than four hundred and four tales respecting the *wiles of women*.

be induced to take up his abode in the city, for so was it written in the holy *Shastras*.

The Rajah, losing no time, sent messengers to induce the ascetic to come to his capital; but the horned saint heeded them not, so the sovereign went in person to the anchorite; but even he could not prevail upon Shringhi Rikh to leave his forest-home and the asceticisms in which he was engaged.

In this difficult crisis, a harlot, gaudily dressed and with her lips reddened with the *pân* she was eating, presented herself before the Rajah and said to him jauntily—

"O king, I will bring Shringhi Rikh to you, on condition that when I do so you will give me one half of your kingdom. If you agree to this I shall make the saint shave off his matted locks and put on a turban, and, having quite subdued him, I shall lead him into your majesty's presence," adding confidently, "With my beauty I can do anything I like."

The worthy Rajah, acting for the benefit of his lieges, accepted these extravagant conditions, and the fair wanton went off to the jungles where the *sadhu* lived. Taking with her a party of beautiful women arrayed in finery and dressed to perfection, she prepared a habitation for herself in the woods, and on the trees around her temporary abode she hung *ludoos* [1] and other delicacies, and, when all her arrangements were complete, commenced singing to the dulcet accompaniment of musical instruments.

The *rishi*, seeing these unaccustomed sights, and hearing sweet sounds, the like of which had never before reached his ears, became astonished, and in his perplexity came to the conclusion that they must be due to visitants from another world. Feeling hungry, he ventured to pluck some of the novel fruits (*ludoos*) he discovered growing on the trees near by. He found them deliciously sweet and quite to his taste, and, wondering how such "fruits" had appeared there, attributed them to the god Indra.

"Perhaps," soliloquised the *sadhu*, "the god has been graciously pleased with my austerities and has come down in person to witness them."

[1] A *ludoo* is a well-known Indian sweetmeat.

While thus reflecting, he noticed a woman beautifully dressed and decked with costly jewellery standing a little way off. So lovely was she that the mere sight of her removed all his cares. He wondered who she could possibly be, and asked himself, "From what distant world is this enchanting visitant?"

Suspending his austerities, he approached the woman, and, filled with wonder, sat down near her; then growing bolder went up to her, and, bowing low, said to her—

"Tell me, who art thou? Art thou the consort of Shiv-ji or of Vishnu? Tell me."

She said, "I am not a goddess, but the wife of Oodaluk *rishi*. Hearing of you—for your fame has spread far and wide—I have come to make you my husband."

Having thus spoken, she lavished flatteries upon him, and in a short time, by exercising her seductive charms upon the recluse, she subdued him to her purpose, and before long brought him away, a willing captive, to the nearest village. When she conducted Shringhi Rikh into the Rajah's domains the rain began to fall, as the Brahmans had predicted, and the hearts of the people rejoiced greatly.

The *rishi* was then married to one of the Rajah's daughters, and continued to live in his father-in-law's territories, which for a long time derived the greatest benefit and good fortune from his presence. However, it came to pass that eventually his residence in the land caused an excess of rain, and it was thought desirable to lure him back to his old mode of life. So the services of the courtesan were once again called into requisition, and she successfully persuaded the *sadhu* to return to his former woodland haunts, where he resumed his long-interrupted austerities.[1]

[1] Faith in the help of saintly *sadhus* during seasons of drought is not extinct amongst the Hindus even of our own times.

"With the progress of the season the area of crop failure in India is becoming narrowed and defined. Northern Bombay, some of the native States in Central India and Rajputana, with adjoining portions of the Punjab, are involved, though it is still doubtful whether the loss of both harvests will be complete over very considerable tracts. There are sufficient food stocks in the country, and rising prices will secure economy in their consumption. Relief measures are ready. One feudatory State discovered

V. The Lost Son Restored.

There was at one time a very great Rajah named Sukret Singh. His Rani's name was Jewankala. To them a son was born; but for some reason or other the infant was not satisfactory to his unnatural mother, so she quietly flung the baby into the sea, and informed her husband that a tiger had carried him off. The Rajah, believing his wife's story, comforted her, saying, "Permashwar (God) will give you more sons." Yet twenty-five years passed after this event, and the Rani was not blessed with another child.

One day about this period—that is, twenty-five years after the disappearance of her infant—the Rani saw a very handsome young man, and, her heart becoming captive to his beauty, she sent a *bichauliya* (a female go-between) to invite him to a clandestine interview. He came at the Rani's request, and gratified her wicked desires. With the cunning of the serpent she confided to her new lover the true story of her baby's disappearance, and how she had falsely stated that he had been carried off by a tiger.

"Now," said the Rani to her paramour, "I want you to understand that you were carried away by a *jogi* in the form of a tiger, that instead of destroying you the *sadhu* reared you himself, and that, knowing you to be a king's son, he had disclosed to you these important facts of your history before going away on a journey to a very distant land."

The Rani thus taught the young man, and he agreed to act in accordance with her wishes.

A day or two afterwards the Rani said to her husband,

a resource denied to the British Government, and thereby secured a special rainfall all to itself while surrounding districts remained drought-stricken. A wandering Brahman of peculiar sanctity was followed by crowds, who gave him no peace till he consented to apply his occult powers to the relief of their parched fields. Worn out by their importunities, the holy man at last sat down and vowed he would not rise till the water flowed over his feet. In two hours the brazen sky was overcast, rain set in, and twelve hours later the Brahman was ankle-deep. The situation was saved—and the man. This, at least, is the report semi-officially furnished by the State to the political officer."—*Saturday Review*, 7th October 1899.

"I have strange but very important news for you. Our baby son, who was carried away by a tiger, was really taken by a *jogi* in the form of a tiger, but he did not devour our child. His *chelas* brought him other children for his feasts, and he spared ours because he was a king's son. I have myself seen and recognised our lost child."

The Rajah, listening with astonishment to these wonderful assertions, said—

"Send for him, and let me hear the story from his own lips."

Thereupon the young man was summoned to the palace and questioned.

"What really happened," said he, "how can I possibly know?—but what the *jogi* told me, that will I truthfully relate." And he proceeded to repeat what the Rani had taught him. She, acting her part well, appeared to be overcome with emotion at the young man's statements, wept false tears copiously, and in the very presence of the Rajah, making her lover her son, embraced him affectionately and, lamenting their long separation, kissed him on the lips again and again. She had a bed made for him in her own room, and could not bear her lost darling out of her sight, even for a few minutes. During the eight watches of the day and night she guarded him from further danger, and enjoyed herself right well.

VI. A Kind-hearted Lady.

In the city of Sirhand there lived a *jogi* named Swarganath and also a certain woman, Sri Chhah Man Mati, who fell desperately in love with him.

One day the *jogi* was in her house when it was made known to her that her husband was on the point of returning home—in fact, was quite close at hand.

Grasping the decidedly serious situation, she thus hastily addressed her lover—

"Take up your sword at once and shout angrily, 'The thief who has robbed me has entered here. You have concealed him; drive him away; I will certainly kill him!'"

At the same time she actually hid upon the premises

the *jogi's chela*, a fellow who used to come with his master as his bodyguard and had been appointed to the post of door-keeper and sentinel during his *guru's* surreptitious visits to the frail, if fair, lady.

While matters were being thus hastily arranged, the husband arrived at his home. The *jogi*, with much simulated wrath, repeated the words he had been taught, but after a short yet furious howl of rage he went away, brandishing his sword in a menacing fashion.

"Dear husband," said the lady, explaining the situation to her bewildered lord, "that *jogi* was burning with anger owing to some mistake made by his *chela*. He was going to kill him, and would have done so but for the asylum I have afforded him. I permitted the poor fellow to hide himself in our house, and thus avoid the consequences of his *guru's* wrath. Now let us release him. He is hidden in that corner," pointing to the place of concealment.

The husband was very pleased with the thoughtful kindness displayed by his charming wife. So the man who had been concealed in the house was quietly hurried off the premises, and went away joyfully to rejoin his worthy *guru*—the amorous *jogi*, very gratified, indeed, that matters had in the end turned out so satisfactorily for himself.

VII. The Father Duped.[1]

There was a Rajah named Nilkate of Popeewutee city. Mangubechater, his wife, was like an incarnation of the goddess of love, and their daughter, named Sri Algunjamuttee, so beautiful that it might be said of her that she excelled the moon in brilliancy and appeared to have been fashioned by the hand of Brahma himself. There was a neighbouring Rajah, Srimantilk by name, too handsome to be described. So incomparable, indeed, was he that the sun, seeing his perfection, became ashamed of himself. Once Sri Algunjamuttee went to a garden to while away

[1] In this and the following tale the text of the originals has been rendered more literally than in the preceding stories, though the grossness of language which is characteristic of so many of these productions has been avoided.

her time with other girls of her own age. There she happened to see Rajah Srimantilk, and became enamoured of him. She was so affected by this sudden passion that when she went home she was like a gambler who had lost all he ever possessed. By a signal from her eyes she summoned to her side one of her young and trusted companions, and, giving her gold and jewels, entreated her to bring about a union between herself and the young Rajah who had so completely captured her susceptible heart.

"If I do not get him," said the love-sick princess, "I shall turn a *yogini*, and, flinging away all my jewels and finery, fly to the lonely forests; or, taking a beggar's gourd in my hand, I shall wander about the world, living upon the alms of the charitable. I want him to be the very apple of my eye, and failing that I shall kill myself. Alas! why have I lived so long to suffer all this torture, all this burning pain?"

When the girl-companion saw her distress, she came close up to her and, laughing, said in her ear—

"Don't fret; I'll send some clever woman to him."

These simple words seemed very sweet to the love-lorn princess in her great trouble.

In accordance with her promise, the girl-friend sent a clever *bichauliya* to Rajah Srimantilk, the princess herself merely saying—

"Do what is necessary, but save my life."

The *bichauliya* followed after the Rajah, who was out hunting. She dressed herself in costly garments, and decked herself out with jewels of rare beauty and value. When the Rajah saw such a lovely creature, a being like a real *peri*, in the midst of the jungle, he was astonished.

"Is this resplendent creature of the race of the Devtas, Gandharbas, Daityas, or Nagas, or is she really human? Let me inquire why she has come here. Is she not lovely?"

Thinking thus, the Rajah approached her, and, viewing her beauty at close quarters, fell in love with her at once.

The *bichauliya*, on her part, handed him a pearl necklace and a letter from her mistress, and while doing so said—

"You, sir, I can see, have fallen in love with my beauty; but she who has written this is a thousand times more lovely than I. Come with me and feast your eyes."

The Rajah, enticed by this glowing description of the charms of the princess, agreed to accompany her faithful messenger. He forgot all about his own affairs, and, filled with the idea of the lovely princess, he put the handsome *bichauliya* into his chariot and drove where she directed him to go. The way was long, but at last they arrived near the palace of the love-sick princess. The Rajah now disguised himself as a *sadhu* and lit his fire within sight of her window. Daily, with the permission of her father, used the princess to come and piously feed the good *sadhu* with her own hands. At night, when everyone was asleep, she would visit him also. In this way the princess was very happy. No one recognised the disguised Rajah or suspected what was going on. One day Sri Algunjamuttee went to her father and deliberately said things which she knew would excite his anger. She succeeded well enough, for the king became so enraged that he ordered his *vazir* to turn her out of doors into the jungle. When she heard this royal command Sri Algunjamuttee pretended to be very unhappy, and cried bitterly, though secretly rejoicing in her heart. The incensed and implacable father's peremptory command, "Take her away at once," was of course obeyed implicitly, and the princess was conveyed to the forest, and left there.

But in a very short time her lover came and joined her, and, after they had enjoyed themselves to their hearts' content, he carried her off to his own city.

VIII. Woman's Cunning.

Jogsain was the name of a certain Rajah, and his Rani's name was Sri Sanyaspati. She had a son born to her, who, when he grew up, was very beautiful. In the city over which Jogsain ruled there was a Jât woman who fell desperately in love with the young prince, and though she used, on one pretence or another, to see him every day, yet she found no opportunity of attaining her wishes. To gain her object, she disguised herself as a *jogi*, and went to the Rajah's palace, giving out that she was well versed in *janter*, *manter*, *tanter* (talismans, spells, and magic rites). Seizing a favourable opportunity, the pretended *jogi* said to the Rajah's son—

"If you will come with me to a lonely place, I shall show you some wonders that will astonish you."

The prince and *jogi* talked over the proposal; the prince's curiosity was greatly excited, and he said—

"I have never been out alone at night, but I will accompany you, since you are a *jogi*, if you promise to raise the spirits of the dead in my presence."

The pretended *jogi* engaged to perform this great miracle to pleasure the king's son, and the two started out together on their strange, unholy business. When they had penetrated, side by side, some little way into the lonely jungles, the *jogi*, turning suddenly towards the prince, and taking him entirely by surprise, said sharply—

"Now do as I bid you, or I will kill you on this spot."

The prince, quite unprepared for such a contingency, became alarmed and lost his presence of mind.

The pseudo-*jogi* thereupon stated her wishes without any circumlocution, and her companion willy-nilly yielded to her wicked desires.

The depth of woman's cunning is unfathomable! God created her; but Himself repents it.

. . . .

The foregoing tales speak for themselves, and, while throwing some light upon the conduct of love affairs in the East, show, amongst other things, that although the Indians feel that *sadhuism* is honourable and respectable, they are none the less quite alive to the great convenience of the *sadhu's* habit, as a disguise, for the successful conduct of amatory intrigues.

CHAPTER VI

SADHUS AS DESCRIBED BY SOME EUROPEAN VISITORS TO INDIA

Greek and Roman Accounts of Sadhus and their Practices—Observations regarding Sadhus and their Peculiarities recorded in the Works of the Jeweller Tavernier, the Physician Bernier, the "Senior Merchant" James Forbes, the Missionary Ward, Colonel Sleeman, and Bishop Heber.

DISTORTION arising from ignorance and prejudice is unavoidably present in all pictures of an alien civilisation drawn by visitors coming from countries remote both geographically and intellectually; yet these pictures have their value, affording as they often do important *facts*—wrongly interpreted, perhaps, but still *facts*—for the formation of a judgment in respect to the growth and development of customs and institutions. For this reason it seems desirable to recall to mind such particulars and impressions in regard to *sadhus* as European travellers, or residents in India of a bygone age, have placed on record for the benefit of their contemporaries and succeeding generations.

With what admiring wonderment the Greeks and Romans regarded India and its strange people after the Macedonian invader lifted the veil which had for ages separated from the Western nations that mysterious land

and its tranquil civilisation, classical literature amply testifies.

Amidst the many *unaccustomed* objects and institutions which attracted the attention of European visitors beyond the Indus, the ascetic philosophers (Brahman and Buddhist) and their peculiar ways were not the least interesting. Appreciative stories of the wisdom of these philosophers—*gymnosophists* the Greeks called them—have come down to us, with descriptions of some of the curious penances to which they subjected themselves. From these narratives we learn that the ascetic sages, who were held in the very highest honour by both the people and their rulers, lived an austere life, often in communities; that they studied self-control, spent much of their time in serious discourses and in imparting wisdom to others, teaching "that the best doctrine was that which removed pleasure and grief from the mind."[1] As to their self-mortifications, the Greek and Roman accounts show that in their nature they were very similar to, though probably not so severe as, those practised in India at later periods. For example, one of these ascetics would lie naked on his back in the open air, enduring all the vicissitudes of scorching sunshine and chilling rain; another would stand for hours on one leg, supporting with both hands above his head a beam of wood some three cubits long; a third would fix his gaze upon the rising sun, and stare at the great luminary all day till he disappeared below the western horizon. And, when afflicted with disease or tired of life, these wise men of India would sometimes erect a pyre and voluntarily perish in the flames in the presence of the multitude.

Having satisfied ourselves, from Greek and Roman sources, of the antiquity of the ascetic practices of the Indian sages, we may, passing over many centuries, profitably take stock, even cursorily, of the facts and impressions regarding *sadhus* which some of the comparatively modern European visitors to India, and official or other residents there, have recorded in their published works.

When M. Tavernier travelled in the Mogul Empire as a dealer in precious stones, about the middle of the seven-

[1] Strabo, M'Crindle's *Ancient India*, p. 71.

teenth century, the land he saw was very different in many important respects from that which had met the eyes of the Macedonian hero.

Many and striking changes had naturally occurred during the two thousand years which had elapsed since the fourth century before Christ. New world-religions had arisen since then, and the followers of the latest born of these creeds—aliens from Central Asia—were masters of a great part of India when the Frenchman travelled there. Yet the *sadhu* was still a prominent figure in Indian life, and Hindu ascetics were, as in Greek times, much in evidence everywhere, for M. Tavernier speaks of the "infinite multitude of *faquirs* that swarm all over India," generally moving about in large parties and quite naked.

These *faquirs*—for so he designates *sadhus* of all sects—were, he tells us, followers or imitators of Ravan, the demon-king of Lanka, who abducted the fair Sita from her hermitage in the woods of Dandaka. This, of course, is incorrect; for though, according to the legends, Ravan had been a great ascetic in his time, and acquired superhuman power by his austerities, none of the ascetic sects set up for being his *followers.* But though Tavernier's knowledge of the origin of the *sadhus* was on a par with that of most European visitors to India up to and including our own time, still he certainly took intelligent note of what came under his own observation in regard to the severe austerities practised by some of them. In the English version of his travels, published in London in 1684, there is a curious engraving illustrating some of these self-inflicted tortures.[1]

This plate appeared to me so interesting for many reasons that I reproduce it (Fig. 6), together with the following explanatory notes by our author:—

No. 1 is the part where the Bramins paint their idols; such as Mamaniva, Siva, Madedina, and others, whereof they have a great number.

No. 2 is a figure of Mamaniva, which is in the pagod.

No. 3 is another pagod near the former. There stands a cow at the door, and within stands the figure of their god Ram.

---

[1] *Travels in India,* part ii. book ii. chap. vi.

HINDU ASCETICS.
(Reproduction of an Old Illustration.)

FIG. 6.

To face page 94.

No. 4 is another pagod, into which the *faquirs* that do penance often retire.

No. 5 is another pagod dedicated to Ram.

No. 6 is a hut into which a *faquir* makes his retirement several times a year, there being but one hole to let in the light. He stays there according to the height of his devotion, sometimes nine or ten days together, without either eating or drinking; a thing which I could not have believed had I not seen it.

No. 7 is a figure of another penitentiary, over whose head several years have passed; and yet he never slept day nor night. When he finds himself sleepy, he hangs the weight of the upper part of his body upon a double rope that is fastened to one of the boughs of the tree; and by the continuance of this posture, which is very strange and painful, there falls a humour into their legs that swells them very much.

No. 8 is the figure of two postures of two doing penance, who, as long as they live, carry their arms above their heads in that manner; which causes certain carnosities to breed in the joynts, that they can never bring them down again. Their hair grows down to their wasts, and their nails are as long as their fingers. Night and day, winter and summer, they go always stark naked in the same posture, exposed to the heat and rain and the stinging of the flies, from which they have not the use of their hands to rid themselves. In other necessities they have other *faquirs* in their company, always ready to assist them.

No. 9 is the posture of another penitent, who every day for several hours stands upon one foot, holding a chafing-dish in his hand, into which he pours incense, as an offering to his god, fixing his eyes all the while upon the sun.

Nos. 10 and 11 are the figures of two other penitents sitting with their hands raised above their heads in the air.

No. 12 is the posture wherein the penitents sleep, without ever resting their arms; which is certainly one of the greatest torments the body of man can suffer.

No. 13 is the posture of a penitent whose arms, through weakness, hang flagging down upon his shoulders, being dried up for want of nourishment.

There are an infinite number of other penitents, some who, in a posture quite contrary to the motion and frame of nature, keep their eyes always turned toward the sun; others who fix their eyes perpetually upon the ground, never so much as speaking one word or looking any person in the face. And indeed there is such an infinite variety of them that would render the further discourse of them more tedious.

True it is that I have hid those parts which modesty will not suffer to be exposed to view. But they both in city and country go all as naked as they came out of their mothers' wombs.

Although the worthy gem merchant evidently did not understand the motives or ideas of these "penitents," as he styles them, his testimony is conclusive as to the fact that *sadhuism* was flourishing in his day. And strange to relate, the contagion of *sadhuism,* indigenous to the soil, seems to have so affected the Muhammadan rulers of India, that, besides the peripatetic Hindu ascetics, Tavernier met bands of almost naked Muslim dervishes wandering over the country, sometimes, as became members of the dominant race, exceedingly haughty and overbearing in their demeanour. One such band, consisting of about forty-seven persons, all well armed, including a few who had held very high positions in the Imperial Court, is specially mentioned by our traveller. Although proceeding on foot, this band of Muslim ascetics had many fine horses led before them, their saddles and bridles adorned with gold and silver ornaments, and they had also ten or twelve oxen to carry their sick. Arriving at the spot where Tavernier had pitched his camp in the most convenient position he could find, the armed and wealthy dervishes desired him to vacate it, as they needed the place themselves, and the Frenchman thought it prudent to yield to their request without demur.

Notwithstanding their pomp and self-assertion, these wandering ascetics lived upon alms obtained by begging, for were they not *faquirs?* However, in all probability it was fear which made the people comply, as did Tavernier himself, with their demands.

This picture of truculent Muslim *faquirs,* affording as it does a striking contrast to that of the mild Hindu ascetics known from the earliest times to our own day, has, as an index of the inwardness of Islam, an obvious value.

The physician François Bernier, who during the reign of the Mogul Emperor Aurangzeb travelled extensively in India, and met M. Tavernier there, does not fail to mention "the vast number and endless variety of *faquirs*" he encountered. Of these the *jogis* seem to have made most impression upon him, not by their religious or philosophical professions, but by their repulsive appearance. From his narrative it is evident that the practice of holding the arms perpetually above the head was a common one with the *sadhus* in his day,—much more common, I should say, than it is at the present time,—but the only feeling which this cruel self-torture seems to have awakened in the mind of the French physician was one of disgust; for, alluding to those who adopt this unnatural attitude, he says, "No fury in the infernal regions can be conceived more horrible than the *jauguis*, with their naked and black skin, long hair, spindle arms, long twisted nails, and fixed in the posture I have mentioned."[1]

Bernier was so far correctly informed that he realised that the object of the *jogis* was union with God; and he relates that one of the *jogis*, evidently a man of some reputation, assured him that he could at pleasure fall into a trance, during which he would be blessed with a ravishing vision of God and transports of holy joy beyond description. Bernier understood that penances were commonly endured for the attainment of some definite advantage in a new birth,—for example, reappearance on earth as a Rajah,—and he was also acquainted with the fact that many *sadhus* set up claims to the possession of magical powers, and that such claims were readily admitted by the people.

The testimony of this enlightened traveller, corroborating that of his contemporary Tavernier, leaves no doubt that two hundred and fifty years ago Hindu religious devotees abounded in the Mogul Emperor's dominions; that they wandered about freely in considerable bands, and walked through large towns stark naked,—"men, women, and girls looking at them," says Bernier, "without any more emotion than may be created when a hermit passes through our streets."

In the course of time a Christian power from beyond the seas supplanted the Muhammadan overlords of India, yet the *sadhu* still held his own under the new and unsympathetic régime.

That sagacious, intelligent, and quaintly, perhaps unctuously, pious Christian, James Forbes, who spent seventeen years in Western India—from A.D. 1766 to 1783—in the Honourable East India Company's service,

[1] Bernier's *Travels* (A.D. 1656–68), pp. 316, 317 (Archibald Constable & Co.).

and having attained the rank of "senior merchant" in the employment of that famous corporation, retired at the early age of thirty-three years with a disordered liver and an ample fortune, did not fail to observe, during his exile in the East, the *sadhus* and *faquirs* of his day.

From his valuable *Oriental Memoirs*, published in 1813, we learn that in the latter portion of the eighteenth century the wandering *sadhus* were in great force throughout the western country. "These gymnosophists," he says, "often unite in large armed bodies and perform pilgrimages to the sacred rivers and celebrated temples; but they are more like an army marching through a province than an assembly of saints in procession to a temple, and often lay the country through which they pass under contribution" (vol. i. p. 68).

Our author was also aware that in their pererrations these peripatetics went "from the confines of Russia to Cape Comorin and from the borders of China to Malabarhill on the island of Bombay" (i. 286), that they had many marvels to relate of the men and places they had seen, and were especially lavish in their praise of beautiful Kashmir (ii. 459). Mr. Forbes found these travelled ascetics more liberal-minded than the stay-at-home Hindus, and confesses that he "spent many a pleasant and improving hour with religious mendicants both Hindus and Mohammedans" (ii. 461).

One of these men, a venerable Brahman, informed Mr. Forbes "that he had lived under different governments and travelled in many countries, but had never witnessed a general diffusion of happiness equal to that of the natives under the mild and equitable administration of Mr. Hastings, at that time Governor-General of Bengal."

"I cannot," adds Mr. Forbes, "forget the words of this respectable pilgrim; we were near a banian tree in the durbar court when he thus concluded his discourse: 'As the burr tree, one of the noblest productions in nature, by extending its branches for the comfort and refreshment of all who seek its shelter, is emblematical of the deity, so do the virtues of the governor resemble the burr tree; he extends his providence to the remotest districts, and stretches out his arms, far and wide, to afford protection and happiness to his people. Such, sahib, is Mr. Hastings!'" (vol. ii. 462).

According to our author, it would seem that the roving propensities of the *sadhus*, however beneficial to themselves intellectually, were not conducive to right living, for many of them led a by no means chaste life, being veritable terrors to husbands wherever they went (ii. 234), and, though they had professedly renounced the world and its vanities, the wandering religious mendicants often contrived, to the great annoyance of the officials, Mr. Forbes included, to carry on, for their own profit, no little illicit trading in valuable objects (ii. 214, 215).

We also learn from Mr. Forbes that "many *yogees* and similar professors" subjected themselves to cruel penances and mortifications. "Some of them," he tells us, "enter into a solemn vow to continue for life in one unvaried posture; others undertake to carry a cumbrous load or drag a heavy chain; some crawl on their hands and knees for years around an extensive empire; and others roll their bodies on the earth from the shores of the Indus to the banks of the Ganges, and in that humiliating posture collect money to enable them either to build a temple, to dig a well, or to atone for some particular sin. Some swing during their whole life, in this torrid clime, before a slow fire; others suspend themselves, with their heads downwards, for a certain time over the fiercest flames" (vol. i. p. 69).

In his travels Mr. Forbes came across the *sadhu* who carries his useless arms above his head, and, reduced to utter helplessness by his voluntary asceticism, is fed by pious Hindu women even of good position. He also saw the men who swing round a lofty pole suspended from a cross-beam by means of iron hooks fixed in the muscles of the back.

A far rarer and more curious form of austerity is thus described: "I saw another of these devotees, who was one of the phallic worshippers of Seeva, and who, not content with wearing or adorning the symbol of that deity, had made a vow to fix every year a large iron ring into the most tender part of his body, and thereto to suspend a heavy chain, many yards long, to drag on the ground. I saw this extraordinary saint in the seventh year of his penance, when he had just put in the seventh ring; the wound was then so recent and so painful that he was obliged to carry the chain upon his shoulder, until the orifice became more callous" (vol. i. p. 70).

Mr. Forbes, intelligent observer and inquirer that he was, ascertained that the Hindu devotees were recruited from all classes of the community "except the caste of Chandala." He did not fail to realise that a high standard of abnegation and self-repression was theoretically demanded of the professed ascetics, and he was prepared to admit that, though the majority of the *sadhus* fell far short of the requirements of the rules of their sects, there were at least some enthusiasts who in solitude and meditation passed blameless lives and were credited with the possession of miraculous powers.

About a hundred years ago, the well-known Christian missionary Ward, visiting Saugor Island at the head of the Bay of Bengal, came across certain Hindu ascetics in the extensive, dreary, and tiger-haunted jungle which covered that place. Two of these were Bairagis from the "Upper Provinces," who lived in the wilderness in separate log huts. When Ward saw them their customary fire was burning on a sandy ridge, and before it, seated on a deer skin, was one of the ascetics, all but quite naked, preparing some *ganjah*, which he presently smoked in his *chillum*. The Christian missionary entered into conversation with the hermit, and learned from him that he had adopted a life of abstraction and isolation from the world neither to expiate any sin nor to secure any reward. He averred that he had no desires and no hopes, but that being removed from the agitations of the worldly life he was full of tranquil joy.

Near a neighbouring temple Mr. Ward discovered two other almost naked ascetics covered with ashes, each one having his long matted hair tied in a knot upon the top

A SOLITARY.

FIG. 7.

To face page 100.

of his head. One of these *sadhus*, quite a young man, was holding up one of his arms; as, indeed, he had been doing for no less than three years. "The nails of his hand," says Ward, "were grown long like the claws of a bird of prey." Inquiry elicited from the devotee the statement that he was indifferent to future rewards, and that the whole of his time was spent in a succession of religious ceremonies and in repetition of the name of God. He had to bathe at least once a day, and a single meal at midday was all that he might partake of. The conspicuous fresh footprints of a tiger becoming the subject of remark, the *sadhu* mentioned, without displaying the slightest emotion, that within the preceding three months six persons had been carried off by tigers, before his eyes as it were, adding, with apparent indifference, that he would himself probably suffer the same fate.

The other ascetic by the lonely temple in the jungle, who it appears held little if any communication with his neighbours, evinced no desire for intercourse with the inquisitive strangers, but remained absorbed in his own devotions. A solitary of this type is depicted in Fig. 7. Referring to the physical state of these ascetics, the Christian missionary remarked, "It appears almost impossible for human beings to manifest a greater disregard of the body" than was shown by these men; and we may add that, whether indicative of wisdom or folly, their painful austerities in a remote fever-and-tiger-haunted swampy jungle were plainly above any suspicion of imposture.

That remarkably well-informed and agreeable writer about the India of the early decades of the last century, Colonel Sleeman, who in his *rambles* met a great many *sadhus* of various sects, formed a correct appreciation of their position in the Hindu social system, and was fair-minded enough to recognise their good qualities as well as the service they could at that time render to the British Government by carrying a good report of it all over the country in their extensive wanderings through the remotest districts of the independent native States. At the same time, Colonel Sleeman did not overlook the curious fact that the very excellence of the British organisation, under which the soldiers' work was being efficiently carried out by one-tenth of the number of men formerly employed by the rival native rulers, was the cause of swelling very considerably the ranks of the religious mendicants.

Colonel Sleeman records from personal knowledge some very interesting incidents connected with *faquirs* and *sadhus*, which, however, need not be reproduced here; [1] but one peculiar feature of *sadhuism* of which he affords us a glimpse is too instructive to be overlooked.

"The Mahadeo sandstone hills," says Colonel Sleeman, "which in the Sathpore range overlook the Nerbudda to the south, rise to between four and five thousand feet above the level of the sea; and in one of the highest parts a fair was formerly, and is perhaps still, held for the enjoyment of those who assemble to witness the self-devotion of a few young men, who offer themselves as a sacrifice to fulfil the vows of their mothers! When a woman is without children she makes votive offerings to all the gods who can, she thinks, assist her, and promises of still greater in case they should grant what she wants. Smaller promises being found of no avail, she at last promises her first-born, if a male, to the god of destruction, Mahadeo. If she gets a son, she conceals from him her vows till he has attained the age of puberty; she then communicates it to him, and enjoins him to fulfil it. He believes it to be his paramount duty to obey his mother's call, and from that moment he considers himself as devoted to the god. Without breathing to any living soul a syllable of what she has told him, he puts on the habit of a pilgrim or religious mendicant, visits all the celebrated temples dedicated to this god in different parts of India, and at the annual fair on the Mahadeo hills throws himself from a perpendicular height of four or five hundred feet, and is dashed to pieces upon the rocks below! If the youth does not feel himself quite prepared for the sacrifice on the first visit, he spends another year in pilgrimage, and returns to fulfil his mother's vow at the next fair. Some have, I believe, been known to postpone the sacrifice to a third fair; but the interval is always

[1] The reader may consult Colonel Sleeman's *Rambles and Recollections*, vol. i. chap. xiii., vol. ii. chap. xxvi.

spent in painful pilgrimages to the celebrated temples of the god."[1]

Bishop Reginald Heber, who made an extensive tour in India during 1824–26, records his surprise at finding that the Hindu devotees were not so common as before his coming to India he had expected to find them (vol. i. p. 111). Of those the Bishop did actually come across he has little if anything to say, and his narrative is singularly deficient in just appreciation or reasonable comprehension of *sadhuism.* From the missionary point of view he certainly recognised the importance of the Hindu ascetics *as hindrances to the conversion of the people to Christianity*, and in this connection refers to one nearly naked man, "walking with three or four others, who suddenly knelt down one after the other, and, catching hold of his foot, kissed it repeatedly."

Amongst other cases which came under his own observation, the Bishop mentions a man who had vowed to use only one leg, the other being shrunken from disuse; a devotee who held his hands above his head till he had lost the power of bringing them down again (vol. i. 110, 111); and a hermit "sitting naked with his hands joined and his eyes half shut" (i. 266).

The Bishop was told about two *yogis* who lived apart, yet quite safely, in a tiger-haunted jungle, and was assured that one of these men was visited every night by a formidable tiger, who came to lick the ascetic's hands and be fondled by him (vol. ii. 265–68); but the story did not make much impression on the prelate.

Heber was also shown, but evinced no great interest in, "a small college . . . of religious mendicants or *viragies*" (ii. 373). Once he came across "a holy *yogi*, his naked and emaciated body covered over with white powder, and an iron implement, like a flesh-hook, in his hand, which is frequently carried by devotees in this part of India (Baroda)" (vol. iii. p. 55).

. . . .

[1] Colonel Sleeman's *Rambles and Recollections of an Indian Official*, vol. i. chap. xv. The practice referred to has, of course, died out or been suppressed.

The foregoing brief references to the recorded experiences and impressions of travellers and others show that the *sadhu*, who is at the present time too prominent a feature in the Indian world to escape attention, has also occupied an honoured place in his native land through all the many and often painful vicissitudes of fortune which it has experienced.

Yet the *sadhu* of to-day is not necessarily the *sadhu* of former times. It is true that nakedness, austerities, and roving habits have been persistent outward characteristics of the Indian *sadhu* through at least five-and-twenty centuries; but it has to be noted that these peculiarities have, by reason of their very obviousness, helped to conceal from the casual observer the fact, which will be established in the next chapter, that the religious ideas of which *sadhuism* is the outward expression have, in the progress of time, been undergoing many important changes.

CHAPTER VII

A VIEW OF THE SUCCESSIVE PHASES OF MODERN HINDUISM AND OF THE ORIGIN OF THE MORE IMPORTANT HINDU SECTS, IN RELATION TO THE DEVELOPMENT OF SADHUISM IN INDIA

SECTION I.—Some fundamental Doctrines of Hindu Theology—Mya—Pantheism—Metempsychosis—Karma.

IT is necessary for a full comprehension of *sadhuism* that the student should approach the subject with some knowledge of the fundamental doctrines evolved in India by the early Brahmanical theologians; and of such doctrines we are happily not left in ignorance.

In presence of the mysterious workings of the phenomenal world and the incomprehensible tragedies of life around them, the bewildered Hindu thinkers, being human and intellectual, were driven perforce to conceive some plausible explanation of the mighty riddle of existence—of being, suffering, decay, and dissolution—which confronted them in its appalling and majestic silence. To solve their profound difficulties for themselves, they naturally fell back upon their imaginations, and, thus far, did not differ much, except in the nature of their fancies, from their brethren of other creeds.[1] But it has to be noted that in their unbounded confidence in their own dream-world the Hindu sages pronounced the *senses* to be the misleading cause of man's ignorance, and arrived at the conclusion that the world, as revealed by the senses, was all pure deception, illusion (Mya), and that consequently the *real world, true knowledge,* could only be reached by neglecting, suppressing, and, as it were, getting behind the senses. To this verdict of Hindu theological philosophy may be traced the preponderance of introspective contemplation, which we find favoured by the various schemes of religious life adopted by Hindu sectaries. Subtle philosophical speculations about the origin and destiny of the world, about spirit and matter, could hardly coexist with the joyous physiolatry of their earlier cult, and this consequently became gradually converted into an abstract nebulous pantheism, which fascinated the Hindu mind, and has coloured all its subsequent ideas —so much so, that even the very recent and delicate scientific researches on what he calls the "response of matter," carried out by a clever and well-known Bengali Professor of Science, Dr. J. C. Bose, have very appropriately led him to say—

"It was when I came upon the mute witness of these self-made records, and perceived in them one phase of a pervading unity that bears within it all things; the mote that quivers in ripples of light, the teeming life upon our earth, and the radiant suns that shine above us,—it was then that I understood for the first time a little of that message proclaimed by my ancestors on the banks of the Ganges thirty centuries ago: 'They who see but one in all the changing manifoldness of this universe, unto them belongs Eternal Truth, unto none else, unto none else!'"

This pantheism, recognising only one indefinite substance or Being from which everything came and into which every-

[1] Guessing at the origin and constitution of the material universe in its wonderfully various aspects is a process by no means confined to the theologians and philosophers, but may be traced, with important differences no doubt, in the host of theories and hypotheses, most of them long since discredited, which science has presented to the world.

thing would return, has, naturally, not found favour with Christians. Professor Caird characterises it as "a gulf in which all difference was lost," adding that "the ethics which could spring from such a faith was only the negative ethics of an asceticism which renounced the world and withdrew from it as an empty illusion."[1]

Long centuries prior to the Christian era two important tenets had taken firm root in India, and they are flourishing there to this day. One of these is belief in metempsychosis (*samsâra*), the other what is known as *karma*. According to the former, death does not release the soul permanently from its connection with matter, for it may have to return again and again, even an endless succession of times, animating other bodies, human, bestial, and even vegetal;[2] while, according to the doctrine of *karma* (the Sanskrit word for action), it is upon a man's actions in this life that will depend the condition or state in which the soul will be reincarnated. After the death of an individual his soul may pass for a time into a place of enjoyment—a heaven of bliss, in fact; but, unless its purification has been complete, it will in the fulness of time be inevitably reincarnated for a new mundane existence. In a word, the present state is the result of past actions, and the future depends upon the present. Now, the ultimate hope of the Hindu should be so to live that his

[1] Caird's *Evolution of Religion*, vol. i. p. 263. In connection with this subject, the following will not be without interest:—"As we read in the Katha Upanishad, 'The self-existent pierced the openings (of the senses) so that they turn forward; therefore man looks forward, not backward, into himself. Some wise man, however, with his eyes closed and wishing for immortality, saw the Self behind.' . . . 'The wise, when he knows that that by which he perceives all objects in sleep and in waking is the great omnipresent Self, grieves no more.' 'As the sun, the eye of the whole world, is not contaminated by the external impurities seen by the eyes, thus the one Self within all things is never contaminated by the misery of the world, being himself without.' 'There is one eternal thinker, thinking non-eternal thoughts, who, though one, fulfils the desires of many. The wise who perceive him within their Self, to them belongs eternal peace, not to others.'"—Caird's *Evolution of Religion*, vol. i. p. 355.

[2] The doctrine of the transmigration of souls was held by the ancient Egyptians. It found a footing in Greece and amongst the Jews—the Kabbalists. The Manichæans recognised it, and some heretical Muslim sects also adopted it.

soul may be eventually freed from the necessity of being reincarnated, and may in the end be reunited to the Infinite Spirit from which it sprang. As, however, that goal is very remote, the Hindu not uncommonly limits his desires and his efforts to the attainment of a "good time" now, and in his next appearance upon this earthly stage.

CHAPTER VII—*continued*

SECTION II.—Modern Hinduism—Principal Divisions—The Sivite Reformer, Sankara Acharya—His Crusade against Buddhism—Sakti Worship—Mahmoud of Guzni's successful Invasion of India—Islam a stimulating Factor in the Origination of new and rival Siva and Vishnu Sects—The Puranas—Ramanuja's Campaign against Sivaism—Basava and his Doctrines—Krishna Worship preached by Madhavacharya—His Theological Views—Ramanand preaches at Benares the Worship of Rama and Sita—Tendency towards Anthropomorphism in the later Sects.

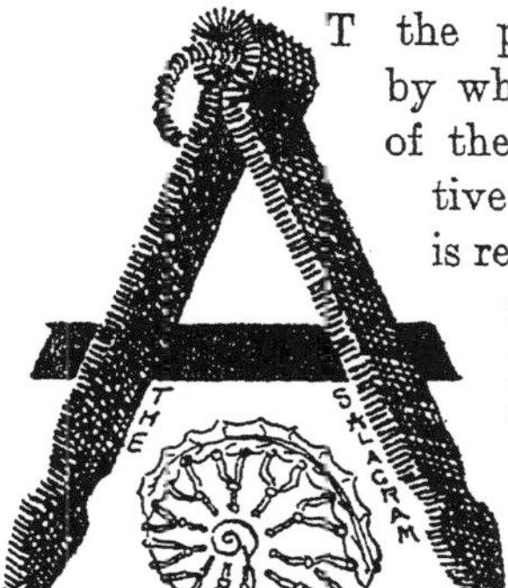

AT the present time Hinduism proper—by which I mean the practical religion of the Hindu people, not the speculative opinions of Hindu philosophers—is represented by a bewildering variety of sects, of which the more important ones at least may be classified with tolerable accuracy under the following main groups :—

1. Saivas, worshippers of the god Siva.

2. Saktas, worshippers of the *female energy* and especially of the goddesses Devi, Durga, and Kali, all consorts of Siva.

3. Vaishnavas, worshippers of the god Vishnu.
   (*a*) In his incarnation as Rama Chandra with his wife Sita.
   (*b*) As Krishna with his wives Lakshmi and Rukmani and his favourite mistress Radha.[1]

[1] It was a peculiarity of the Egyptians, that, like the present Hindus, they were divided as it were into sects, each of which adopted some one deity out of the Pantheon for the exclusive object of worship, paying no

Towards the close of the eighth or the beginning of the ninth century A.D. Siva worship attained a prominent position and considerable success, mostly through the exertions of an unmarried Brahman named Sankara Acharya, who carried on a vigorous crusade against Buddhism. It would seem that he countenanced *every* form of Hinduism, but, "whatever Sankara's own faith may have been, his followers are practically Sivites." [1]

Of the religious peculiarities of this transition period we have fortunately many interesting particulars in a work entitled *Sankara Vijaya*, by one Ananda Giri, a reputed disciple of Sankara himself. The broad divisions of Saivas, Saktas, and Vaishnavas can all be recognised as existing at that time, but the sects described by Ananda Giri can hardly, if at all, be identified with those of the present day; and it is noteworthy that in no portion of the *Sankara Vijaya* "is any allusion made to the separate worship of Krishna, either in his own person or that of the infantine forms in which he is now so eminently venerated in many parts of India, nor are the names of Rama and Sita, of Lakshmana or Hanuman, once particularised as enjoying any portion of distinct and specific adoration." [2]

Siva, regarded by his special followers as the Supreme Being, commands their adoration in many different and even seemingly contradictory characters; but he is usually worshipped under the impersonal symbol of the *phallus* or *lingam*, an undoubtedly very ancient Oriental cult, though not confined exclusively to the East. The spiritualisation, exaltation, and even deification, of natural desire, of the sexual instinct in fact, has been in the East from the earliest times an object of certain sect founders, impressed, no doubt, and fascinated by the mystery of generation. And so it has come about that this mystery, which the West

regard to all the rest. As in modern Hinduism Vishnu and Siva have engrossed the religion of the country, so in Egypt of the first Christian century Anubis and Cnuph had become the sole objects of Egyptian veneration.—King's *The Gnostics and their Remains*, pp. 101, 102.

[1] *Hindu Castes and Sects*, by Dr. J. M. Bhattacharjee, p. 375.

[2] *Sketch of the Religious Sects of the Hindus*, by Professor H. H. Wilson, pp. 11, 12.

has regarded with the greatest suspicion and dread, has been invested by the subtle mysticism of the Orient with the sanctifying garment of religion.

In connection with the cult and practices of the Sankarite ascetic sects, it should be borne in mind that although Siva is regarded by the Hindus as the Destroyer, yet throughout India he is worshipped under the symbol of the *lingam*, because in the endless round of births and deaths to which, according to the doctrine of metempsychosis, all sentient beings are subject, it is easy for the mystic to see in destruction only the precursor of renewed existence.[1]

I.

I am the god of the sensuous fire
  That moulds all nature in forms divine;
The symbols of death and of man's desire,
  The springs of change in the world are mine;
The organs of birth and the circlet of bones,
And the light loves carved on the temple stones.

II.

I am the lord of delights and pain,
  Of the pest that killeth, of fruitful joys;
I rule the currents of heart and vein;
  A touch gives passion, a look destroys;
In the heat and cold of my lightest breath
Is the might incarnate of Lust and Death.

* * * * * *

V.

And the strong swift river my shrine below,
  It runs, like man, its unending course,
To the boundless sea from eternal snow;
  Mine is the Fountain, and mine the Force
That spurs all nature to ceaseless strife;
And my image is Death at the gates of Life.

(From Sir Alfred Lyall's "Siva.")

Under the influence of the Hindu admiration of the ascetic life, Siva, the Great God (Maha-dev), stands forth in the later Hinduism of the Puranas as the *great ascetic* (Mahatapah, Mahayogi), a fact of especial significance in

[1] For the modern *lingam* worship the principal authorities are the Skanda, Siva, Brahmanda, and Linga Puranas.

connection with the subject of the present work. "In this character he appears quite naked (*digambara*), with only one face like an ordinary human being, with ash-besmeared body and matted hair (whence his name Dhurjati), sitting in profound meditation under a banian tree, and often, like the contemplative Buddha, under a canopy formed by a serpent's head. There he is supposed to remain passionless, motionless, immovable as the trunk of a tree, perhaps rooted to the same spot for millions of years." [1]

With Siva are also commonly associated his consorts and his bull Nandi.

Siva, as Professor Wilson points out, is stated to have "appeared in the beginning of the Kali age as *sweta* for the purpose of benefiting the Brahmans. He resided on the Himalaya mountains and taught the *yoga*." Now the word *sweta* means white, and all images of Siva, as well as pictorial representations or living presentments of the god, are always coloured white.

The legend referred to will account for the fact that Siva is especially the god of the Brahmans.

Sankara Acharya's crusade against Buddhism originated in Southern India, but Sankara himself preached his doctrines far and wide, travelling from Malabar, where he was born, to the valley of Kashmir in the Himalayas, where he died at the early age of thirty-two. He has been raised by his followers to the dignity of an incarnation of Siva. "His sanctity was in such repute that he was held to have worked several miracles — amongst others, transferring his own soul for a time into the dead body of a King Amru, that he might become the husband of the king's widow for a brief period, and so learn by experience how to argue on amatory subjects with the wife of a Brahman named Mandana, who was the only person he had never conquered in argument. This is described in a poem called Amaru-Sataka, to which a mystical interpretation is given." [2]

[1] *Brahmanism and Hinduism*, by Professor Sir Monier Williams, p. 83 (third edition).

[2] *Ibid.* p. 56.

Sankara's aim in life seems to have been to destroy Buddhism in India and to revive and establish an old Brahmanic cult. His chief doctrine was the essential unity of the Divine Spirit and the human soul. He held, indeed, that all nature is but a manifestation of the Universal Soul, takes its origin from that soul, and is eventually absorbed therein. In order to impress this doctrine upon his mind, "the Sivite is required by his religion to assert every now and then that he is Siva";[1] Sivoham—I am Siva.

For the attainment of final emancipation, *mukti*, Sankara held that realised knowledge of the oneness of the Âtman, or self, with the Absolute, or Brahman, was essential.

The nature of Hindu views on this subject may be somewhat elucidated by the following dialogue from the *Nadir unnikat*, a book in Persian, written in the middle of the seventeenth century, explanatory of the tenets of the sect known as the *Baba Lalis*:—

"Are the soul, life, and body merely shadows?—The soul is of the same nature as God, and one of the many properties of universal life—like the sea, and a drop of water; when the latter joins the former, it also is sea.

"How do the Paramâtma (supreme soul) and Jivâtma (living soul) differ?—They do not differ, and pleasure and pain ascribable to the latter arises from its imprisonment in the body—the water of the Ganges is the same whether it run in the river's bed or be shut up in a decanter.

"What difference should that occasion?—Great; a drop of wine added to the water in the decanter will impart its flavour to the whole, but it would be lost in the river. The Paramâtma, therefore, is beyond accident, but the Jivâtma is afflicted by sense and passion. Water cast loosely on a fire will extinguish the fire; put that water over the fire in a boiler, and the fire will evaporise the water. So the body being the confining cauldron, and passion the fire, the soul, which is compared to the water, is dispersed abroad.

[1] *Hindu Castes and Sects*, by J. N. Bhattacharjee, M.A., D.L., p. 371.

The one great supreme soul is incapable of these properties, and happiness is therefore only obtained in reunion with it, when the dispersed and individualised portions combine again with it, as the drops of water with the parent stream; hence, although God needs not the service of His slave, yet the slave should remember that he is separated from God by the body alone, and may exclaim perpetually, Blessed be the moment when I shall lift the veil from off that face. The veil of the face of my beloved is the dust of my body.

"What are the feelings of the perfect *faquir*?—They have not been, they are not to be, described; as it is said, a person asked me, What are the sensations of a lover? I replied, When you are a lover you will know."[1]

Sankara founded at least four important monasteries,[2] and established various orders of wandering friars, to be referred to later on; but, unlike Buddha, he did not admit nuns to his orders.

Sakti worship, that is, the worship of the *female* energy in nature, having the *yoni* and *yantra* for its accepted symbols, is not perhaps as old in India as the phallic cult of Siva; but we know it was flourishing there in the eighth and ninth centuries A.D., and has a very considerable following at the present time. The written authorities upon which this cult is based are certain Puranas—for example, the Brahma Vaivartha, Skanda, and Kalika; but the most important Scriptures of the Saktas are the Tantras, which they regard as a fifth Veda.

As worship of the goddesses Devi, Durga, and Kali, the Sakti cult prevails, sometimes combined with the grossest immoralities, mostly in the eastern portions of India,—Behar, Bengal, and Assam,—where emotionalism and mysticism are very prominent features of the national character; the instance under consideration being a good example of the fact that, where these mental qualities are found in excess, they usually coexist with a deficiency of self-control which may lead to sexual depravity. However,

[1] Wilson, *Religious Sects of the Hindus*, pp. 225, 226.

[2] At Sringiri in Mysore, Badrinath in the Himalayas, Dwarka in Kattiawar, and Jagganath in Orissa.

as the Sakti cult naturally produces no ascetics, it is outside the scope of this book.

Since as far back as 636 A.D. successive waves of Mussulman invasion had been beating with more or less effect against the western boundaries of India. In A.D. 1024 Mahmoud, the Muhammadan ruler of Ghazni, after eleven successful invasions of India as far as Gwalior and Kanauj, returned once more, attracted this time by an avaricious desire to secure the enormous wealth of the famous temple of Somnath in Guzerat. Mahmoud had already destroyed the temples of Thaneswar and Nagarkote, but Somnath, on account of the fame of its sanctity and riches, was a prize which excited his fanaticism as well as his cupidity. Situated by the Arabian Sea, close to the sacred land where Krishna ruled and died, the temple of Somnath appealed to the most cherished religious feelings of the Hindus; but, though desperately defended, it fell into the hands of the invader, who contemptuously shattered in pieces the object of worship there—a gigantic *lingam*—and carried off in triumph the hoarded treasures of centuries of Hindu piety.

"The *linga* worship of Siva, we know," says Professor Wilson, "was everywhere the predominant form of the Hindu faith when the Mohammedans first invaded India,"[1] and anyone at all acquainted with the extensive and restless rovings of the Indian *sadhus* can easily imagine how quickly the news of that terrible and striking catastrophe, the destruction of Somnath, must have been carried throughout the length and breadth of India by the wandering Sivite friars and other peregrinating ascetics of the day. The news as it sped through the land must have struck dismay everywhere, and awakened painful doubts in millions of hearts, as when the sack of the Eternal City by Alaric and his Goths in the fifth century gave a shock to Roman pride and the pagan cults of the empire from which they never recovered.

An ominous storm-cloud was gathering over Hindu

[1] Preface to his translation of *Malati and Madhava*.

India, throwing a dark shadow of distrust over old cherished beliefs. It was indeed just one of those critical periods in the history of a nation when universal searchings of hearts give rise to revisions of long-established faiths and to the formulation of new religious hopes and aspirations. In the gloom of those troublous days the Vishnu Puranas, with their extravagant legends for the glorification of their chosen divinity, seem to have been compiled, somewhere about the middle of the eleventh century, from old traditions, coeval, no doubt, with Sivaism and Buddhism.

During the hundred years which followed the compilation of these Puranas the Muhammadan power was being consolidated in the Punjab, and a feeling of unrest at the imminent peril which threatened Hinduism must have been experienced throughout the remainder of India. Such political conditions are always favourable to the advent of prophets, reformers, and new religious systems. In due time, therefore, appeared a rival to Sivaism in the form of a Vishnu cultus.

Sivaism, as already stated, had received a great impetus from the teaching and preaching of Sankara Acharya, but had no doubt been discredited in men's minds by recent events.

The prophet of the new Vaishnava (Vishnuvite) religion was Ramanuja, a Brahman of Southern India, who about 1150 A.D. commenced his campaign against Sivaism, teaching a monotheism hardly distinguishable from pantheism. Instead of the much venerated *lingam*, symbol of Mahadev, he presented to the Hindu world, as objects of special adoration, Vishnu,[1] Krishna, and Rama; also their respective wives, Lakshmi, Rukmini, and Sita. Contrary to the views of Sankara, he taught that the human soul was distinct from the Supreme Spirit, and retained its identity and separate consciousness even when absorbed in the

[1] The god Vishnu, according to the Puranas, has appeared on the earth in nine different incarnations, one of these being Rama Chandra, and he is to appear once more as Kalki "at the end of the present age of sin for rescuing the land of the Aryas from their oppressors."—Bhattacharjee's *Hindu Castes and Sects*, p. 415.

Supreme Being. "As a matter of fact, he believed in three distinct principles, namely—

1. The Supreme Spirit, 'Para-brahma or Iswara.'
2. The separate spirits of men, 'Chit.'
3. Non-spirit, 'Achit.'"[1]

And it may be added that he recognised the merit of good works for the attainment of final exemption from further transmigrations.

Ramanuja's conflict with the worshippers of Siva was carried on with a great deal of vehemence, and he was himself obliged to seek refuge from his enemies in the court of the Jaina King of Karnata. Two distinct sects claiming to be his spiritual descendants, styling themselves Vada-galais and Ten-galais respectively, are to be found at present in Southern India. Ramanuja's followers affirm that their prophet was an incarnation of the divine serpent Sesha.

Like other Indian reformers or heresiarchs, Ramanuja established ascetic orders in connection with his sect known as the Sri Vaishnavas, and founded a large number of monasteries.

Lingam worship, as organised and extended by Sankara and his immediate followers, was not, however, to be yet ousted by its rival. Within a century of the promulgation by Ramanuja of his Vishnu cultus, a new movement in favour of Sivaism was set up by Basava in the southern Mahratta country. Though a Brahman by birth, Basava "denied the superiority of the Brahmans, and tried his best to abolish the distinction of caste."[2] He also opposed many ancient orthodox practices—cremation, for example—and even questioned the inspiration of the Vedas.

According to his followers, Basava was an incarnation not of Siva, but of Siva's bull Nandi, who was sent down especially to revive the Sivite cultus.[3] To Basava are attributed many remarkable miracles. After his work on earth was accomplished he disappeared into the Sangameswara *lingam*, and thus returned to the heaven whence he came.

[1] *Hindu Castes and Sects*, by Dr. J. N. Bhattacharjee, p. 435.
[2] *Ibid.* p. 396.
[3] Professor H. H. Wilson's *Religious Sects of the Hindus*, p. 143.

Basava established an ascetic mendicant order in connection with his sect, named Jangamas or Lingaits because they wear a *lingam* enclosed in a metal casket suspended from the neck by a cord. The order referred to is well known in Southern India, but representatives of it are rarely met with in the country north of the Vindhyahs, although some are established at Benares.

But the political clouds continued to gather overhead, the danger to Hinduism still increased. Islam was steadily triumphing. What better course was open to the Hindus than to forget their sectarian differences and unite together in the worship of the divine Krishna, the central figure of that great Hindu epic, the Mahabharata,[1] and the very god Vishnu[2] himself, in whom all Hindus could find their ideals satisfied. And so in the thirteenth century Madhavacharya, a Kanarese Brahman, born in A.D. 1199, vigorously preached the special worship of Krishna, but, unlike Ramanuja, without displaying any hostility whatever to Sivaism, his object being to effect a union of Sivites and Vishnuvites under a new religious banner.

To this end the images of Siva, Durga,[3] and Ganesh[4] are worshipped along with those of Vishnu in the temples of the sect established by Madhavacharya.

As in the present time the Krishna cult seems to be in especial favour amongst the Indian people, and as its spread in certain forms must affect the practice of austerities, it seems desirable to consider the popular beliefs respecting this god.

In the Mahabharata he is a warrior king, wise, subtle, and full of guile. He is also the Supreme Being, and unmistakably reveals himself as such. Some of the earlier Puranas represent him in the same light. But

[1] An epitome of the Mahabharata forms a portion of my *Great Indian Epics* (George Bell & Sons).

[2] "Krishna is regarded by some as the eighth incarnation (of Vishnu), but according to the more orthodox view he was Vishnu himself, and was not a mere incarnation."—Dr. Bhattacharjee's *Hindu Castes and Sects*, p. 415.

[3] The wife of Siva.

[4] The god of wisdom, son of Siva and Parvati, represented as a short corpulent man with four hands and the head of an elephant.

later and more favourite legends devoted especially to his youthful years dwell upon the dangers to which in infancy his life was exposed from the jealous fears of his royal uncle, expatiate upon his personal beauty, and revel in the sensuous details of his various amours with the *gopis* (milkmaids), amongst whom the most favoured was Radha, a married woman passionately devoted, body and soul, to her divine lover. Their loves, not unmixed with jealousies and tears, as sung by the poets of India, have met with ecstatic appreciation, while an attempt has been made by the more sober-minded to cover their unblushing carnality under a diaphanous veil of devotional mysticism.[1] Whither all this dallying with warm voluptuous passions and sensuous images would inevitably lead the frailer devotees does not need to be explained.

When the Krishna cult *originated* is very doubtful. Its roots may be very ancient, but there can be no doubt that it was in a new form that it appeared in India in the thirteenth century.

Madhavacharya, the prophet who preached Krishna, believed, like his predecessor Ramanuja, in the independent existence of the human soul, and denied the possibility of its absorption into the Universal Spirit either in this life or after death. He held that there is one Eternal Supreme Being, Vishnu, and that Siva, Brahma, and all the other gods are subject to decay and dissolution; that there are two eternal principles, God and the Human Soul, or rather souls, the former independent, the latter dependent. "With regard to the visible world, he taught that its elements existed eternally in the Supreme Being, and were only created by Him in the sense of being shaped, ordered, and arranged by His power and will."[2]

The sect established by Madhava has, like the rest, its own mendicant orders and its own monasteries.

The success of Vaishnava doctrines in Southern India led to their promulgation in the Gangetic valley, princi-

[1] With this process we in the West are familiar in the very far-fetched interpretation which has been put by Christian theologians upon the glowing sensuousness of the Song of Songs.

[2] Professor Sir Monier Williams, *Brahmanism and Hinduism*, p. 131.

pally through the preaching and teaching of a Brahman named Ramanand, who lived at Benares in the thirteenth or fourteenth century. It is said that Ramanand, one of Ramanuja's successors, having travelled extensively over India, returned to one of the monasteries of his sect, when some priest or other raised the objection that in his wanderings he could not possibly have observed the rule of the Ramanuja sect, requiring meals to be strictly private. On these grounds Ramanand was required to eat apart from the rest of the brethren. In resentment he founded a new sect, and, to show his contempt for caste distinctions, freely admitted into it men of all castes, *even the lowest*; and this was probably a prudent or even necessary concession to popular feeling, more than ever unwilling to accept the old yoke, since Islam was prepared to receive all into its communion on a footing of equality.

Ramanand's followers were taught to pay especial reverence to Rama and his wife Sita; for, with political dangers looming on the horizon, what more natural than to turn one's thoughts to the faultless prince who, while an incarnation of deity, had been in his human character a wandering ascetic in the forests of Central India for no less than fourteen years, and withal a successful warrior, capable of avenging a wrong even when the evil-doer was the terrible ten-headed demon-king of the Rakshasas.[1]

Again, what more charming and more admirable character could be found to arouse the love and homage of all good men than that ever-faithful and tender wife, the peerless Sita.

The cult instituted by Ramanand was an example of the worship of God *incarnated in human form*, similar to that which we have in Christianity—a religion which had already become familiar to the Indian people; for Roman Catholic missionaries had long been established amongst them.

If Sivaism was to be superseded by Vishnuism, surely

[1] The story of Rama is the subject of the famous Sanskrit epic, the Ramayana, of which I have given an epitome in my *Great Indian Epics* (George Bell & Sons).

the object of adoration should be a god-man like Rama, a model son and an exemplary husband, but above all a redoubtable warrior and a leader of avenging hosts.

There are both monks and nuns connected with the sect of the Ramanandis, who have flourishing monasteries throughout Northern India.

CHAPTER VII—*continued*

SECTION III.—Modern Democratic Reformers—Kabir, his peculiar and important position as a Reformer—Vallabhacharya sets up the Worship of Krishna as Bala Gopala—Chaitanya the Mystic preaches the Worship of Krishna *cum* Radha—Baba Nanak and his Teaching—The Sikhs—Dadu and his Sect—Ram Charn and the Ram Sanehis founded by him—The Rajput Princess Mirabai a Devotee of Krishna—The Trend of Latter-day Hinduism—Brief Summary.

UP to this time all the heresiarchs—for such they really were—mentioned in this sketch, from Sankara Acharya to Ramanand, were Brahmans and men of education.

Although they belonged to the privileged caste of the hereditary priesthood, democratic tendencies became more and more apparent in the sects which successively arose under their guidance, the latter of these exhibiting a very marked disregard for caste distinctions. At the same time, anthropomorphic leanings are plainly manifest in the extensive and popular worship of the Kshatriya warriors Krishna and Rama.

In Kabir we have a low-caste man unacquainted with Sanskrit literature, and a reformer of such a strikingly new type amongst Hindu religious leaders that he calls for more than a passing notice. This man, there is reason to believe, may be numbered amongst the principal disciples of Ramanand, though he was no slavish follower of the master. It is related that Ramanand lived at Benares in the strictest seclusion. He stayed all day indoors, and only at about two o'clock in the morning went down to the Ganges to have his bath and perform his devotions. Kabir, the low-caste weaver, could never obtain access to the great teacher, because the master's followers and disciples drove him contemptuously away. He knew, however, that Ramanand went nightly to the sacred river for his bath, and so he used to lie in the path and watch him as he passed. One night Ramanand, on his way to the Ganges, stumbled against Kabir, and instead of asking who he was, or making any apology, merely said, as he passed along, "Ooth! Ram ko Ram bolo!" (Rise up! say Ram to Ram!).

Kabir was delighted, and went about telling everybody he met that Ramanand had accepted him as his *chela*, and had communicated the initiatory *mantra* to him. The disciples of the great teacher questioned him about this, and not without sundry reproaches. Ramanand denied all knowledge of the man. Kabir on his part maintained the truth of his statement, and desired to be confronted with his *guru*. He was conducted before Ramanand, and related what had occurred. The master was pleased, and said, "Yes, he is my *chela*! What greater *mantra* is there than the name of God?" This is one story, and, though not identical with the one given in the Dabistan, does not differ very materially from it. But, according to the *Bhakta mala*, Kabir's mother was at her own request brought by her father to see Ramanand, who, without taking note of the fact that she was a widow, saluted her with a benediction, to the effect that she might be favoured with a son. Of course the saint's words, once uttered, were irrevocable. The virgin widow in due time gave birth to a male child, and, overwhelmed with shame, secretly abandoned the infant, who was found by a weaver and his wife and reared as their own offspring.

Judging from the works attributed to him and his

immediate disciples, he was a pronounced mystic,[1] gifted by nature with a great power of emotional influence. But, mystic though he was, Kabir's worldly wisdom led him to advise his disciples to conciliate all men.

> "Shabse hiliye, shabse miliye,
> Shabka lijiye nam;
> Han-ji han-ji shabse kijiye,
> Wasa apna gam,"

which jingling couplet may be sufficiently rendered—

> "Mix with all, with all associate,
> Each man's name borrow free;
> Let 'Yes, sir!' on your lips be ever,
> But bide 'neath your own roof-tree."

Kabir, though a monotheist after the Indian fashion, did not deny the existence of the Hindu deities; but he considered that their worship was not necessary, and he was clearly anti-idolatrous in his views. What was a new thing in Hinduism, Kabir insisted that *purity of heart* was all-important, and ceremonies or modes of worship of little account.

Thus said the teacher: "To Ali and Rama we owe our existence, and should therefore show similar tenderness to all that live: of what avail is it to shave your head, prostrate yourself on the ground, or immerse your body in the stream? Whilst you shed blood you call yourself pure and boast of virtues that you never display. Of what benefit is cleaning your mouth, counting your beads, performing ablutions, and bowing yourself in temples, when, whilst you mutter your prayers or journey to Mecca or Medina, deceitfulness is in your heart. The Hindu fasts every eleventh day, the Mussulman during the Ramazan. Who formed the remaining months and days that you should venerate but one? If the Creator dwell in tabernacles, whose residence is the universe? Who has beheld Rama seated amongst the images, or found him at the shrine to which the pilgrim has directed

[1] Mysticism, Dr. Max Nordau says, "is the expression of the inaptitude for attention, for clear thought, and control of the emotions, and has for its cause the weakness of the higher cerebral centres."—*Degeneration*, p. 536.

his steps? The city of Hara is to the east, that of Ali to the west; but explore your own heart, for there are both Rama and Karim."[1]

A characteristic story told of Kabir, extracted from Shea and Troyes' translation of the Dabistan, may not be out of place here.

"Kabir showed always great regard for the *faquirs*. One day a number of dervishes came to him. He received them with respect in his house. As he possessed nothing, to show his generosity and munificence to them, he went from door to door to procure something; but, having found nothing, he said to his wife, 'Hast thou no friend from whom thou mayest borrow something?' She answered, 'There is a grocer in this street who threw an eye of bad desire upon me; would I from this sinner demand something, I should obtain it.' Kabir said, 'Go immediately to him, grant him what he desires, and bring something for the dervishes.' The woman went to the lewd grocer and requested the loan of what she required. He replied, 'If thou comest this night to me, thy request is granted.' The woman consented, and swore the oath which he imposed upon her to come, after which the grocer gave her rice, oil, and whatever these men might like. When the *faquirs*, well satisfied, went to rest, a heavy rain began to fall, and the woman wished to break her engagement; but Kabir, in order to keep her true to her word, having taken her upon his shoulder, carried her in the dark and rainy night through the deep mud to the shop of the bad grocer, and placed himself there in a corner. When the woman had entered into the interior part of the house, and the man found her feet unsullied, he said to her, 'How didst thou arrive without thy feet being dirty?' The woman concealed the fact. The grocer conjured her by the holy name of God to reveal the truth. The woman, unable to refuse, said what had taken place. The grocer, on hearing this, shrieked and was senseless. When he had recovered his senses, he ran out and threw himself at Kabir's feet. Afterwards, having

[1] Sabda the 56th, quoted in Professor H. H. Wilson's *Sketch of the Religious Sects of the Hindus*, pp. 52, 53.

distributed among the poor whatever he had in his shop, he became a *viragi*." [1]

The cardinal precepts of Kabir are the obligations of *humanity and truth*, the desirability of retirement from the world, and, above all, "implicit devotion in word, act, and thought to the *guru*, or spiritual guide." This last precept, which did not originate with Kabir, and is by no means peculiar to his sect, has taken strong hold of the Indian mind, and has led to *guru*-worship of a decidedly objectionable type.

Much of Kabir's teaching was so greatly to the taste of his Muhammadan countrymen that they actually claimed him as a true Muslim. It is narrated that after his death both Hindus and Muhammadans contended for the possession of his body, each desiring to do honour to the saint; but, while they disputed, Kabir himself appeared in their midst, and directed them to look under the cloth which was supposed to cover his mortal remains, and after saying this instantly vanished. When the coverlet was lifted a heap of sweet-scented flowers was discovered, and nothing more. The contending parties, astonished and awestruck, shared the blooms between them, and dealt with them according to their respective funeral ceremonies.

One half of the flowers was burnt by the Hindus, the other half was buried by the Muslims, and a cenotaph erected over it.

It is impossible to overlook the fact that Kabir stands out in prominent contrast with the Hindu sect-founders who had preceded him, being a low-caste man and uneducated, and that in him the influence of Islam and perhaps also of Christianity are clearly traceable. The importance of Kabir in the more recent religious history of India is not to be gauged by the number of his professed followers—the *Kabir-panthis*—for they are not a very considerable body; but Kabir's teaching has largely influenced that of subsequent sect-founders—Guru Nanak, for example.

The books recognised by his followers as embodying

[1] The Dabistan of Mosun Fani, translated by Shea and Troyes, vol. ii. pp. 189, 190.

the teachings of Kabir are known collectively as the Khas Grantha, and consist of some twenty works in Hindi verse, some of them of considerable size.

The followers of Kabir regard him as an incarnation of the deity, and pay him divine honours, and of course many miraculous circumstances connected with his life and doings are narrated.

Monasteries for the accommodation of *Kabir-panthis* exist in many places, and their mendicant friars may be met with all over Northern India.

The age of Martin Luther was a time of considerable religious activity in India, for there were no less than three founders of leading Hindu sects who were contemporaries of the great European reformer, all three belonging to northern parts of India—viz. Vallabhacharya preaching at Benares, Chaitanya at Nadya in Bengal, and Nanak in the Punjab.

Vallabhacharya (or Ballavacharya) was born at Benares in 1479 A.D. of Brahman parents, and in his mature years set up in his native city the worship of Krishna, not as he is represented in the Mahabharata—shrewd statesman and brave warrior—but as Bala Gopala, the cowherd boy who indulged in amorous dalliance with the frail milkmaids of Bindrabun. Philosophically, Vallabha held that the human soul was a spark of the Divine Essence, and though separated from was yet identical with it. His system, which has attained great popularity and has led in practice to the grossest profligacy, is of great interest, because, unlike his sect-forming predecessors, Vallabha *discountenanced* all mortifications of the flesh, maintaining that the body should be reverenced and not ill-used. His revolt against the old ideas and deeply rooted sentiments of his own people curiously resembles the recoil from sacerdotalism, and particularly asceticism, which occurred contemporaneously in Europe under the stimulus of the spirit which led to that great epoch known as the Renaissance.

At Nadya, the chief seat of Sanskrit learning in Bengal, Chaitanya (A.D. 1484–1527), a high-caste Brahman, initiated a religious movement of considerable importance.

At the time of Chaitanya's advent the political state of Bengal was, from the Hindu point of view, gloomy in the extreme,[1] and the religion of the people seems to have been for the most part nothing but undisguised licentiousness. Surely a reform of morals was essential before any amelioration of political conditions could be hoped for. "The bacchanalian orgies of the Tantrics," writes a Bengali, "and their worship of a 'shamefully exposed female,' provoked the abhorrence of Chaitanya and roused his energy to remove the deep blots upon the national character. He commenced his labours by holding meetings of his immediate friends. At these meetings he expounded the life and acts of Krishna. Passages in Bhagbut which everyone understood in a literal sense he construed figuratively; and, by striking upon the emotional chord of our nature, he thought of putting down sensualism by sentiment. In a little time his enthusiasm affected hundreds, and gathered round him a body of disciples."[2]

We have ample biographical details of Chaitanya, and from these it is evident that his was one of those highly neurotic, emotional temperaments, bordering upon madness, which are characteristic of what it is the present fashion to call the "higher degenerates." More than once, indeed, the border line of sanity seems to have been passed by him, and he met his end by walking into the sea at Puri in a fit of mental aberration. The essence of the Nadya reformer's teaching has been thus summed up by a Bengali Brahman: "Chaitanya taught that *bhakti*, or fervent devotion, was the only road towards God, and that *bhakti* was of the following kinds:—

1. The devotion of a servant to his master.
2. The devotion of a friend to a friend.
3. The devotion of a parent to a child.
4. The devotion of a lady to her lover."

[1] "About the time when Sree Gauranga (*i.e.* Chaitanya) appeared, Bengal had nearly lost its independence. The ruler was a Mohammedan, and, though the Hindus succeeded from time to time in occupying the throne, they were obliged to embrace Mohammedanism in order to retain their sovereignty."—*Lord Gauranga, or Salvation for All*, by Shishir Kumar Ghose (Calcutta, 1897), vol. i. Introduction, p. ix.

[2] *Travels of a Hindu*, by Bholanath Chunder, pp. 29, 30.

Chaitanya recommended Radha worship, and taught that the best form of devotion was that which Radha, as the beloved mistress of Krishna, felt for him.[1] The reformer also inculcated the necessity of strict vegetarianism and total abstinence from intoxicants. He prohibited animal sacrifices, and even communication with all who performed such sacrifices. The remarriage of widows found favour with him.

Men of all castes, even the lowest, and Muhammadans also, were admitted into his sect by Chaitanya. "Three of his principal disciples, namely, Rup, Sanatan, and Haridas, were Islamites."[2]

An innovation made by Chaitanya was religious musical processions known as *sankirtans*. How powerfully music—dreamy, sensuous, subtle music—may sway the emotions of men, even to ecstasy, is well known in the history of all religions, even Islam; so it is not to be wondered at that the *sankirtans* of Chaitanya, appealing strongly to highly impressionable natures, aided the spread of his teaching very much, and have become an exceedingly popular feature in recent religious movements in India. Chaitanya was fond of theatricals, and, once playing with other amateurs, took the part of Rukhmini, the chief wife of Krishna.

The history of religion shows how readily in all countries emotional natures import the ideas of sexual relationships into their mystical longings for union with the Divine Being—a tendency which even the strong hand of a guiding central authority has not always been able to restrain from developing into objectionable practices.[3]

[1] Bhattacharjee's *Hindu Castes and Sects*, p. 469.

[2] *Ibid.* p. 464.

[3] *Christian Mysticism*, by W. R. Inge, pp. 139, 140. Writing of St. Catherine of Siena, "the spouse of Christ," Mr. John Addington Symonds says, "'Cristo amore. Cristo amore.' The reiteration of the word 'love' is most significant. It was the keynote of her whole theology, the mainspring of her life. In no merely figurative sense did she regard herself as the spouse of Christ, but dwelt upon the bliss, beyond all mortal happiness, which she enjoyed in supersensual communion with her Lord. It is easy to understand how such ideas might be, and have been, corrupted, when impressed on natures no less susceptible, but weaker and less gifted than St. Catherine's."—*Sketches in Italy and Greece*, iii. p. 53.

Now Chaitanya, unhampered by any controlling authority, preaching earnestly in a warm climate to a highly emotional people, commended with success the worship of Krishna *cum* Radha; and such a combination, in spite of subtle hermeneutists explaining it as a mystical union, has not failed to lead to extravagant profligacy amongst the more ardent followers of the cult.[1]

Chaitanya, it may be mentioned, was anticipated by another leader, Nimbaditya, who founded a sect known as the Nimats, with headquarters at Muttra. It is almost unnecessary to say that the prophet of Nadiya was in the eyes of his disciples nothing less than an incarnation of Vishnu, and even in his lifetime a temple was erected, in which his image—an almost naked mendicant painted yellow—was the object of worship.

The sect founded by Chaitanya nearly four hundred years ago is still flourishing, and seems latterly to have been making great progress. Bindrabun, on the banks of the Jumna, identified as the spot where Krishna carried on his intrigues with the *gopis*, owes its existence and its present flourishing state to Chaitanya and the sect which originated with him. The prophet himself left no issue, but he had two Brahman coadjutors in his life's mission; and their descendants, now known as *gossains*, are the acknowledged and venerated spiritual heads of the sect.

Writing with reference to the Vaishnavas of Bengal, and the Chaitanites in particular, Professor H. H. Wilson says—

"Of all obligations, however, the *guru padasraya*, or servile veneration of the spiritual teacher, is the most important and compulsory. The members of this sect are not only required to deliver up themselves and everything valuable to the disposal of the *guru*, they are not only to entertain full belief in the usual Vaishnava tenet, which identifies the votary, the teacher, and the god, but they are to look upon the *guru* as one and the present deity, as possessed of more authority even than the deity, and as one whose favour is more to be courted and whose

[1] An account of the more disreputable Chaitanite sects of Bengal is given in Dr. Bhattacharjee's *Hindu Castes and Sects*, pp. 480–83.

anger is more to be deprecated than even that of Krishna himself." [1]

The Chaitanites, who have long manifested a marked hostility to the Brahmans, have their own mendicant orders and their monasteries, many of them flourishing institutions.

In the wake of the successful teaching of Chaitanya we have the Radha Ballabis, who afford a curious and instructive instance—not, it is true, confined to Hinduism—of the manner in which worship is gradually transferred from the principal divinity to others associated with him even in a distinctly subordinate capacity. The sect referred to was founded, it is said, at the end of the sixteenth century, with headquarters at Bindrabun in Northern India, the object in view being to concentrate attention upon the worship of Radha, even in preference to that of Krishna himself; the faithful and devoted human mistress thus superseding, as it were, in men's veneration her divine but fickle lover.

Nanak.—A spiritual descendant of Kabir was Baba Nanak, a Hindu of the Kshatriya caste, who was born in the Punjab in A.D. 1469, and died there in 1539. From his earliest youth Nanak displayed a strong leaning towards the society of *sadhus*, a disinclination for regular work of any kind, and a passion for a wandering life. He is said to have travelled extensively over India, and to have visited Persia and even Mecca.

Needless to say, many miracles are attributed to him.[2] His opinions and teachings—vague and mysterious—are embodied in the Adi Granth ("The First Book"), a collection of prayers, or rather rhapsodies, compiled some fifty years after his death by one of his successors, Guru Arjan Dev. From these it may be gathered that Nanak acknowledged the existence of the Hindu divinities, over whom, however, he placed a Supreme Being, Akal Purkh, the *Formless One*.

From passages in the Japji composed by Nanak himself, it may be gathered that his philosophical ideas

[1] *Hindu Castes and Sects*, p. 103. [2] *Vide supra*, pp. 31–33.

differed little, if at all, from ordinary Hindu pantheism, his Supreme Being having no separate, conscious existence. But so much was Nanak under the influence of Islam that he often refers to God in terms which might be appropriately used by a Muhammadan or a Christian. And he was so far emancipated from the power of Hindu traditions and practice that he dissuaded his disciples from the worship of idols and the observance of Hindu religious ceremonies. Born and reared under a powerful Muhammadan government, Nanak endeavoured, like his predecessor Kabir, to assimilate his doctrines to those of his masters without abandoning the faith of his fathers; and he strove to conciliate the dominant class by maintaining that there was no material difference between Hindu and Muslim, this syncretism being only too natural on the part of the religious Hindu in the face of the powerful bigotry and proselytising energy of the Islamic rulers.

Nanak claimed that the Supreme Being was his *guru*, and had appointed him the *guru* of mankind. All castes were admitted into his sect, now well known as the *Sikhs* of the Punjab. One of his earliest disciples, Mardana, was a Mussulman by birth.

Nanak was succeeded by nine *gurus*, and under the last of these—Govind Singh (A.D. 1675-1708), who compiled a second Granth known as the Granth of the Tenth Reign—the peaceful religion of Nanak was transformed into a militant creed. Stimulated by this new cult, the *Sikhs* developed later on into a powerful political organisation. This remarkable metamorphosis was due to resentment at the religious persecutions and oppressive exactions carried on by the Muhammadan rulers of India, and was powerfully aided by the favourable opportunity for revenge, loot, and self-aggrandisement afforded by the very palpable decay of the Muslim power in India during the eighteenth century.

The *Sikhs* of Govind Singh are permitted to eat flesh, though not beef, and may drink ardent spirits and bhang, but are prohibited from using tobacco in any form.

On the whole, *Sikhism* seems to have been an effort, prolonged, but by no means quite successful, to do without the gods of the Hindu Pantheon and their Brahman priesthood, to discard idolatry, and to shake off the fetters of caste. At the period of its greatest divergence from Hinduism, the *Sikh* sect stands forth as a democratic brotherhood, believing in a sort of vague Indian pantheism disguised as monotheism. Now, however, many shades of opinion prevail amongst the *Sikhs*, and many very Hindu practices find favour amongst a large proportion of the brotherhood.

Sikhism has given rise to several mendicant orders, and a goodly number of flourishing monasteries known as Akhâras, belonging to the sect, exist in the Punjab and Northern India.

Dadu (A.D. 1550–1600).—Within a few years of the death of Baba Nanak, a very low-caste man of the name of Dadu founded in Rajputana a new non-idolatrous sect of Rama worshippers, and after his mission on earth was completed he ascended to heaven from the hill Naraina in Jeypore territory, where stands the principal monastery of his sect, known as the Dadu Panthis.

Ram Charn, belonging to the first half of the eighteenth century, was another reformer who, resolutely opposing idol worship, embroiled himself with the Brahmans, and was in consequence subjected to much persecution at their hands. The Ram Sanehi sect founded by him is of austere habits, and freely admits to its fellowship Hindus of all castes. All members of the sect are vegetarians, and are required to abstain from intoxicants as well as from narcotic drugs and tobacco.

Rama is the special god of the sect. Both men and women take part daily in his worship, though the two sexes are not permitted to do so at the same time. The religious services of the Ram Sanehis are said to have a strong resemblance to those of the Mussulmans.

Two mendicant orders belong to the sect, which has its principal monastery at Shahpur in Rajputana.

In addition to the number of examples of Hindu heresiarchs already given in this volume, one female sect-founder, the Rajput princess Mirabai, may also be mentioned.

Of this lady it is related in the Bhakta mala[1] that on account of her refusal to abandon the worship of Krishna, at the command of her husband, the Rana of Udaypur, she was expelled from the royal palace, but in consideration of her rank was allowed a separate residence. The worship of Ranachor, a form of the youthful Krishna, was the one which had captivated the imagination of the princess, and, as a reward for her devotion to the divine object of her adoration, she was eventually, in a miraculous manner, received into the image of her especial deity, and thus, in appropriate fashion, disappeared from the world.

An idea of the transcendental views held by this lady (and by Krishna-Radha worshippers generally) may be gathered from the following anecdote told of her :—

"When Mirabai, the Rajput princess, who left everything for her love for Krishna, visited the renowned Rup Goswami of Brindaban, one of the chief *bhaktas* of Sree Gauranga (Chaitanya), Rup, an ascetic of the highest order, refused to see her on the ground that he was precluded from seeing the face of a woman. As a fact, Mirabai was a most beautiful young princess, and he had not much faith in her pretensions. Hearing the message of Rup, Mirabai replied, 'Is he then a male? If so, he has no access to Brindaban. Males cannot enter there, and, if the goddess of Brindaban comes to know of his presence, she will turn him out. For does not the great Goswami know that there is but one male in existence, namely, my beloved Kanai Lal (an endearing name of Krishna), and that all besides are females?' Rup now understood that Mirabai was really a staunch devotee of Krishna, and so agreed to see her."[2]

What peculiar religious customs spring from such opinions, the following extract shows :—

"*Sukee-bhava*.—These mendicants, born in the western

[1] See Professor Wilson's *Sketch of the Religious Sects of the Hindus*, pp. 85–87.

[2] *Lord Gauranga, or Salvation for All*, by Shishir Kumar Ghose, vol. i. Introduction, p. xl. (Calcutta, 1897).

provinces and composed of Bramhuns and other castes, are followers of Krishna, and, though men, put on the dress and ornaments and assume the manners of women, professing the same attachment to Krishna as the milkmaids are said to have had when Krishna was on earth. They paint and adorn with flowers an image of Krishna, and dancing around it, in imitation of the milkmaids, worship it daily."[1]

A small sect called Mirabais, acknowledging the leadership of the Rajput princess, is said to be still in existence in Western India.

Taking a retrospective survey of Neo-Brahmanism as sketched in the foregoing pages, one cannot help being impressed with the following facts. Although the worship of Vishnu under the forms of Krishna and Rama spread far and wide, although the primitive phallic cult of Siva also flourished contemporaneously, although men in their anxiety paid homage impartially at the shrines of *both* these gods of the Hindu triad, and in Eastern India invoked, with many strange rites, the goddesses Durga and Kali, yet the Muhammadan Empire went on extending irresistibly, until at length it became paramount in India. Islam, indeed, with its uncompromising monotheism and its abhorrence of idolatry, made itself powerfully felt throughout the land, while numbers of the subjugated became converts to the vigorously proselytising creed of the conquerors, under which invidious distinctions of caste were not maintained.

Amidst the wreck of Hindu States the question of the preservation of Hinduism itself became of vital importance. Diverse methods of achieving this great object naturally suggested themselves to differently constituted minds. Hinduism might be made softly alluring, by some means or other, so as still to retain the allegiance of a disillusioned race, no longer confident in the support of its gods and its arrogant priesthood; or the national religion might be reformed to suit the new order of ideas awakened by the presence and claims of Islam; or it might be modified so as to resemble, outwardly at least, the Muslim faith, and thus avoid contempt and evade persecution.

[1] Ward's *Hindus*, p. 296.

Three distinct effects arose from the circumstances and conditions to which attention has just been drawn.

1. The rise of sects combining the worship of Radha, the favourite mistress of Krishna, with that of her divine lover—a combination too naturally suggestive of sensuality, and one lending itself readily to the establishment of practices calculated to attract followers by their veiled or open immorality. To this class belong the sects of the Nimats, the Radha Vallabhis (sixteenth century), and the Chaitanites (sixteenth century) of Bengal.

2. The appearance of conciliatory syncretic Hindu sects intended, at any rate by their *original* founders, to bridge over the differences between the religions of the Hindus and their Muslim rulers—to reconcile them, in fact. In this category may be placed the sects formed in Northern India by Kabir (sixteenth century) and by Guru Nanak (sixteenth century), though the latter sect was under subsequent spiritual leaders developed along very different lines from those adopted by the founder.

3. The formation of Hindu sects opposed to idolatry: for example, the Ram-worshipping Dadu Panthis (A.D. 1550–1600) and Ram Sanehis (A.D. 1718), both of Rajputana.

During the decay of the Muhammadan and the rise of the British power in India, the process of sect-formation has been as active as ever. New and potent factors, such as Western education and aggressive Christianity, have come into play in the disintegration of immemorial beliefs and practices and the formation of new ones. None of all the main types of post-Buddhist Hinduism can be said to be actually dying out; indeed, under the complete religious freedom of British rule they all appear to give signs of renewed vitality. Many recent sects are of a decidedly objectionable type; but, whether respectable or otherwise, nearly all furnish a contingent of mendicants to swell the hordes of the privileged itinerants who swarm over the country.

Under the new conditions of life obtaining in India, and in response to intellectual stimuli of European origin, there have recently appeared in our own time certain small theistic, non-idolatrous sects, like the *Brahmo-samaj*, whose chief prophet, the eloquent Keshub Chunder Sen, was a *sudra*; and the *Arya-samaj*, founded by a Mahratta Brahman named Dayanand, a man of commanding talents and personality. The former of these sects is well known in Europe and America, through its founder and some of its prominent apostles having visited the West and lectured there; but the Brahmo cult has still a quite insignificant following, perhaps because, by denying the authority of the Vedas, it has practically drifted away from Hinduism. The *Arya-samaj*, though hardly a purely religious sect, adhered to the Vedas, as *interpreted by Dayanand*; but it favours certain practices which are certain, in the course of time, to undermine its morals, though possibly these very practices might prove an attraction and help to swell the numbers of the new sect.

It remains to note the fact that political circumstances and national aspirations have also, in recent times, called into being the dangerous sect of the *Kukas* in the Punjab, and have led quite lately to the very significant deification in his own country of the Mahratta chieftain Seva-ji (A.D. 1627–80), famous for his successes against the Muhammadans, and for the establishment of the practical supremacy of the Mahrattas in Southern India.[1]

And so the kaleidoscope of Indian religious sects presents at every succeeding period new groups and combinations. For each sect, old or new, it is an absolute necessity that it should have its own temples, to accommodate the material representations of its chosen divinities and to lodge the priests who conduct the worship of the idols and accept the gifts presented to them. Moreover, if the sect is to spread and flourish, it must have its own missionaries, who, in conformity with immemorial Indian traditions, should be wandering ascetics. Nor could it have been difficult, at any time, to find such men in

[1] Under the auspices of certain Indian politicians, the Sivaji festival was, for the first time, celebrated in Calcutta in June 1902, and was the occasion for many significant speeches by no means calculated to promote harmonious relations between the rulers and the ruled in India.—*Vide The Englishman*, Calcutta, 26th June 1902.

abundance owing to the many causes predisposing to world-weariness, renunciation, and abstention from labour which have been ever present in India.

Hinduism is certainly very old, and its foundations lie deep down in the hearts of the Indian people, but even my brief sketch of its history must have made it abundantly clear that, contrary to the prevailing impression, it has undergone vast changes in the course of time, and that it is still as plastic as of old, because neither now nor at any previous stages of its development, especially since the Buddhist revolt, has it been subject to that organised *control* of a centralised authority which circumstances rendered possible in Europe; hence new sects have arisen, and have expanded in a way which was not *tolerated* by the strong arm of the ecclesiastical authorities in Christendom.

The Aryan nature-gods have certainly long ceased to be worshipped. Indra, Kuvera, Yama, Varuna, Garuda, and Soma have likewise fallen into the background of oblivion. It is true that the Brahmans have managed to secure long-continued veneration for their tutelary deity Siva, but the people have enthroned two Kshatriya heroes, Krishna and Rama, as the especial objects of their veneration; the former, for many reasons, being the more popular of the two, and likely, in one aspect or other, to maintain his place for ages to come in the hearts of the Hindus.

With the striking changes which the religion of the Hindus has steadily undergone there have been concomitant mutations in the attitude of the worshippers towards the unseen powers.

Within the pale of Brahmanism the worshipper relied on complicated rites and ceremonies, on sacrifices, spells, pilgrimages, and almsgiving—all these being conducted by or under the strict guidance solely of the Brahman priesthood, who practically controlled his destinies, and without whom there was no possible salvation. Buddhism, rejecting such sacerdotal aids, required its followers to trust to complete detachment from the world as the safest and surest means of securing happiness here and spiritual deliverance hereafter; and Buddhism expected each man or woman to work out his or her own emancipation. In modern Hinduism, which succeeded Buddhism, the Brahmans never recovered such an ascendant position as they had enjoyed in earlier days, for the ascetic saints and sages had acquired too much consideration and authority to be suppressed or set aside. And at the same time new ideas had taken hold of men's minds, causing them to place less reliance than of yore in the old ceremonial rites, and leaving them to place their trust and hope in passionate devotion to or *faith* in a chosen god. A great and mighty change this, a momentous revolution. But since for most men the divinity is too high, too remote, too transcendent for this devotion, the Hindu has in many cases accepted as substitute for the chosen deity his supposed representative, his very incarnation, the living *guru*, the saintly *sadhu* to whom he actually pays his adoration.[1] Only the wilfully blind could fail to see the parallelism between these developments and those which have occurred in other more familiar creeds.

In respect to that most important subject, *caste*, it may be said that the appearance of each new sect has been signalised by a renewed struggle against the disabilities imposed by caste, but with little practical result beyond the formation of new castes or sub-castes; which is by no means to be wondered at, since the time-honoured system has, naturally, the unflinching, whole-hearted support of the superior classes, and particularly of the still powerful Brahmanical priesthood.

Recently that most intellectual of rulers, the German Emperor, was reported to have said "that the germ of every sectarian movement is political, so is the germ of every political movement a question of the material welfare of the people;" and there is profound truth in this statement. How frequently in Europe and elsewhere unfavourable political conditions have led to general despondency, and thereafter to religious revivals and the birth of

[1] How completely even a highly educated and practical man can subordinate himself to a living *guru* is well exemplified in the case of an ex-Postmaster-General of the North-West Provinces, cited in Professor Max Müller's *Life and Sayings of Rama Krishna*, pp. 20–22.

heretical sects or new monastic orders, is a matter of history. The fact being admitted that the political background of each period cannot but colour the minds of the populace and its leaders, it becomes a factor of too much importance to be passed over entirely; *hence* the place given to it in the foregoing brief outline of the rise and progress of modern Hinduism seems to need no special justification.

As supplementary to the above condensed account of the appearance from time to time of new gods and novel conceptions in Hinduism, and of the genesis of the more prominent sects under the leadership of religious reformers, the important fact must not be overlooked that, whatever the doctrinal views and ultimate hopes of subtle theologians and earnest religionists may have been, there have never, at any period, been wanting multitudes of Hindu people indisposed to undergo austerities or personal discomforts of any kind, and yet none the less desirous of securing a prosperous time in this life, a better time in the next mundane existence, and eventually also eons of bliss in the various heavens of the gods. And this worldly-minded class has, on account of its wealth and influence, been too important and useful a factor in the community to be really slighted by the prophets and the priesthood, however much such professors of religion might rail against riches as such. Renunciation, as preached by most founders of sects or religions, if universally practised, could obviously only end in national extinction; hence it follows that, to preclude such a disaster, there must always be a class of *workers* whose special function it is to produce and provide the necessaries of life for themselves and also for those who, abstaining from all labour, desire to live on alms.

And indeed, wherever religion recommends or enjoins renunciation, it also proclaims, with no uncertain voice, that liberality to the poor—meaning more particularly the religious poor—and the priestly classes will be unstintingly rewarded here and hereafter. Mendicity, on the colossal scale in which it has existed in India time out of mind, could only be possible on the condition of widespread and whole-hearted charitableness on the part of laymen of all classes; hence it is not surprising to find charity lauded in the Hindu Scriptures as the special virtue of this present age, known to Hindus as the *Kali Yuga.*

"In the *Krita Yuga,*" says Vrihaspati, "the prevailing virtue is declared to be religious austerity; in the *Trita,* divine knowledge; in the *Divapara,* sacrifices; and in the *Kali Yuga,* charity, compassion, and restraint of passions.

"Manu, however, beginning with the use of almost identical words, constitutes charity alone the supreme virtue in the degenerate *Kali Yuga*—

"'In the *Krita Yuga* the prevailing virtue is declared to be religious austerity; in the *Trita,* divine knowledge; in the *Divapara,* sacrifices; in the *Kali Yuga,* charity alone.'"[1]

[1] *The Hindu Law of Endowments,* Tagore Law Lectures, 1892, by Pandit Prannath Saraswati, M.A. and B.L., p. 15 (Thacker, Spink, & Co., Calcutta).

CHAPTER VIII

HINDU ASCETIC SECTS AND THEIR SUBDIVISIONS

SECTION I.—Introductory Remarks—The Multiplicity of Hindu Sects by no means Abnormal—Jain Monks or Yatis interviewed—Their Opinions and Habits.

THERE are, as might have been expected, a large number of Hindu sects. Professor Wilson gives a list of forty-three of them, and adds that in popular works on the subject ninety-six heresies are ordinarily recognised. It is needless to say that even this figure would not nearly represent the actual number existing at the present time. Amongst the sects studied and described by Europeans are some whose tenets and practices have filled pious Westerns with supercilious wonderment or holy horror; but, if we are to be just, it must be admitted that such abnormalities may be found, if looked for, in the by-paths of every religion, not excepting the Christian. All religions in the course of their existence give rise to a multitude of heretical separatists. In the case of Christianity, heresies appeared from apostolic times, and some sects holding opinions entirely subversive of morality as we understand it came into existence very early indeed;

for example, the Antinomians, who held that the moral law was not binding upon Christians. Sects possessed of little inherent vitality died of natural exhaustion, but many, both in the early centuries and in the Middle Ages, such as the Gnostics, Manichæans, Nestorians, Albigenses, Hussites, and others, were forcibly and relentlessly suppressed by Church and State authority. Since the successful revolt against the power of the Papacy in the sixteenth century, a very considerable number of dissenting Christian sects, some with ideas in regard to political and sexual morality far removed from those ordinarily accepted by the established Churches, have appeared and secured a footing for themselves.[1]

Similarly, Hinduism in its long history has produced a great variety of peculiar sects, and, as it differs from Christianity in not having had a powerful, well-organised, and resolute central authority to *guide* for *centuries* its theological development, the heresies—often characterised by great freedom and originality of doctrine and much latitude in practice—have, in most cases, been able to run a normal course, and have sometimes grown to be almost semi-independent religions.

It seems superfluous to state that the foregoing remarks and comparisons are merely intended to remove the erroneous impression which prevails, rather widely, that there is something abnormal in the multiplicity of religious sects to be found in India.

Amongst the still existing Indian sects, the Jains, so interesting in themselves, and also as a link with Buddhism, claim precedence of attention. This ancient sect,—it is hardly an independent religion now,—whose origin is perhaps antecedent to that of Buddhism, and therefore may date back earlier than the sixth century B.C., exhibits much of the spirit, the precepts, and the discipline of monasticism as established or organised by Gautama Buddha, a full description of which may be read in Mr. Spence Hardy's comprehensive work entitled *Eastern Monachism.* As, how-

[1] Amongst sects of quite recent date originating in Protestant countries may be named the Swedenborgians, Mormons, Shakers, Irvingites, Darbyites, Sandemanians, Perfectionists, Agapemonites, and Christian Scientists.

ever, I do not desire to deal with the Jain system in any detail, may I invite the reader to make the acquaintance of the Jains—monks, nuns, and laymen—by following me as I describe for him my impressions of certain religious meetings of that most ancient sect held in the autumn of 1898, at which I had the privilege of being present.

Jain Monks or Yatis.—A few high steps rising from the mud of the narrow overcrowded lane brought me into a dark hall, which gave access to a straight and steep flight of brick stairs not a yard wide between its bounding walls. I ascended these stairs, and, after passing through a low restricted doorway at the top, found myself on the flat terrace roof of the main building—an ordinary house such as may be found in the native quarters of any city in Upper India. This flat roof, however, had been partially built upon along three sides, the rooms thus formed being all doorless and practically open towards the central uncovered space. The effect was as if three verandahs opened upon an ample central hypæthral court. For privacy and convenience in a hot tropical climate, nothing could be more admirably conceived. In one of the rooms, or verandahs, which might have been eighteen or twenty feet long and eight or ten feet wide, there were assembled a number of well-to-do persons—merchants, shopkeepers, and others—sitting upon cotton carpets and floorcloths. At one end was a raised platform made of rough planks, and on it was seated an elderly Jain monk of some importance, with two or three others in attendance. I had been expected, so a small cane chair covered with a white cloth had, with thoughtful kindness, been placed for me near the senior monk, on his right hand, neither on the platform nor under the roof, but just outside.

The whole of the platform was not of uniform height; the part where the principal monk sat was higher by a few inches than the part occupied by the juniors. There is no equality in this world; there never was, and there never will be! No furniture could be seen in the room, but, as a concession to the imperious demands of the new age, a big-faced clock occupied a conspicuous place on the wall. Behind the monks, and partially concealed from view by the platform on which they sat, was a group of women, amongst whom were at least forty nuns. The monks presented a peculiar appearance. Clean-shaven were they all—head, face, and eyebrows. Each man wore a sort of bib of three or four folds of white cloth, not under his chin, but *over his nose and mouth*, held in place by strings passed above the ears and tied behind the head. These were characteristic outward symbols of the most important of Jain tenets, — absolute respect for life in all its forms, — and are worn in order to obviate the possible accidental and unintentional destruction of even the minutest organisms by being drawn into the nose or mouth in the ordinary process of respiration. Hence they are really *life protectors*. But an inconvenient article like this could be used by ordinary people only on purely ceremonial occasions, and not always then, for several men in the room, instead of wearing their bibs, carried them in their hands. A picture of a Jain *yati* appears at the commencement of the chapter.

The nuns, of course, had their mouths and noses covered, and were, besides, so completely veiled as to show little of their faces but a pair of eyes.

Only the principal monk spoke, and fortunately he was by no means disinclined to be communicative. He interested me greatly by his serene yet pathetic gravity and a gentle dignity which seemed to pervade his every word and movement. He sat cross-legged on the platform, clothed in two white cotton sheets—one round his loins and the other about his shoulders. No beads, bangles, or armlets, nor marks of any kind, either ornamented or disfigured his person. The two cotton sheets were, as he told me, all the clothes he might wear or possess, with the exception of *half* a blanket in the winter time. Many other interesting particulars about his order did the venerable *yati* communicate to me; and, though these may be found in European books on Jainism, I was pleased to receive them from him, and I reproduce them here.

During the four months of the rainy season known as the *chamasa*, the Jain monk may seek shelter and repose in a *dharmsala* of his order, which is a guest-house established by lay Jains for the accommodation of the monks; but for eight months in every year he must wander over the country barefooted and bareheaded, as friars of his order have done since at least five hundred years before the birth of Christ. He may on no account avail himself of any mode of conveyance, whether horse, carriage, boat, or railway car; nor may he ever sleep in a bed. And year after year they wander about, these gentle monks, without staff or scrip, armed only with soft besoms of cotton threads to tenderly brush away minute insects that might happen to be in danger of destruction under the pressure of their persons whenever fatigue necessitates some rest for their wearied limbs. Many of these besoms were in evidence amongst the audience, and each monk present was provided with one for his own especial use. The only other property any of these men may possess is a wooden alms-bowl in which to receive food. Monks who can read may carry about with them their sacred books in the Prakrit character. Some of these books were shown to me, beautiful specimens of caligraphy, all in detached leaves protected by a couple of thin wooden boards. Metal must on no account be touched by the monks, except perhaps in the form of a needle, which may be borrowed when required, but must be returned the same day before the sun goes down.

Since the most important guiding principle of their lives is to avoid hurting, leave alone killing, any living thing, it is obvious that they do not partake of flesh meat of any kind whatever; but they carry their self-denial further, for they never taste *fruit* and drink no wine of any sort. From sunset to sunrise they must, on no pretext whatever, eat or drink anything. Jain *sadhus* should never bathe, for if they draw water from tank or well they are sure to be the cause of death or suffering to living creatures. They may not drink any water but what has been used for culinary purposes: for example, water in which rice or vegetables have been boiled, or warm water used for rinsing out cooking-pots. *Such* water was not drawn *for them*, or stored *for them*; it had been *used* already, so the act of drinking it could bring no sin to them. They may even use such water for sponging themselves. That is the nearest approach to a bath that is permissible under any circumstances.

Jain monks are not to light a fire, for fear of killing any living thing that may be lodging in the fuel.

When engaged on their annual tramp the monks go to the houses of Hindus, but preferably to those of their own sect, generally known as Bhabras, where they ask for a bit of bread which may be over from the last meal and about to be thrown away.

The lay members of the sect loyally support the wandering monks and nuns, some curious rules regulating the intercourse between them. One of these ascetics visiting the house of a lay member may enter boldly without announcing his or her presence, and may help himself to what food is available; but if the fire is alight in the room the ascetic should take nothing, and so also when the pots and pans happen to be in contact with one another.

Women must on no account be touched by Jain monks, nor even may their garments come in contact without serious defilement, only to be atoned for by fastings and penances. And of course the same rule applies, *mutatis mutandis*, to the case of Jain nuns.

When the Jain monk dies, his fellows apprise any members of their sect who may be near at hand of the event; but they themselves pass on. It is for the stranger to cremate or bury the corpse, or leave it to its fate. What matters the body when the soul has deserted it?

There was a suspicion of vanity in the manner of the old monk as he stated and explained to me these facts about his order, and I felt that he needed this sustaining spiritual pride to help him along his difficult way, not less difficult for being voluntary. His personal appearance gave the impression of great suffering, and his attendants all had the same appearance, contrasting very much indeed with the ordinary *sadhus* of other sects. And wherefore this austere rejection of the world's goods, wherefore all this self-inflicted misery? Is it to attain a glorious heaven hereafter, a blessed existence after death? No!

It is, as the old monk explained to me, only to escape rebirth—for the Jain believes in the transmigration of souls—and to attain eternal *rest.*

"It is *sin* in this life," said the *yati,* "and the consequences of sin in previous existences that clog and disfigure the pure spirit. These have to be got rid of if the soul is to be set free. Suppose," he went on, "we have a pot of impure butter: how do we purify it, how do we separate extraneous stuff from the pure substance? We heat the *pot which contains it*, and then the *ghee* and the impurities part asunder, the latter falling to the bottom of the vessel. So we must heat (*i.e.* afflict) the body, which is the pot containing both the pure spirit and the attendant impurities, till on the furnace of asceticism one is completely separated from the other. Hence our fastings and our self-denials, all to secure exemption from future rebirths and to attain blessed *narvana.*" And as he said this, the serenity of the old monk's countenance and his placid eyes seemed an assurance that he himself was well on the way to the longed-for goal.

After courteously answering my many questions, the old man read to the assembly some selections from the Jain sacred books and expounded the same. He then addressed his audience, and in the course of his sermon plainly indicated his disbelief in the existence of God. A discussion afterwards arose between him and a pandit who accompanied me, with, as might have been expected, a resultless display of Sanskrit learning and subtle dialectics.

I am quite sure that the uncompromising atheism of the *yati* was not shared by all his hearers; for a day or two afterwards a Jain layman, who had been present at the meeting, came to me and explained what he, and probably a majority of the sect, understood to be the functions of God in the universe. He said that the Creator (evidently accepting His existence) was by no means the cause of or responsible for the wickedness and suffering in this world. Each individual soul received the reward or punishment due to its own acts. God through His sacred law warned all men against the consequences of evil-doing, and showed them the right way; *but He did not interfere in the affairs of the world.*[1] Yet the more He and His commandments were remembered the better for each separate soul. It was like this: A man's house is on fire, and he asleep. A stranger comes and wakens him up. It is for the owner now to see to the safety of his own property. So through life it is God's warning voice in the sacred books that informs us that our house is on fire. Each man must, however, look to his own safety and comfort, here and hereafter, and expect no *divine interposition* in his favour.

Religion amongst Jains who accept these views would therefore seem to exclude the idea of prayer for help. It would resolve itself into a constant recollection of the divine commands and warnings, and, I have no doubt, of appreciation of the goodness of God in having given these warnings for the benefit of short-sighted mortals in their earthly pilgrimage. Still, as few men would be content with such a religion, the Jains have come to regard some twenty-four of their own saints[2] practically as principal deities, and nowadays many, perhaps the major portion of the sect, venerate also the higher gods of the Hindu Pantheon.

Whatever point of view we may take, it is still a matter for wonder that the impulse which set the Jain *sadhus* in motion has lasted for five-and-twenty centuries; that *yatis*, bareheaded and barefooted, naked, or with just two cotton sheets to cover them, have wandered through India for eight months every year for two or three thousand years, not seldom without any reliance upon or even belief in God, mortifying the frail flesh, and all this in order to ensure a cessation of the evils of rebirth—wandering ceaselessly to attain rest and final annihilation; wandering blamelessly, generation after generation, while dynasties

[1] It is not without interest that in this twentieth century the well-known surgeon, Sir Henry Thompson, has, after twenty years of study, arrived at much the same conclusions as my Bhabra friends, viz. that the omniscient and omnipotent Power which rules the universe *does not interfere in the affairs of mankind.* Only the great modern surgeon goes further still, affirming that the Omnipotent has left mankind *without the guidance of any revelation whatever.*—*The Unknown God* (Frederick Warne & Co., 1902).

[2] Known as Jinas or Tirthankaras.

have come and gone, and nations have risen, decayed, and vanished.

And, while the men have taken up the task of working out their own emancipation, the women have not been backward in the same cause, but since times immemorial have, always in couples, wandered like the monks over the country, resting like them during the *chamasa* in the nunneries of their sect. Many of the women who join this mendicant order have no doubt done so in middle age, disillusioned and tired of life. But quite young girls also follow the path of asceticism. For example, I learned, on the very best authority, of a married girl of only sixteen years of age, who, having a strong religious bent, told her husband a short time previously that henceforth he would be *to her as a brother*—a very significant expression in the mouth of an Indian woman. Her husband accepted her decision, and with her consent arranged a second marriage. When the new wife arrived, the first one, prepared to renounce the vanities of this life, sold her jewels to the value of two thousand rupees, gave a feast and presents to the Brahmans, and, adopting the life of a *Punjni*, left her home for ever. The ceremony of entering the ascetic order was attended with a good deal of personal inconvenience. The girl's luxuriant black hair had to be plucked out by the roots; not a vestige of eyebrow or eyelash was left. After that, she tied a cloth over her mouth to prevent the possible destruction of minute organisms, and, armed with a besom of cotton threads, started with some others of her sex on a round of pilgrimages or wanderings.

I have often met these nuns on the road, and once quite fifty of them marshalled in order. They must have been coming from or returning to a nunnery in the neighbourhood.

Sometimes the adoption of the monastic life is made the occasion for a special demonstration, which always includes a procession. The postulant, or perhaps more properly the novice, is decked out in the best of clothes and the costliest jewels, and carried through the town in whatever mode of conveyance he or she may select.

PROCESSION IN HONOUR OF THE VEILING OF A JAIN NUN.

FIG. 8.

To face page 150.

When the round is made, the candidate is taken to some appointed place, and there, after being disrobed and clad in the simple vestments of the order, takes the prescribed vows, and receives from the senior *sadhu* present the *mantra* of the order. The illustration (Fig. 8) represents such a procession in Ludhiana on the occasion of a *Grihasti* woman becoming a Jain nun or *sadhui.*

The Jains are divided into two principal sub-sects—one called *Swetambara* (white-robed), the other *Digambara* (sky-clad—*i.e.* naked). A *yati* or monk of the latter denomination does not attach any particular importance to the *chamar* (the besom) or the *puttika* (mouth veil), and is not permitted to carry an alms-bowl. He must receive his food in the palm of his hand.[1] The *Swetambaris* and the *Digambaris* are each subdivided into four orders. The Jain laity belong almost exclusively to the trading community and the Baniya caste.

[1] *Hindu Castes and Sects,* by Jogendra Nath Bhattacharjee, M.A., D.L., pp. 553–55 (Calcutta, 1896).

CHAPTER VIII—*continued*

ASCETIC SECTS AND THEIR SUBDIVISIONS

SECTION II.—Principal Hindu Sects: Saivas, Vaishnavas, and Sikhs—Particulars regarding Sanyasis, Dandis, Paramahansas, Brahmacharis, Lingaits, and Aghoris.

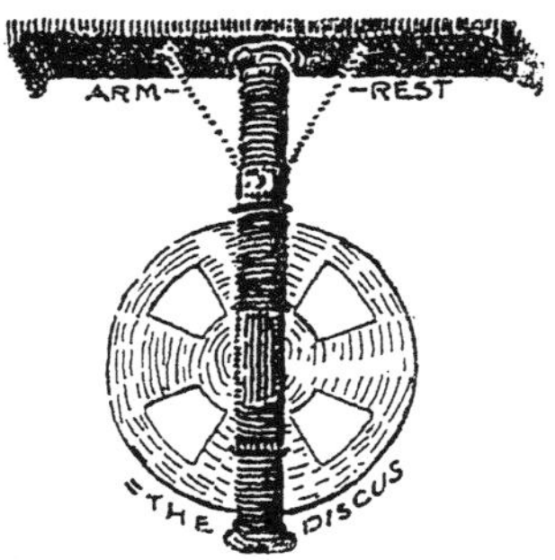

HE Hindu ascetic sects which make up the great bulk of the wandering *sadhus* of India, more particularly Northern India, and which I propose to notice as typical examples, are the following:—

Saivas, or worshippers of Siva—

1. Sanyasis
2. Dandis
3. Paramahansas
4. Brahmacharis

} followers of Sankaracharya.[1]

5. Lingaits, followers of Basava.
6. Aghoris.
7. Yogis.

Vaishnavas, or worshippers of Vishnu—

1. Sri Vaishnavas, followers of Ramanuja.
2. Madhavas, followers of Madhavacharya.
3. Ramanandis, followers of Ramanand.
4. Kabir Panthis, followers of Kabir.
5. Ballavacharyas, followers of Ballavacharya.
6. Chaitanites, followers of Chaitanya.

[1] Acharya means teacher, or more properly religious teacher.

Sikhs, followers of Nanak—

1. Udasis.
2. Nirmalis.
3. Nihangs or Akalis.

The petty sects known as Dadhu Panthis, Ram Sanehis, and Mirabais, referred to in the last chapter, do not call for any further notice here.

1. The Sanyasis.[1]

The followers of Sankara, while paying special honour to Siva, do not, as a rule, reject the other gods of the Hindu Pantheon, nor do they deny the truth of the *Shastras* generally. Hence the order is a rather mixed one, containing many Vaishnavas and even Tantrics. It is nevertheless a pretentious sect, claiming that its members are alone the true *sadhus* of India, probably because the closing and strictly ascetic period in the lives of the "twice-born" castes (as laid down in Manu's ordinances) is known as the *sanyasi* stage.

It is generally held that the *Sanyasis* are divided into ten sub-orders, the Dasnamis, named as follows :—

(1) Giri.	(6) Parvat.
(2) Puri.	(7) Sagar.
(3) Bhârti.	(8) Tirath.
(4) Ban.	(9) Ashram.
(5) Auran (Aranya).	(10) Saraswati.

But it would seem that the last three names on the list belong properly to the order of the *dandis*.

All Hindus, even Sudras and outcasts, may join this order, though it is generally held that some of the sub-orders, such as the Ban, Auran, and Saraswati, admit Brahmans only. At the annual spring saturnalia low-caste men actually become *Sanyasis temporarily* during the continuance of the festival. At such times they undergo

[1] It would appear that in Benares the *Sanyasis* are commonly known as *gosains*.—*Hindu Tribes and Castes as represented in Benares*, by the Rev. M. A. Sherring, part iii. chap. ii.

a variety of self-inflicted tortures, such as passing thick metal skewers through their tongues or the flesh of their arms or sides.

Such facts prove conclusively the democratic character of the order and its freedom from the caste prejudices of Hinduism. Granting this, it was still quite startling to read in the *Pioneer* of Allahabad, early in 1899, that an elderly, educated, and well-to-do American lady of French extraction had come to India as a *sanyasin* under the name of Swami Abhayanda, having been admitted to the Puri sub-order by Swami Vivikananda, the Bengali *sadhu* who went to the Congress of Religions at Chicago as the representative of the Hindus of India. The lady, it would appear, had studied the Upanishads and been converted to the pantheistic doctrines of the Vedanta philosophy. "Her original intention," says the *Pioneer,* "was to beg her way through India. She had a basket for the purpose instead of the customary bowl. But she has been persuaded to relinquish this intention. She wears a high-necked dress of the plainest possible cut and of a yellow colour."

All *Sanyasis* may eat together, and the majority accept food from any Hindu. They may not partake of flesh meat or spirits. They rub ashes over their bodies, wear salmon-coloured robes, and a tiger skin when they can get one. About sect marks on the forehead they affect indifference, though some paint an eye, like the central eye of Siva, just above the nose. All wear, as a distinguishing badge, a necklace of rudraksha berries, or, failing that, at least one such berry. The hair of their heads, and their beards also, are allowed to grow freely. In their hands they usually carry a conch, or a pair of iron tongs—the latter a very useful article indeed; for whenever they are seated they light a fire and proceed to smoke *ganja*.[1]

Sanyasis pointedly discard those outward symbols of Hinduism—the *jeneu* (sacred thread), and the *chundî* or *shikha,* a tuft of hair ordinarily worn on the crown of the head.

When, after a period of probation, the postulant wishes

[1] The dried hemp-plant, used for smoking like tobacco.

[Photo by Col. Constable.

SANYASIS AT A RELIGIOUS GATHERING.

FIG. 9.

To *face page* 154.

to be received as a *chela*, he must bring an offering including a *lingam* and a rudraksha berry to the *Sanyasi* whose disciple he wishes to become. Four *Sanyasis* are required for the initiatory ceremony. In their presence the candidate has to make a declaration of his determination to observe the rules of the order, to renounce the world and its vanities—in fact, to abandon all worldly affections and desires; for the *Sanyasi*, as the Bhagavad-gita says, is one who "does not hate and does not love anything."

The chief of the four officiating *Sanyasis*—the selected *guru*, in fact—whispers into his ear the *mantra* of the order; another confers a new name upon him, together with a surname selected from the first seven distinctive appellations of the sub-orders given on a previous page; the third rubs him over with ashes; the fourth breaks his sacred thread if he have one, and cuts off his scalp-lock, thus symbolising his complete severance from worldly life and ordinary Hinduism.

After his initiation the new *chela* is expected to serve his principal *guru* (preceptor) for a time, in order to learn wisdom from him, to make certain pilgrimages, and to follow the rules of the order. When the period of probation has expired, more ceremonies have to be performed, including the *shradh*, or post-funeral rites, of the new *Sanyasi*.

The rules laid down for the guidance of the *Sanyasi* have been variously stated to me; but the following six prohibitions and six commandments, as learned from one of the order, may be regarded as a fair specimen of the injunctions they are expected to observe.

Six Prohibitions.

1. Do not sleep on a couch, under any circumstances.
2. Do not wear white clothes.
3. Do not speak to or even think about women.
4. Do not sleep during the daytime.
5. Do not at any time ride on a horse or other animal, or in any vehicle whatsoever.
6. Do not allow your mind to be agitated in any way.

Six Commandments.

1. Leave your abode *only* for the sake of begging necessary food.
2. Say your prayers every day.
3. Bathe every day.
4. Contemplate daily the likeness or image of Siva.
5. Practise purity and cleanliness.
6. Perform the formal worship of the gods.

When death overtakes him the *Sanyasi* is buried in a grave like a pit, with a side receptacle in which the body is made to sit up facing east or north-east with its arms supported on a wooden rest (*byragun*). *Sanyasis* have *no* after-death or burial ceremonies, no *shradh* ceremonies like ordinary Hindus, these having been performed when the *Sanyasi* was finally admitted to the order; and even the formal feasts which are given on such occasions by the other ascetic sects, such as Bairagis and *Yogis*, are omitted.

One morning at about ten o'clock I overtook a strange procession—strange even for India—wending its way slowly along the Lahore Mall between the Chief Court and the Cathedral. A loud brass band led the way, discoursing music—European music, too; for it was not difficult to make out the tune of the once-popular song—

> "Just before the battle, mother,
> I was thinking most of you."

Behind the musicians came some three or four men carrying smoking censers of sweet incense. They were marching in front of a litter borne on the shoulders of a few men. It was a very unusual-looking litter, the front being in the form of a moresque arch. There was a cloth hood over it, but it was open on three sides, so that the occupant could be plainly seen except from behind. And the occupant was a dead *sadhu*, sitting in vacant contemplation with his legs crossed in the approved manner. He was tied to the upright back of the litter and was covered with strings of flowers, which formed a sort of floral veil over his face but could not conceal the hideousness of death, as the unconscious head rolled helplessly from side to side, keeping time, in a sort of grotesque mockery, to the measured step of the bearers as they marched slowly along the wide road.

On one side of the litter was a hired landau with some respectably dressed natives, who may or may not have been part of the procession, and on the other a slovenly policeman in yellow trousers and blue tunic lolling in a one-horse carriage known as an *ekka.* A little confused crowd, in which the female element predominated, brought up the rear; while a number of urchins, stimulated by curiosity, accompanied the cortège and pointed out the dead man to one another. I ascertained that the party was on its way to a selected spot where the *sadhu,* a *Sanyasi,* would be buried in a circular grave, sitting upright and covered over with salt. This funeral procession brought to my recollection a similar one I had seen many years previously at Rajamundry, in the Madras Presidency. On that occasion the dead *sadhu* was placed in a sitting position in his grave, a quantity of salt was piled up about him, and earth thrown in till the body was nearly covered up. Then upon the top of the shaven head, still exposed to view, a large number of cocoanuts were broken in order to crack the skull and afford the imprisoned soul a means of exit from the now useless body. The fragments of the cocoanuts which had been used for the liberation of the dead man's soul were, I remember, eagerly sought for by the bystanders.[1]

It should be mentioned that the practice of burial rather than cremation, in the case of these and certain other *sadhus,* is due to the sentiment that the bodies of such sainted personages do not need to be purified by fire.

Nearly every *sadhu,* however ignorant he may be of letters, or however regardless in practice of what are usually held as the essentials of a moral life, is aware of, and, on occasion, can parade wise maxims, instructive stories, and pithy parables intended to point the way to virtue or dissuade from vice. Amongst *Sanyasis* there is not found

[1] The funeral ceremonies of a Brahman *Sanyasi* are described in part ii. chap. xxxvi. of the Abbé Dubois' *Hindu Manners, Customs, and Ceremonies.*

any dearth of such ethical guides; as, for example, the so-called "twenty-four *upa gurus*" or *assistant gurus* of the famous *muni* Dattatreya, which I learned from the mouth of a *Sanyasi*, and which, although quaint and artless, seem sufficiently interesting and characteristic for partial reproduction here.

Out of the twenty-four *upa gurus* I select the following:—

1. *The Earth.*—The lesson to be learned from this *guru* is patient endurance. As the uncomplaining earth suffers injuries and affronts without any sign of resentment, so should the *sadhu* be unperturbed by any ill-treatment and indignities he may be subjected to.

2. *The Heavens* (*Sky*).—Into the serene sky ascend the glad sounds of mirth, the fierce roar of battle, the beating of drums, and the clash of swords; but it retains none of them: the *sadhu*, in the midst of the turmoil of life, should, in like manner, retain no impression of the events about him, be they joyous or mournful.

3. *Fire.*—As flame always tends to *rise*, even if the lighted torch be reverted, so should the aspirations of the *sadhu* always be to higher things; and as the pure flame feeds indiscriminately on all sorts of fuel, the living timber of the forest as well as the refuse of the dung-heap, so ought the *sadhu* to accept willingly whatever food is given to him, never reflecting upon its value, nor whether it is stale or fresh.

4. *The Pigeons.*—Dattatreya once watched a pair of pigeons build a nest and rear a couple of young ones. When the young were tolerably grown they used to make short excursions on the wing, but one day were ensnared by a fowler. The mother bird returning saw the fate of her brood, and in her anxiety to help them got caught in the net herself. Her mate, coming on the painful scene, lost command of himself, and seemed from his excited flutterings as if he too would get ensnared, and so it soon happened.

Now, this incident should be a warning to the *sadhu* as to what he should *not* do. Family ties, however tender, are only transient, and should not affect him, lest they bring him to the unfortunate end of the miserable pigeons in the net of the fowler.

5. *The Ocean.*—The ocean does not rise when the rivers flow into it, nor diminish if water be drawn from it, so the *sadhu* should not swell with pride if a number of disciples, attracted by his fame, gather round him; nor, on the other hand, should he be concerned in the least degree if they all depart and leave him companionless.

6. *The Harlot.*—A courtesan was sitting one evening decked in her best clothes waiting for a visitor. She was all the while wishing that someone would come to her who would pay her with a liberal hand. A stream of people passed by, but not one called in. Midnight at last arrived, and now the disappointed woman pondered, "If I were only to give as much thought to God as I do to unprofitable wickedness, what blessings might He not vouchsafe to me!" From that moment the harlot changed her mode of life, and, turning from evil desires, adopted a religious life; a fact from which the *sadhu* should learn that even the most depraved of mortals may seek God, and become entirely changed in heart.

7. *The Brahman Girl.*—There was once a Brahman who, as required by Hindu custom, had given his daughter in marriage to a man of his own caste. The girl was, however, still residing in her father's house when a member of her husband's family arrived unexpectedly. The child-wife was alone, and, having requested the visitor to be seated, retired modestly into the inner apartments to prepare some food for him. There was no flour in the house, so she proceeded to pound some wheat in an *oklee* (mortar). Her *choorees* (bangles) made a clatter as she pursued her labours, and she felt ashamed of thus seeming to attract the stranger's attention. She removed some of the bangles, but still the clatter went on; she took off a few more, but the tinkle of the metal rings did not cease, until she had *only one* left on her wrist. Then there was peace and quietness. Thus it is in life. The *sadhu* should live alone if he desire serenity and contentment of mind.

8. *The Bhringhi.*—This creature is said to carry dead insects to its nest, and then, by humming persistently

into their ears for a day or two, to bring them back to life again.[1] "What a lesson for the *sadhu*!" thought Dattatreya. Surely he should, by persistent teaching, bring men who are dead in sin and worldliness back to God and spiritual life.

2. The Dandis.

This sect is recruited exclusively from the Brahman caste, yet it discards the sacred thread. It derives its name from the *danda*, or staff, which each member is required to carry.

Theoretically, *dandiwallahs* should not settle down in one place for a *single* day, and even the *danda* should not be allowed to *rest*, but should be stuck erect in the ground or be suspended from a tree.[2] In practice, however, these rules are neglected, and large numbers of *dandis* are to be found at any time in Benares, where an important *ghât* or bathing place on the Ganges is named after them. The *dandis*, I have been assured, do not worship Siva, but only their own *danda*. If this be correct, the explanation is probably that the *danda* is regarded by them as the phallic emblem of the god.

Dr. J. W. Bhattacharjee says the *dandi* is not required to worship any god, and that after initiation "he is supposed

[1] My inquiries respecting the very interesting insect referred to have not met with success. Indians have not been very careful observers of nature, and it appears to me that the habits of some of the solitary wasps may possibly have given rise to the belief which gives Dattatreya an opportunity for a lesson in holiness to the *sadhus*. These solitary wasps (*ammophila*, for example) are known to sometimes sting their prey into unconsciousness before carrying them to their nests to serve as food for the family, and it may well happen that some of these victims revive in the nest and might seem to have been restored to life by their captors.

[2] In regard to the *danda*, Sir Monier Williams in his *Buddhism* (Preface, p. xiii) says: "Finally, there is the *danda* or staff held in the left hand, and used by a *Sanyasi* as a defence against evil spirits, much as the *dorje* (or *vajra*) is used by Northern Buddhist monks. This mystical staff is a bambu with six knots, possibly symbolical of six ways (*gati*) or states of life through which it is believed that every being may have to migrate—a belief common to both Brahmanism and Buddhism. The staff is called *sudarsana* (a name for Vishnu's *cakra*), and is daily worshipped for the preservation of its mysterious powers."

to pass into the condition of a god, and he himself constantly expresses his belief in such transformation by repeating the Soham formula," which is *Sevoham*, signifying, "I am Siva."

The *dandis* wear salmon-coloured clothes, which may be dyed once only. Some, however, go about the jungles quite naked. They are not allowed to touch fire, money, or metal in any form. Their food may be obtained from the houses of Brahmans, but they may ask for it only when there is no smoke or fire in the house and the grinding mill is still; in other words, when the family has already taken its meal. The *dandiwallah* should not ask for food when anyone else, even a dog, is waiting for it.

Initiation.—The *shagird* (postulant) who wishes to become a *chela* is first obliged to fast for three days, living only on milk. On the fourth day there is a grand *hawan* (a ceremony in which *ghee* and other combustible substances are consumed in the fire as a sacrifice to the gods). After this he is shaved, head and all, with the exception of a few hairs on the crown. Then the candidate has to stand waist-deep in water—a river, a tank, or any deep reservoir will answer the purpose. With his own hands the postulant then plucks out the few hairs which had been allowed to remain on the top of his head. His sacred thread is removed and burnt, the ashes thereof being eaten by the neophyte. While in the water he receives the *mantra* of the order from his *guru* or preceptor, and also a new name with one of the following surnames: Tirtha, Assama, Bharati, or Sarswati.

When he steps out of the water he is handed a staff and a gourd, and is robed in five bits of salmon-coloured cotton cloth, one piece being wrapped round the head. Rules for his guidance in life are explained to him: for example, that he must not touch fire, may take but one meal a day, must get his food from the houses of Brahmans only, and so on. He is admonished not to possess any property at all, to use either a gourd or an earthen vessel for his water and food, and to cling to the banks of the Ganges. He is further enjoined to preach to the people and to practise virtue.

Dandis as a rule bury their dead, or commit the body to some sacred stream.[1]

On receiving news of the death of any relative, the *dandiwallah,* who must be fatherless and motherless, wifeless and childless, before he can join the sect, has only to bathe and to wash his clothes and *danda*. No further ceremonies or observances are required of him.

3. Paramahansas.

A learned Indian Sanskritist explained to me that the name of this sect is derived from the words *parama,* meaning much or great, and *hansa,* a certain (mythological) animal which can separate water from milk ; whence, as my pandit said, it would seem that the *Paramahansa* is one who can distinguish truth from falsehood.[2]

Sanyasis, dandis, and other ascetics who have undergone a probation of usually not less than twelve years, may be admitted to this superior order, in which both Sivites and Vishnuvites merge their religious differences in a comprehensive *self-worship,* based on the presumption of each *Paramahansa's* identity with the Divine Spirit.

Such high pretensions have of necessity to be supported by some visible proof of superiority to physical discomfort and the weaknesses that flesh is heir to ; and so it happens that some members of this sect go about naked

[1] These practices would seem to be a necessary consequence of the strict prohibition of the use of fire by these sectaries.

[2] Ordinarily *hansa* means a *goose,* a signification which, in view of the pretensions of the members of the sect, may at least be noted. Kabir the mystic says, " The goose and the paddy bird are of one colour and frolic in the same pool ; the goose extracts the milk from the water, and the paddy bird drinks the mire."—Wilson's *Sects of the Hindus,* p. 55.

A more fanciful interpretation of the word *hansa* is to be found in the following extract :—

" In the science of breath the technical symbol for inspiration is *sa,* and for expiration *ha.* It is easy to see how these symbols are connected with the roots *as* and *ah.* The current of the life-wave spoken of above is technically called *hansachasa,* that is, the motion of *ha* and *sa.* The word HANSA, which is taken to mean God, and is made so much of in many Sanskrit works, is only a symbolic representation of the two eternal processes of life—*ha* and *sa.*"—*The Science of Breath,* by Rama Prasad, M.A., F.T.S., London, 1890, p. 22.

in all weathers, some affect to live without eating food of any kind, others observe strict silence and do not indicate even by a sign any physical need or suffering. There may be impostors among them, but honest ascetics are certainly not wanting; and so great is the respect and admiration which the self-denial of these *sadhus* commands from the Hindus, that they are seldom if ever allowed to experience the full measure of the physical evils which would, in ordinary course, be attached to their voluntary asceticisms.

Amongst the *Paramahansas* are scholars well versed in Sanskrit learning. These are usually to be found in monasteries.

Paramahansas bury their dead, or float their bodies away upon some running stream.

4. Brahmacharis.

In the ideal scheme for the conduct of life prescribed by the Hindu lawgiver Manu and summarised on p. 15, it will be found that the period of early youth is to be devoted to vedic study, the student, living on alms, being known as a *Brahmachari*. But *Brahmacharis* of this sort have practically disappeared from India; those who now go by the name belong either to an inferior ministering order created by Sankara to serve as helps and companions to *Sanyasis* and *Paramahansas*, or they form a class apart amongst the Tantric sects of Bengal.

5. Lingaits.

Being strongly opposed to Brahmanism, the distinguishing badge of this sect is a *lingam* fastened to the neck or arm by a thread which "is called the *linga sutram*, as opposed to the *yajna sutram* or sacred thread of Brahmans."[1] The mendicant monks of this sect, known as *vaders*, meaning masters or lords, go about with small bells attached to their arms or carried in the hand to advertise their presence. They receive from the

[1] Dr. J. N. Bhattacharjee's *Hindu Castes and Sects*, p. 397.

lay *Lingaits* the most extravagant veneration and even worship.

The *Jangamas*, who are occasionally seen in Upper India, are stated by Dr. Bhattacharjee to be "the priestly *Sudras* of the sect." They are married men not given to austerities, and go about well clad, as will be seen from the illustrations at the commencement of the Preface and at p. 52 of this volume. In regard to the name of the sect, "it is said that, when Shiv (Siva) at his marriage desired to give alms to Brahmans, no Brahmans appeared; the god thereupon tore open his leg (*janga*) and produced therefrom a man whom he called Jangama, to whom he gave his alms,"[1] and this man, no doubt, was the father of the sect. At Kedarnath in Garwal they have a temple and monastery of their own.

In Southern India, especially in the Malabar and Coromandel districts, the *Lingaits* are very numerous. According to the Abbé Dubois, they abstain from animal food, bury their dead, and "do not recognise the laws relating to defilements which are generally accepted by other castes." They practise no post-burial rites.[2]

6. Aghoris.

Regarding the existence and practices at the present day of this ancient and repulsive sect, the following extract from a newspaper conducted entirely by Indians affords information:—

"The loathsome story of a human ghoul from Patiala shows that the influence of the *Aghorpanthi* has not yet completely died out in this country. It is said that for some time past human graves have been found robbed of their contents, and the mystery could not be solved until the other day, when the police succeeded in arresting a man in the act of desecrating a child's grave some forty miles distant from the capital (Patiala). The ghoul not only did not conceal the undevoured portion of the corpse

[1] *Report on the Census of the Punjab*, by E. D. Maclagan, I.C.S., p. 116.

[2] *Hindu Manners, Customs, and Ceremonies*, part i. chap. ix.

he had with him, but told his captors the whole story of his gruesome career. He is a low-caste Hindu named Ram Nath, and is, according to a gentleman who saw him, 'a singularly mild and respectful-looking man,' instead of a 'red-eyed and ravenous savage,' as he had expected to find him from the accounts of his disgusting propensities. He became an orphan at five, and fell into the hands of two *sadhus* of his own caste, who were evidently *Aghorpanthis*. They taught him to eat human flesh, which formed the staple of their food. The meat was procured from the graves in the villages they passed through. When Ram Nath was thoroughly educated in this taste the *sadhus* deserted him. Since then he has been living on human carrion only, roaming about the country like a hungry vulture. He cannot eat cooked food, and therefore gets two *seers* of raw meat from the State every day. It is also reported that Sirdar Shamshere Singh, private secretary to the Maharajah, has now forbidden to give him anything but ordinary jail food, with a view to 'reforming him.' The ghoul is, however, determined to starve rather than eat what he has not been accustomed to." [1]

Strange as it may seem, the disgustingly repulsive habits of the *Aghoris* are a direct and legitimate, if horrible, outcome of a desire to push the pantheistic doctrines of the Vedanta philosophy to their logical conclusions in a certain direction. "If everything in existence is only a manifestation of the Universal Soul, nothing can be unclean!" So argues the *Aghorpanthi*, and he proves the uncompromising sincerity of his convictions by his repellent acts.

Cases, few and far between, of necrophilism, anthropophagy, and coprology are not unknown to mental pathologists in Europe; but it is, perhaps, only in India that such perverted instincts could be made the basis of a *religious* sect.

The *Aghorpanthis* can date back to a considerable antiquity, but, though never at any time of importance numerically, have not escaped the notice of Europeans in India. Of these cannibal *sadhus*, Moor, who identifies

[1] The *Tribune* (Lahore), 29th November 1898.

them, no doubt incorrectly, with the *Paramahansas*, writes as follows in his Hindu Pantheon :—

"However difficult it may be for an English reader to believe the hitherto unrecorded story of the flesh-abhorring Hindus, not only do other castes of the Hindus, but even of the Brahmins themselves, eat flesh, and one sect at least eat human flesh. They do not kill human subjects to eat, but they eat such as they find about the Ganges and other rivers, and near Benares they are not unusually seen floating down the river on a corpse, and feeding upon its flesh; and the human brain is judged by these epicurean cannibals to be the most delicious morsel of their unsocial banquet. They are called *Paramahansa*, and are by no means a low despicable tribe; but, on the contrary, are esteemed, at any rate by themselves, a very high one. Whether the exaltation be legitimate, or assumed by individuals in consequence of penance or holy and sanctified acts, I am not prepared to state; but I believe the latter, as I have known other instances where individuals of differing sects, by persevering in extraordinary piety, or penance, have been deemed incapable of sin."

The present headquarters of the *Aghorpanthis* appear to be at Mount Abo. Some of them claim to acquire magical power by eating human flesh. "The fact is," says Dr. J. N. Bhattacharjee, "that as Brahmanism inculcated cleanliness and the eating of wholesome food, the *Aghoris*, who formed one of the sects setting up 'opposition shops' as it were, insisted on the utmost degree of filth, and hoped to gain alms by horrifying the people and not by gaining their respect." [1]

I am not prepared to say how much truth there may be in this opinion, but certainly there is no denying that the *Aghoris* are only too successful in extorting money from people who have a supreme dread of them, and would much rather accede to their demands than see them carry

[1] *Hindu Castes and Sects*, pp. 393, 394. On the subject of these *Aghorpanthis* the reader may refer to Ward's *Hindus*, p. 296, and Mr. W. Crookes' *Popular Religion and Folk-lore of Northern India*, vol. ii. p. 172.

out their threat of eating in their presence disgusting offal or foul carrion.

Women known as *Aghorinis* are often associated with these ghouls, and are as filthy as and even more shameless than their male companions.

CHAPTER VIII—*continued*

SECTION III.—Yogis and Yoga Vidya—Yogis attracting attention in the West—Philosophico-religious Ideas underlying Yogaism—Emancipation of the Soul the supreme Object of Hindu religious Aspiration—Yoga Vidya teaches how Union of the individual Soul with the All-Spirit may be accomplished—Details and probable Origin of the Discipline and Practices of Yoga Vidya—The Pretensions of the modern Yogis—History, Customs, and Rules of the Yogi sect.

JUDGING from current literature of a certain class, the *Yogis*[1] and their doctrines have, in recent years, somehow attracted attention in both Europe and America, and *yoga* teachings have come to be regarded as the highest expression of transcendental Hinduism. In the United States, notwithstanding their superlative industrialism, there is a growing class of publications in which prominence is given to such subjects as the rationale of concentration, psychic breathing, subliminal consciousness, the perception of the *Self*, *rapport* with the Universal, and also, without disguise, the *Raja Yoga* system of India.

The *Yogi*, moreover, has been accepted in the West as the type or representative of the religious ascetics of India. It is therefore very desirable that the ideas and practices of the *Yogis* should be set forth here as fully and clearly as may be consistent with brevity.

Hindu philosophico-religious ideas, involved as they

[1] The *Yogis* are in the vernaculars of Northern India ordinarily called *jogis*.

are in a tangled labyrinth of mystic speculations, present very serious difficulties to the student, particularly as there are naturally many systems of Hindu philosophy and, of course, a multiplicity of teachers to be reckoned with. Yet there are some more or less widely accepted fundamental notions which when stripped of confusing details are not beyond ordinary comprehension, and, as they serve to elucidate the practices of the *Yogis*, will now be noticed. At the same time, it may be added that, amongst the many fantastic dreams which have been presented to mankind as authoritative explanations of the universe, these Hindu speculations are not without dignity, beauty, and originality.

According to the fundamental notions of Hindu philosophy to which I refer, every living man is made up of an individual soul, a subtle invisible body, and a gross body. The soul is of the same essence as the All-Spirit, although temporarily detached, as it were, from it in some mysterious way. It is by its nature incorruptible and unchanging. The subtle body (*sûkshma-sarîra*),[1] however, is not so, and while in connection with the gross body is influenced, affected, and modified through the senses by the play of the primal forces of nature. The impressions thus made upon the subtle body, the dispositions engendered in it by the influences to which it is exposed, affect its nature, so that, even when separated after death from its grosser

[1] "In the Sâmkhya-philosophy this *sûkshma-sarîra* appears as *linga-sarîra*, or the sign-body. *Sthûla-sarîra*, or coarse, material body, consists, according to some Sâmkhya teachers, of the five or four coarse elements (*bhûtas*), according to others of the earth only, and is made up of six coverings—hair, blood, flesh, sinews, bones, and marrow. The subtle or inner body, sometimes called the vehicle or the *âtivâhika-sarîra*, is formed of eighteen elements: of (1) Buddhi, (2) Ahamkara, (3) Manas, (4–8) the five Tanmâtras or *sûkshma-bhûtas*, and (9–18) the ten senses. This body is of course invisible, but without it the coarse body would be useless. It forms what we should call our personality, and causes the difference in the characters of individuals, being itself what it has been made to be by former works. All fitness for reward and punishment attaches to it, not to the *Purushas*, who are all alike and unchanging, and it likewise determines by means of its acquired dispositions the gross bodies into which it has to enter from life to life, till final freedom is obtained by the *Purusha*; and not only the gross body, but the subtle body also, is reabsorbed in Prakriti."—*The Six Systems of Indian Philosophy*, by Professor F. Max Müller, p. 395.

counterpart, it still retains the taint of its corporeal existence—that is to say, the affinities, proclivities, and tendencies developed in it during its earthly sojourn. Now, in the ordinary but eternal interaction of the complex forces of nature—the *pranas* and *tatwas*—these acquired qualities bring about the reincarnation of the subtle invisible body along with the soul to which it is united. But for the soul, rebirth is a most undesirable event, a most terrible hardship. Escape, however, from this dire calamity is fortunately possible, provided the subtle body be only freed from the influence of the senses, so that it may lose all attachment to things mundane—all earthward tendencies, as it were. But who is to accomplish this? Who is to set the *sûkshma-sarira* free from the trammels of worldly affections? It is the soul alone that can do it; it is the soul which must work out its own salvation.

Before it, then, lies the task of weaning the subtle body completely from the hopes and fears, the affections and desires, of earthly life. To regain its freedom it must succeed in effacing the impressions made upon the subtle body during its earthly life, in annulling the attractions of carnality and destroying the forces which make for rebirth. It may take ages and strenuous efforts in many successive lives to accomplish this; but, when it is finally attained, the *sûkshma-sarîra*, after the dissolution of the gross body, will have no tendency to return to this earth, but will be merged in the soul, and that again, released from every hampering impediment, will become reunited with the All-Spirit.

A presentment of the relations of the soul, the body, and the Great Spirit, which evidently appeals to the peculiar voluptuous sentimentalism of the Bengali nature, deserves a passing notice—

"The soul," says a recent writer, Babu Shishir Kumar Ghose, "is attached to the body, and naturally feels a great attraction for it. But its real partner is the Great Spirit of the universe. The soul of man is likened to a woman, whose lover is the body, but whose husband is the Great Soul, viz. God. But she, the soul, undutifully forsakes her wedded husband and cleaves to her gallant, the body. The object of the practice of *yoga* is to detach the woman (the human soul) from her lover (the human body), reunite her with her lawful husband, the Great Soul, Brahma, or the Great Spirit. . . .

"One way of attempting to detach a faithless woman from her lover is to reason with her; another way is to make her gallant disagreeable to her. The *Advaitabadees* follow the methods mentioned just now, in order to detach the soul (woman) from her gallant, the body. (1) They reason with their souls[1] and persuade them to believe that their undue attraction for the body cannot conduce to their happiness, for the body does not endure for ever. And (2) they practise all sorts of mortifications upon their bodies, and thereby prevent the soul to derive any pleasure from its union therewith. The soul, thus driven to detach herself from the body, is slowly and gradually led towards the Great Spirit, for the purpose of being united thereto."

The accomplishment of the supreme object of Hindu religious aspiration, as explained in the foregoing paragraphs, may give occupation to the soul in many successive transitory lives; but if a struggle in the right direction be steadily maintained in any one life here below, it makes the task in succeeding lives all the easier, since the tendencies cultivated in one embodied existence are more easily trained in the next one, and so on, till they are finally *established*.

Evidently the endeavour towards perfection, that is, towards the emancipation of the soul, involves the cultivation of apathy (*vairagya*), with the crushing out of all human affections, desires, and lusts, and the complete detachment of the mind from all earthly things.

This conclusion gives us the key to much of the higher religious ideas of the Hindus, and also makes

[1] "They reason with their souls!" There is a queer confusion of ideas here, a *new third* party intervening between the soul and the body to *reason with and persuade* the former. Yet the above extract is not without value, illustrating as it does the very sensuous imagery by which alone even philosophical doctrines can be brought home to the comprehension of minds steeped in the ideas of the Sakta worshippers.

intelligible their universally accepted doctrine of *karma*, according to which, as explained in a previous chapter, all actions good or bad must bear their fruit at some time or other in the present or in future lives; a doctrine which certainly makes for morality, and accounts intelligibly for the striking and apparently unjust inequalities which human society and individual history present.

After the foregoing explanation, it will be easily understood that everyone desirous of effecting the final emancipation of his soul and its reabsorption into the All-Spirit should follow practices calculated to wean the mind from the distractions and seductions of its earthly environment.

These general principles being accepted, some eager minds impatient of delays, some emotional natures in love with the Infinite, have deemed it possible to effect a mystical union between the individual soul and the All-Spirit, *even while the former is imprisoned in its corporeal frame*; and for the attainment of this, the highest of desirable objects, is the system devised by Patanjali and accepted as authoritative by the *Yogis*.

The word *yoga* means union, and first occurs in the later Upanishads.[1] *Yoga Vidya* is a complex system of philosophical doctrines and practical exercises for promoting or effecting union between the individual soul and the All-Spirit.

"As described by Svâmin Râma-Krishnânanda in the Brahmavâdin, p. 511 *seq.*, it consists, as practised at present, of four kinds: Mantra, Laya, Râja, and Hatha-yoga. *Mantra-yoga* consists in repeating a certain word again and again, particularly a word expressive of deity, and concentrating all one's thoughts on it. *Laya-yoga* is the consecrating all one's thoughts on a thing or the idea of a thing, so that we become almost one with it. Here again the ideal image of a god, or names expressive of the Godhead, are the best, as producing absorption in God. *Râja-yoga* consists in controlling the breath so as to control the mind. It was observed that when fixing our attention suddenly on anything new we hold our

[1] Weber's *Indian Literature*, p. 239.

breath, and it was supposed, therefore, that concentration of the mind would be sure to follow the holding back of the breath, or the *prândâyâma*. *Hatha-yoga* is concerned with the general health of the body, and is supposed to produce concentration by certain postures of the body, by fixing the eyes on one point, particularly the tip of the nose, and similar contrivances." [1]

Yogi properly means one who practises *yoga* with the object of uniting or blending his soul with the Divine Spirit or World-Soul.

Very curiously, however, the practice of *yoga* is not undertaken by all *Yogis*, nor is it confined to the professed *Yogi*. The efficacy of the system is an article of faith so universally accepted throughout India, that other sectarians, including laymen, even married men and householders, resort to it when so inclined, and it may be added that the founder even of the quite recent theistic sect known as the *Brahmo Samaj*, Babu Keshab Chundra Sen, practised *yoga*.

Now union with the All-Spirit, if accomplished by any individual soul, must surely enhance its susceptibilities and powers. Hence, as I have explained in another book, the *Yogis* naturally claim, and the Hindu world readily concedes to them, a far-reaching knowledge of the secrets of nature and almost unlimited sway over men and natural phenomena.[2]

"When this mystic union is effected," says Professor H. H. Wilson, "the *Yogi* is liberated in his living body from the clog of material incumbrance, and acquires an entire command over all worldly substance. He can make himself lighter than the lightest substances, heavier than the heaviest; can become as vast or as minute as he pleases, can traverse all space, can animate any dead body by transferring his spirit into it from his own frame, can render himself invisible, can attain all objects, become equally acquainted with the past, present, and future, and is finally united with Siva, and consequently exempted from being born again upon earth. The superhuman faculties

[1] Professor Max Müller's *The Life and Sayings of Ramakrishna*, p. 8.

[2] *Indian Life, Religious and Social* (T. Fisher Unwin, London).

are acquired, in various degrees, according to the greater or less perfection with which the initiatory processes have been performed."[1]

A recent Indian exponent of *Râja-yoga* has summed up the object of the system in the following comprehensive statement: "The *Yogi* proposes to himself no less a task than to master the whole universe, to control the whole of nature."[2]

Every *Yogi* does not set up for being a thaumaturgist, since such a pretension might easily be tested to the confusion of the pretender. The claim and the concession are rather in favour of the system and of any who act up to its rules. There are, however, some sceptics who maintain that "*yoga* cannot be effective in this *kali yuga*, or age of sin."[3]

The apparent origin and development of the practical system or method of the *Yogis* is deserving of attention. Starting from that obviously most important vital function, respiration, some Hindu sages appear to have observed and reasoned somewhat in the following way. The air inhaled is evidently the life, or at least contains the vital principle in some subtle form; for deprivation of air means death, and with the last expiration the living body becomes a corpse. Now this air penetrates the corporeal frame, and is easily discoverable in the chest, the stomach, the bowels, and elsewhere. But this life-breath is apparently not stagnant. It possesses some sort of motion, being drawn into the chest through the nostrils and exhaled through the same apertures. Some of the larger and more obvious structural details of the lungs with its branching tubes may have been noticed, and possibly also the chambers of the heart with the great connected vessels suggesting channels for the movements of *prana*, the vital air, and of centres for its concentration.

Reflecting, in their own peculiar way, on the mysterious process of respiration, which was supposed to be a law of

[1] *Sketch of the Religious Sects of the Hindus*, p. 131.

[2] *Râja-yoga*. Lectures by Swami Vivekananda, p. 11 (Longmans & Co., London).

[3] *Hindu Castes and Sects*, by Dr. J. N. Bhattacharjee, p. 402.

the entire universe, on the undoubted presence of air in many parts of the body, and on the meagre stock of anatomical facts known to them,—possibly also guided by some dim conception of fluid circulation in the body,—the founders of *Yogaism* have concluded and taught that along with the air the primal forces of nature, represented by subtle ethers, circulate in the human body in a multitude of vessels (*nadis*) springing from the navel.

The uses and functions of these imaginary *nadis* conveying the subtle ethers through the material system are, as we might expect, confidently, if somewhat indefinitely, described. If we are to believe these purely speculative anatomists, the *nadis* divide and subdivide as they proceed, till the sum-total of them, of different degrees of magnitude, number just 72,000. According to other equally competent authorities, the number of these *nadis* comes up to 727,210,201, and they have their root in the heart and not the navel. Intersecting at various points, these ramifying vessels form plexuses known as *padmas* or *kamalas* (lotuses), which act as centres of force for the performance of the physiological functions. Centres of moral and intellectual powers also exist in the system. Thus we read in the Vishram-opnishat—

"1. While the mind rests in the eastern portion (or petal), which is white in colour, then it is inclined towards patience, generosity, reverence.

"2. While the mind rests in the south-eastern portion, which is red in colour, then it is inclined towards sleep, torpor, and evil inclination." [1]

Upon this foundation of pure assumption is built a *science* for regulating and guiding the currents of the *pranas* and *tatwas* at will, along the multitudinous *nadis* of the human organism, so that they might produce the least harmful effects upon the mind, minimise the evil done by the fact of the soul and the subtle body being sojourners in a fleshy tenement, and thus bring the soul to a realisation of Self; or, in other words, *to perceive its identity with the Supreme Self*.[2]

[1] *The Science of Breath*, by Rama Prashad, M.A., pp. 42, 43.

[2] Max Müller's *Ramakrishna*, p. 46.

The practices actually described in conformity with the *science* above referred to for the attainment of *samadhi*[1] are such as tend to abstract the mind entirely from surrounding objects or events, favouring thereby a condition of self-hypnotism or trance.

With what insight the exercises have been devised by the adepts who prescribed them will be apparent when it is stated that these involve long-continued suppressions of the breath, and the performance of the functions of respiration by peculiar and minutely prescribed modes of inspiration and expiration through the right and left nostrils respectively; that they include posturing in no less than eighty-four different attitudes; also the frequent, even millionfold, mental repetition of the mystic syllable *om*, the prolonged concentration of visual attention on near objects—for example, the navel or the tip of the nose—combined with an equally severe strain imposed upon the auditory nerves in protracted efforts to listen to sounds in the ears themselves.

Then there is *meditation*, the nature of which may be illustrated by the following example:—

"Imagine a lotus upon the top of the head, several inches up, and virtue as its centre, the stalk as knowledge. The eight petals of the lotus are the eight powers of the *Yogi*. Inside the stamens and pistils are renunciation. If the *Yogi* refuses the external powers he will come to salvation. So the eight petals of the lotus are the eight powers, but the internal stamens and pistils are the extreme renunciation of all these. Inside of that lotus think of the Golden One, the Almighty, the Intangible, He whose name is Om, the Inexpressible, surrounded with effulgent light. Meditate on that."[2]

There is no reason to deny that by *such* meditations, and by the practices referred to above, carried out in solitude, a state of self-hypnotisation might be attained,

[1] In Professor Max Müller's *Indian Philosophy* (p. 141) *samadhi* is defined as "meditative absorption." According to Swami Vivekananda, it means super-consciousness. By Sir Monier Williams it is used as the equivalent of *trance*.

[2] *Râja-yoga*, by Swami Vivekananda, pp. 91, 92.

with mental hallucinations more or less permanent,[1] and that even an ecstatic state might be induced. Now ecstasy, particularly religious ecstasy, is a well-known phenomenon, and is associated with many Christian saints: as St. Theresa, St. Philip of Neri, and others. It means such a suspension of consciousness as to cause obliteration, temporarily, of all sense relations with the material world, and is accompanied with beatific visions in which pain is curiously blended with unutterable bliss.

What modern science has to say in elucidation of *ecstasy* may be judged from the following extract from Dr. Max Nordau's well-known work *Degeneration*, and such light as it throws upon the subject will doubtless be welcome to the reader in connection with the claims which we are now considering of the disciples of *Yoga Vidya*.

"The degree of exclusiveness and insistence in the predominance of any presentation is in proportion to the degree of morbid irritability in the particular tract of brain by which it is elaborated. Where the degree is not excessive, there arise obsessions which the consciousness recognises as morbid. They do not preclude the coexistence of healthy functioning of the brain, and consciousness acquires the habit of treating these coexistent obsessions as foreign to itself, and of banishing them from its presentations and judgments. In aggravated cases these obsessions grow into fixed ideas. The immoderately excitable portions of the brain work out their ideas with such liveliness that consciousness is filled with them, and can no longer distinguish them from such as are the result of sense-impressions, the nature and strength of which they accurately reflect. Then we reach the stage of hallucinations and delirium. Finally, in the last stage, comes ecstasy, which Ribot calls 'the acute form of the effort

[1] Amongst the weird tales of Edgar Allan Poe is one entitled "Berenice," in which the unhappy mental disorder associated with the habit of *attentive* and *continuous* contemplation of some *trifling* object or *unimportant* subject leads to consequences replete with the most painful horror. This strange story, displaying rare insight into a certain unhealthy phase of mental activity, is aptly suggestive of the abnormal results which certain *Yogi* practices must often lead to.

after unity of consciousness.' In ecstasy the excited part of the brain works with such violence that it suppresses the functioning of all the rest of the brain. The ecstatic subject is completely insensible to external stimuli. There is no perception, no representation, no grouping of presentations into concepts, and of concepts into judgments and reasoning. A single presentation or group of presentations fills up consciousness. These presentations are of extreme distinctness and clearness. Consciousness is, as it were, flooded with the blinding light of mid-day. There therefore takes place exactly the reverse of what has been noticed in the case of the ordinary mystic. The ecstatic state is associated with extremely intense emotions, in which the highest bliss is mixed with pain. These emotions accompany every strong and excessive functioning of the nerve-cells, every extraordinary and violent decomposition of nerve-nutriment. The feeling of voluptuousness is an example of the phenomena accompanying extraordinary decompositions in a nerve-cell. In healthy persons the sexual nerve-centres are the only ones which, conformably with their functions, are so differentiated and so adapted that they exercise no uniform or lasting activity, but, for by far the greatest part of the time, are perfectly tranquil, storing up large quantities of nutriment, in order, during very short periods, to decompose this suddenly and, as it were, explosively. Every nerve-centre which operates in this way would procure us voluptuous emotion; but precisely among healthy persons there are, except the sexual nerve-centres, none which are compelled to act in this manner, in order to serve the purpose of the organism. Among the degenerate, on the contrary, particular morbidly excited brain-centres operate in this way, and the emotions of delight which accompany their explosive activity are more powerful than sexual feelings, in proportion as the brain-centres are more sensitive than the subordinate and more sluggish spinal centres. One may completely believe the assurances of great ecstatics, such as St. Theresa, a Mohammed, an Ignatius Loyola, that the bliss accompanying their ecstatic visions is unlike anything earthly, and almost more than a mortal can bear. This latter statement proves that they were conscious of the sharp pain which accompanies nerve-action in over-excited brain-cells, and which, on careful analysis, may be distinguished in every very strong feeling of pleasure. The circumstance that the only normal organic sensation known to us which resembles that of ecstasy is the sexual feeling, explains the fact that ecstatics connect their ecstatic presentations by way of association with the idea of love, and describe the ecstasy itself as a kind of supernatural act of love, as a union of an ineffably high and pure sort with God or the Blessed Virgin. This drawing near to God and the saints is the natural result of a religious training, which begets the habit of looking on everything inexplicable as supernatural, and of bringing it into connection with the doctrines of faith."[1]

Taking all the facts into consideration, I should be inclined to conclude that from a remote past many of the phenomena now classed under the general term hypnotism were known to the Indians, and that the more ardent emotional religionists amongst them, stimulated by powerful neurotic impulses, experienced, more frequently perhaps than in other lands, the indescribable joys of the ecstatic state, and lost themselves—lost their very identity—in the marvellous world conjured up in their trance-visions. Once discovered, once experienced, these mysteries, and these strange voluptuous enjoyments, would be so peculiarly congenial with the character and psychology of the Indians, that the more emotional amongst them would be powerfully attracted towards these occult phenomena. In their ardour to gain admittance to the unknown world, whose echoes reached them, eager men would set themselves the task of systematically overcoming the intervening obstacles, and out of such strivings, doubtless, arose the *science* of *Yoga Vidya.* If in ecstasy the Christian saint believed himself to be in mysterious communion with Christ or the Virgin, it is only natural, and in accordance with his beliefs, that the *pantheistic* Hindu, when he reached the state in which he became "insensible to external stimuli,"

[1] *Degeneration*, by Max Nordau, pp. 63, 64 (William Heinemann, London, 1895).

should, in the inner glorious world of his own imaginings, *find himself* (that is, his own soul) in complete union with the Universal Spirit.

Thus far, at any rate, *Yogaism* is quite intelligible; but the pretensions of the *Yogis* to superhuman power have no justification whatever, and have for ages been a fertile source of profitable imposture most detrimental to the healthy development of the Indian people.[1]

Since all religions, philosophies, and sciences which have secured wide acceptance, need for their continual existence in each succeeding age to be interpreted as far as possible up to the level of the new ideas and increased knowledge of the times, we may expect that the same service has been performed for *Yoga Vidya.*

What can be done by an ardent advocate to explain, in the phraseology, and by the light of modern scientific facts and theories, the extremely crude and visionary notions of the *Yogis,* may be learned by a perusal of the lectures of Swami Vivekananda on *Râja-yoga,* delivered at New York in 1895–96.[2]

In these lectures are given, with the aid of the modern conceptions of vibrations, wave motions, electrical currents, and so forth, a statement of the rationale of *Yoga Vidya,* which is ingenious if not convincing. In this contemporary elucidation of *yoga* science we find the *Susumna nadi* identified with the spinal cord, and that the two other most important organs of the body are the brain (*sahasrâra,* the thousand-petalled) and the *mûlâdhâra*-plexus, the latter triangular in form and situated at the base of the vertebral column, being the seat of the *kundalini,* a mysterious reservoir of pent-up force, which is thus defined: "the coiled up, the sleeping Divine power in all beings." The aim and object of all the *yoga* practices is, according to the Swami, to successfully tap this reserve of force, *through the susumna* (which is naturally closed and can be opened by the *Yogis* only),

[1] In another book I have described the complete discomfiture and exposure, to my knowledge, of one of these *Yogi* pretenders to supernatural power.—*Indian Life, Religious and Social,* pp. 36–41.

[2] Longmans & Co., London.

causing the stored-up energy of the *kundalini*, thus set free by the *Yogis'* practices, to flow into the brain. When this difficult feat is accomplished, *samâdhi*, or a superconscious state, is reached, in which "no more will you need to go to books for knowledge; your own mind will have become your book containing infinite knowledge."

However edifying Swami-ji's explanations may be, it is, to say the least, rather curious that the *Yogi* should derive his transcendent *enlightenment* from an organ in the neighbourhood of the coccygeals.

Leaving these purely imaginary anatomical and physiological details, we may profitably turn our attention to a consideration of the actual results of the working of the system known as *Yoga Vidya*, and in doing so shall find that however profound may be the desire of the *Yogi* for the union of his soul, hereafter or in the present life, with the All-Spirit, his own nature craves importunately for advantages less remote, less transcendent, and, in response to this desire, the "science of breath," *i.e.* the regulation of the circulation of the *pranas* and *tatwas*, has, in the hands of the teachers, resulted in the usual childish developments and gross irrationalities of which Hinduism affords such ample evidence.

"20. A knowledge more secret than the science of breath, wealth more useful than the science of breath, was never seen or heard of.

"21. An enemy is killed during the power of the breath, and also friends are brought together; wealth is got during the power of breath, and comfort and reputation during the same.

"52. Any charity given by the wise while the breath is in the left nostril, multiplies krores upon krores[1] of times in *this* world.

"53. Let the *Yogi* look into his face, with one mind and with attention, and thus let him know entirely the motion of the sun[2] and the moon.[2]

[1] A krore equals ten millions.

[2] The *sun* and *moon* here referred to are certain subtle currents in the human body influenced by the luminaries named, and are also referred to as *positive* and *negative*.

"54. Let him meditate upon the *tatwa* when the *prana* is calm, never when it is disturbed; his desire will be fulfilled, and he will have great benefit and victory.

"55. To those men who practise, and thus always keep the sun and moon in proper order, knowledge of the past and the future becomes as easy as if they were in their hand.

"225. In distant warfare the moon is victorious, in near places the sun. When the foot raised first in going belongs to the flowing *nadi*, complete success is the result.

"226. In beginning a journey, in marriage, in entering any town, etc., in all auspicious acts, the flow of the moon is good.

"227. Putting the enemy's army towards the empty *nadi*, and one's own towards the full, when the *tatwa* is congenial, one might conquer the whole world.

"228. Let me give battle in the direction towards which the breath flows, victory is certain even if Indra be in front.

"306. Going to a lonely place and standing with the back towards the sun, let a man look with attention into the neck of the shade he throws on the ground.

"307. Let him see this for as long a time as he can calmly repeat the words, '*Om Kram parabrahman namah*,' for 108 times. Then let him look up into the sky. He will thus see Shankara (the figure of a being capable of appearing in many colours).[1]

"308. By doing this for six months, the *Yogi* becomes the lord of those who walk on earth; by two years he becomes absolutely independent and his own master.

"309. He obtains the knowledge of the three times and great bliss. There is nothing impossible for the constant practiser of *yoga*.

"328. When the mouth, nose, eyes, and ears are stopped by the fingers, the *tatwas* begin to take their rise before the eyes.

[1] This point has been referred to in my *Indian Life, Religious and Social*, pp. 41, 42.

"329. He who knows their colour, their motion, their taste, their places, and their signs, become in this world equal to *Rudra.*"

These extracts from a book entitled *The Science of Breath and the Philosophy of the Tatwas*,[1] are, I fancy, quite as much as, if not more than the patience of ordinary readers can endure, and they are certainly amply sufficient to illustrate how even the finest speculations of the Hindu mind—those, for example, with which we commenced this chapter—may become, in practice, mere fatuous puerilities.

The superhuman power claimed by the modern *Yogi* who dares to court public attention is naturally something very limited, indeed modesty itself, when compared with the pretensions of the sect as a whole. The following few instances will probably satisfy the curiosity of the reader on this subject.

In his *Sketch of the Religious Sects of the Hindus*, Professor H. H. Wilson quotes from the *Asiatic Monthly Journal* for March 1829 an instance of a Madras *Yogi* who used to give exhibitions of what was described as "sitting in the air," and, as already stated in Chap. III., Dr. Honigberger furnishes authentic details of the burial, without any harmful results, for no less than forty days of a *Yogi* at Lahore in the time of Maharajah Ranjit Singh.[2] What stories circulate in India at the present day about *Yogis* and their doings will be understood from the following extract from an Indian newspaper:—

"Great excitement is being caused amongst the simple hill folk in some of the villages to the south of Simla by a certain wandering *Yogi.* The man's last reported feat is really something beyond the ordinary. He is said to have burnt himself alive on a large pyre in front of a whole wondering village, and then ten days later to have appeared in the same village alive and unhurt. The hill people firmly believe this story, which they say must be true, as the *Yogi* can give them a detailed account of the

[1] Translated from the Sanskrit by Rama Prasad, M.A.

[2] *Thirty-five Years in the East,* by Dr. Honigberger, Physician to the Court of Lahore, pp. 126–130, London, 1852.

topography of heaven. This, of course, settles the matter. It is manifestly impossible for any man to describe heaven unless he has been there to see." [1]

The instances above cited were all public performances; and I may add that *Yogis* have always been given, more than other Hindu sectarians, to exhibitions intended to impress the people and win their admiration.

So strong has this tendency been that it will be within the memory of many, that, as mentioned in a previous chapter, a few years ago a Punjabi, one Bava Lachman Das, professing to be a *Yogi*, gave a number of exhibitions at the Westminster Aquarium of his wonderful skill as a posturist, eliciting a good deal of attention on account of the strange and seemingly impossible feats he performed in contorting his arms and legs into most grotesque and unnatural positions.

We have thus far considered the doctrines and pretensions of the *Yogis*; it remains now to give some particulars about the origin and working of the sect as such. Of the *Yogi* sect as it now exists one Mahandranâth was probably the real founder, though the fame of his disciple Goraknâth, who is identified with Siva himself, has eclipsed that of the master. Of Goraknâth nothing authentic is known, though his name is associated with legends dating from a remote past to comparatively modern times.[2]

[1] *Civil and Military Gazette*, Lahore, May 1895.

[2] "And here mention may be made of a modern deified Hindu teacher or sage, named Gorakh-Nath, who is said to have gone from India into Nepal, and is worshipped there as well as at Gorakh-poor and throughout the Punjab. Very little is known about him, and he belongs more to Hinduism than to Buddhism. Some say that he was a contemporary of Kabir (1488–1512), and, according to a *Janamsâkhi*, he once had an interview with Nanak, the founder of the *Sikh* sect. Such legendary accounts as are current are wrapped in much mystery. One legend describes him as born from a lotus. Others describe him as the third or fourth in a series of Saiva teachers, and the founder of the *Kanphata* sect of *Yogis*. The remarkable thing about him is that he succeeded in achieving an extraordinary degree of popularity among Northern Hindus and among some adherents of Buddhism in Nepal. His tomb is in the Punjab, and he is to this day adored as a kind of god by immense numbers of the inhabitants of North-Western India under the hills."—Sir Monier Williams' *Buddhism*, pp. 193, 194.

"The most flourishing epoch of the *Samkhya-yoga* belongs," says Professor Weber, "most probably to the first centuries of our era, the influence it exercised upon the development of Gnosticism in Asia Minor being unmistakable; while further, both through this channel and afterwards directly also, it had an important influence upon the growth of the Sufi philosophy." [1]

The *Yogis* as we find them at the present time pay especial respect to Siva, who is regarded by some of them as the *first Yogi*, and they also honour Bhairon or Bhairava, a god or demigod, usually represented pictorially with a club in one hand, a bottle in the other, and a dog in attendance at his heels. Members of all castes may become *Yogis*. There are several sub-orders, but the more prominent of these appear to be the *Jogeeshurs* or *Kanphatis* and the *Augars* or *Oghars*. All *Yogis* wear rosaries of rudraksha berries. They eat meat, and drink ardent spirits; it is indeed required of them to do so, and the result, in many cases, is the formation of habits of inebriety. *Yogis*, when clothed at all, wear orange-yellow garments. They have their hair plaited with threads of black wool, and coiled on the top of the head. They do not cremate, but bury their dead in a sitting posture facing the north. The *Kanphatis* wear ear-rings (*mundra*), often huge ones, made of jade, glass, or even wood, by which token they may be readily recognised. Their sect-names end in *nâth*.

The *Augars* or *Oghars*, whose sect-names end in *dâs*, are usually recruited from the lowest castes, and do not seem to command the respect of the people. The *Augar* does not wear ear-rings, but usually carries a *nádh* or small wooden pipe suspended from his neck by a black thread. This pipe he sounds in the morning and in the evening, and also before eating or drinking anything. *Yogis* often keep dogs.

A *Yogi* is shown in the illustration, Fig. 10, lightly clad, smeared with ashes, and wearing the *nádh* suspended from his neck. Besides the gods Siva and Bhairava, *Yogis* pay especial honour to nine *nâths* or immortal

[1] *Indian Literature*, p. 239.

saints, who dwell at ease in the inaccessible fastnesses of the Himalayas. Their names are—

1. Goraknâth.
2. Machandernâth.
3. Charputnâth.
4. Mangalnâth.
5. Ghugonâth.
6. Gopinâth.
7. Prannâth.
8. Surathnâth.
9. Chambanâth.

They also hold in special veneration eighty-four *Siddhas* or perfect *Yogis*, some of whom are believed to be still upon the earth. "The distinctive emblem of the *Siddha* worshippers is a silver *singhi* or cylindrical ornament worn on a thread round the neck." [1]

Yoga, with its practices and pretensions, has recently been attracting attention outside India, and the *Nâths* and *Siddhas* just referred to, the immortal men-gods of the *Yogis*, have probably been the prototypes of the wonderful *Mahatmas* of certain European and American theosophists of our day.

There is no denying the fact that *yoga* is practised by many earnest men of unquestionably high character, yet, unfortunately, it cannot be affirmed of a majority of the twentieth-century *Yogis*, who in the guise of ascetics peregrinate the country, living on the pious credulity of the masses, that they are anything better than ignorant worthless impostors, and even dangerous characters.

[1] *Census Report of the Punjab*, 1891, by E. D. Maclagan, I.C.S., p. 115.

A YOGI FROM MIRZAPUR.

FIG. 10.

To face page 186.

CHAPTER VIII—*continued*

SECTION IV.—Vaishnava Sects: Sri Vaishnavas, Madhavas, Ramanandis, Kabir Panthis, Ballavacharyas, and Chaitanites.

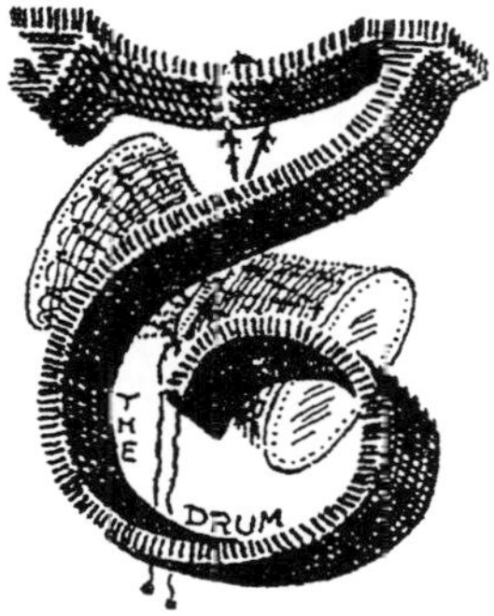

THE sects now to be noticed all devote themselves specially to the worship of Vishnu, but differ from one another primarily in paying adoration to him in his human incarnations either as Ramachandra or as Krishna. As a rule they are all vegetarians, and abstain from spirits.

Rama worshippers may or may not associate his consort Sita with their god. Krishna worshippers usually adore his consorts, or his mistress Radha, along with their chosen deity.

1. The *Sri Vaishnavas*, as followers of Ramanuja are called because they worship Sri or Lakshmi as the consort of Vishnu, are found almost exclusively in the Deccan, where they have flourishing monastic establishments.

The most marked peculiarity of these sectarians is their scrupulousness in regard to food. Nothing must be eaten by a Ramanujite that has not been prepared by himself and in strict privacy. When actually taking his meal, the householder of this sect must be clad either in woollen or silk but not cotton garments. There are two sub-sects, the *Vadagalas* and the *Tengalas*. On the forehead the Ramanujas have painted certain white lines, which in the case of *Vadagalas* resemble a W, in that of the *Tengalas* a Y. They also paint a red streak up and down between the white lines. Members of this sect also adorn themselves with patches of *gopi-chandana* and red lines on the breast and arms. These patches are intended to represent the conch, discus, club, and lotus, emblems of Vishnu, while the red line stands for Sri, or Lakshmi, the wife of Vishnu.

Not uncommonly, members of both sexes have these emblems branded on their persons with red-hot metal stamps.

The necklaces and rosaries of the mendicant orders are made of *tulasi* wood or of lotus seeds, their robes are dyed of a reddish colour. Some call themselves *dandis*, and habitually carry a staff, but, unlike the Sivite *dandis* already described, they do not throw off the sacred thread.

2. *Madhavas*.—This sect, founded, as already stated, by Madhavacharya (A.D. 1199–1278), is confined to Southern India. The monks are celibates, and live in monasteries. They wear a single orange-coloured wrapper. Like the Sivite *dandis*, they discard the sacred thread, carry a staff and a water-pot, and shave their heads. They also brand upon their breasts and arms the symbols of Vishnu. The sect mark on the forehead is composed of two perpendicular lines painted with *gopi-chandana*, and one *black* line between them traced with the charcoal of incense burnt before the image of Vishnu. The black line terminates in a round yellow spot of turmeric. All castes may be admitted to this sect, but their *gurus* or preceptors are always Brahmans.

3. The *Ramanandis*.—This flourishing Vishnuvite sect, which is spread all over Northern India, is known also under the name of *Ramawat* or *Ramat*. It was founded by Ramanand somewhere about the end of the fourteenth or beginning of the fifteenth century.[1]

All *Ramanandis* bear on their foreheads the distinguishing Vishnu sect mark, the *trifala*, which consists of three

[1] Professor H. H. Wilson, *Sketch of the Religious Sects of the Hindus*, p. 31.

upright lines—the centre one red, and the side ones white. They also wear necklaces and rosaries of *tulasi* beads.

The *Ramanandis* have large and wealthy monasteries in Upper India. There are four sub-sects or orders, all celibate. (1) *Achari*, (2) *Sanyasi*,[1] (3) *Khaki*, (4) *Bairagi*. The *Acharis* wear silken and woollen garments, the *Sanyasis* salmon-coloured cotton clothes, while the *Khakis* usually go about naked, their bodies powdered with dust and ashes and their hair and nails unclipped. The *Bairagis* are probably the most numerous order of this sect; their name is commonly applied to all Vishnuvite mendicants, hence they seem to deserve special notice.

The name is derived from *bai*, without, and *râg*, attachment, *i.e.* without attachment to the world, and is applied even to the Bengali followers of Chaitanya.[2]

Hindus of all castes are permitted to become *Bairagis*, and, as a matter of fact, the sect is recruited from all castes, *including the Brahmans*. Evidently, Ramanand's sectarian movement was one opposed to, and no doubt intended to be subversive of, the established, rigid, and immemorial caste system.

Bairagis do not wear coloured clothes, they allow their hair to grow long, and paint upon their foreheads the *trifala*, consisting of three upright lines radiating slightly from the top of the nose, the central line being of a red colour, and the other two white or yellow. As stated in a previous chapter, the central red line is said to typify Vishnu, the lines on the left and right respectively Brahma and Siva. *Bairagis* wear necklaces and carry rosaries of basil (*tulasi*) beads. They do not eat meat or drink spirits, but are commonly addicted to bhang. All, whether of the three "twice-born castes" or not, put on the sacred thread and wear a tuft of hair on the crown of the head—practices which would seem intended as assertions of the equality of all Hindus, effected by a

[1] The use of this name to designate quite distinct sects or orders is, to say the least, somewhat confusing to the inquirer.

[2] *Travels of a Hindu*, by Bholanath Chander, p. 35.

process of levelling up to the higher strata in the caste system.

As a head-covering the *Bairagi* often uses a *Ram nam ka safa,* which is a piece of cotton cloth with the names of Rama and Sita stamped on it, and usually obtained from Muttra or Bindrabun.

Bairagis are supposed to be celibates, but the "monks of this order have generally a large number of nuns attached to their convents, with whom they openly live as man and wife."[1]

A most elaborate ritual has been laid down for the guidance of *Bairagis* in the daily routine of the indispensable business and duties of life, prescribing in minute detail how, for example, the ascetic should wash, bathe, sit down, perform *pranayam* (stoppage or regulation of respiration), purify his body, purge his mind, meditate on Vishnu, repeat the Gayatri as composed for the special use of members of the sect, worship Rama, Sita, Lakshman, Bharata, and Satringah, together with Rama's bows and arrows, and, lastly, the monkey god Hanuman.[2]

So many observances are prescribed and so much repetition is enjoined that it is evident that the object in view was to give the *Bairagi* enough to fully occupy his thoughts and his waking hours. Of course the mystic union of the worshipper with his deity is an object kept prominently before him in these religious exercises, especially in his meditations, and he is required to realise that Rama and himself are *one,* not *two.* The *Bairagi* is expected to pay at least one visit to Dwarka in order to be branded on his right arm with the Vishnu symbols—the discus, the conch, the club, and the lotus.

4. The *Kabir Panthis.*—Kabir having practically recommended his followers to be all things to all men, and to conciliate the world at large by outward conformity with prevailing customs, it has come about, quite naturally, that

[1] *Hindu Castes and Sects,* by Dr. J. N. Bhattacharjee, p. 445.

[2] The history of these personages, as narrated in the famous Sanskrit epic the Ramayana, has been epitomised in my *Great Indian Epics* (George Bell & Sons, London).

the *Kabir Panthis* have no distinctive dress or ceremonies. As far as they do affect peculiarities of any kind, they follow those of the *Ramats*, wearing *tulasi* beads and having the *trifala* painted on their foreheads. Monks of this sect may be met with all over Northern and Central India.

It would seem that the *Kabir Panthis* hold, in opposition to the generally accepted Hindu ideas, that the Creator "has body formed of the five elements of matter, and that He has mind endowed with the three *gunas*, or qualities of being—of course of ineffable purity and irresistible power; He is free from the defects of human natures, and can assume what particular shape He will; in all other respects He does not differ from man, and the *pure* man, the *Sadh* of the Kabir sect, is His living resemblance, and after death is His associate and equal." [1]

5. The *Ballavacharyas*, well known in Western India, worship Bala Gopala, the cowherd boy. All Hindus, *Sudras* included, may join the sect, but men of the lowest castes, such as *dhobis* (washermen), *mochis* (shoemakers), *darzis* (tailors), and *napits* (barbers), are not received into it.

Asceticism is practically unknown amongst the Ballavites, since they hold "the doctrine that the spiritual progress of the soul is possible only by keeping the body and its powers in a sound condition." [2] This being the case, a consideration of their peculiarities lies outside the scope of the present book.

6. The *Chaitanites*.—Even the lowest castes are admitted into this sect. *Chaitanite* mendicant monks are generally called *Bairagis*. Both males and females are admitted, the former being addressed as Babaji and the latter as Mataji. These Babajis and Matajis commonly live together as husbands and wives, though the former affect the usual garments of ascetics and the latter those of widows.

In all religious systems the celibate state has, with good reason, been looked upon as one of supreme

[1] Wilson's *Religious Sects of the Hindus*, p. 51.
[2] *Hindu Castes and Sects*, by Dr. J. N. Bhattacharjee, p. 458.

self-sacrifice, and therefore as a holy state; but it is so entirely unnatural that, when embraced as a rule of life by sects, orders, or professions, it has never been lived up to. What steady and protracted opposition was experienced in the Christian Church before celibacy could be enforced amongst Christian ecclesiastics, and what gross immoralities and scandals compulsory celibacy led to, are well known.[1]

"The *Chaitanite* nuns," says Dr. Bhattacharjee, "are recruited chiefly from the superannuated unfortunates of the town. The order is joined also by some of the unchaste widows of the lower classes."[2]

There are, however, some of the *Chaitanite Bairagis*, the so-called *Brikats* (men disgusted with the world), who profess celibacy and live in monasteries, of which a great many have been erected by the liberality of the richer lay members of the sect.

The dress worn by the *Chaitanite* monks is generally white, but a yellow colour is sometimes adopted. Like other *Vaishnavas*, the *Chaitanites* paint perpendicular lines on their foreheads, generally with *gopi-chandana*; they also, by means of engraved stamps dipped in moist *gopi-chandana*, print upon their arms and breasts the names of their deities and often the word *gora*, which is a corruption for *goura*, one of the many names of their prophet. Their rosaries and necklaces are made of beads cut from the *tulasi* plant, which is held in high veneration by them.

The *Chaitanites* are strict vegetarians, and avoid the use of all intoxicants. They are required to abstain from communion with those Hindus who offer animal sacrifices.[3]

There are amongst the followers of Chaitanya various sub-sects well known for their immoralities. For example, the *Spashta Dayakas*, amongst whom the monks and nuns live together in the same monasteries, with results which

[1] On this subject Mr. H. C. Lea's full and learned work, *Sacerdotal Celibacy*, is probably the best one in English.

[2] *Hindu Castes and Sects*, p. 467.

[3] Ward's *Hindus*, pp. 125, 126.

may well be imagined; the *Sahajas*, who hold that every man is Krishna and every woman Radha, and consequently approve of promiscuous intercourse; and the *Bauls*, who, going one step further, maintain that "sexual indulgence is the most approved form of religious exercise."[1]

[1] Dr. Bhattacharjee's *Hindu Castes and Sects*, p. 483.

CHAPTER VIII—*continued*

SECTION V.—Three Sikh Mendicant Orders: Udasis, Nirmalis, Akalis.

IN the last chapter I noted the more essential characteristics of *Sikhism*, and also the fact that at the present time it is manifesting a tendency, real if hardly perceptible, to re-adopt many of the practices of Hinduism, out of which it gradually emerged in the fifteenth, sixteenth, and seventeenth centuries, under the stimulus of political conditions which have long since ceased to exist.

Of the mendicant orders which sprang out of *Sikhism* I have selected the *Udasis*, *Nirmalis*, and *Akalis* for notice here, more especially on account of the peculiar and picturesque circumstances to which the latter two owe their beginnings.

The *Udasis*.[1]—This order of *sadhus*, which is an extremely numerous one in the Punjab, was founded by Siri Chand, eldest son of Baba Nanak. Siri Chand lived to see the sixth *Sikh guru*, Har Govind, and, when he was over a hundred years old, he adopted

[1] *Udasi* = grief, dejection.

Gurditta, a son of the last-named *guru*, to succeed him as abbot of the order of the *Udasis*. But Gurditta, being a sporting character and a married man, was disqualified from being a proper head of the brotherhood. He therefore made over the spiritual leadership of the order to four men who were to act as his *mosands* or deputies, and these four became the founders of the four principal suborders, called *dhuans*, or hearths, into which the *Udasis* are divided.

It is stated that, when Siri Chand's claims to succeed his father Baba Nanak in the *guruship* were passed over by his venerable parent in favour of Angad, one of his most devoted followers, the disappointed son threw ashes on his head and person, in token of his grief and abasement; and to this day the *Udasis* hold ashes in great esteem in memory of this painful event, the ashes, for ceremonial purposes mixed with calcareous earth, being sometimes made into large balls several inches in diameter.

Udasis are usually decently clad in salmon-coloured clothes. They wear a pointed cap on the head and a black cord known as a *sālee* round the neck. They carry a *jholi* or bag hanging from the shoulder, and a *toomba* or dried pumpkin which serves as a water-pot. A black *āsan*, or small carpet, often forms a part of their travelling outfit. Some wear a mass of matted hair on their heads, others go almost clean-shaven, there being apparently no general rule on this matter. The use of flesh, spirits, and tobacco is denied to the *Udasis*. Many members of the order are good Sanskrit scholars. When a *chela* is admitted into the order, he is adjured to avoid those two deadly temptations: *gold* and *women*. The initiatory ceremony is brought to a conclusion by the *chela* drinking the water with which his *guru's* feet have been washed. He is then taught certain portions of a hymn known as the *jap-ji*, and dismissed with this final admonition—

> "Chārān sādh ke dho dho peyo
> Urap sadh ko apna jeyo."

(Drink the water with which the *sadhu* has washed his

feet, and give up your soul and body to the *sadhu*, *i.e.* the *guru.*)

The *Nirmalis* (the pure).—The circumstances under which this order originated are, I should say, unique. In A.D. 1691, or thereabouts, Govind Singh, the tenth and last *guru* of the *Sikhs*, celebrated with unusual pomp at Anandpur the gay Hindu saturnalia known as the *Holi.* Visitors were attracted thither from considerable distances, and amongst others came a young and beautiful Hindu widow named Anup Kaur, a *Khatrani* by caste, and a resident of Lahore. Guru Govind Singh, who was only twenty-five years of age and a particularly handsome man, captivated the susceptible heart of the young widow, and she resolved to try her arts upon him. It appears that at this period the chief object of Govind's life was to induce, I might almost say *compel,* the goddess Devi to appear to him and promise him her assistance against the Muhammadan rulers of the land, who were carrying on a bitter religious persecution of the Hindus. For the attainment of the end he had in view, Govind had gathered many Brahmans together,—for, like all Hindus, he believed that if the *appropriate* religious ceremonies were *correctly* carried out, the goddess, however reluctant, would be constrained to make her appearance.

It is well known to the Hindu that besides the Brahmans there are others who, by the practice of painful austerities, have become possessed of great, sometimes unlimited, power. These thaumaturgists are to be found only here and there, it is true, amongst the *sadhus* of various sects who abound in India. To the *sadhus,* therefore, Govind frequently resorted for advice and assistance in his endeavours to propitiate the goddess Devi. Having come to know this, a happy idea entered the head of the love-sick Anup Kaur. She would personate a *sadhu,* enter into close relations with Govind, and, in the end, attract and ensnare the object of her passion.

In pursuance of this plan, she disguised herself as a *sadhu,* and, being possessed of ample means, she easily secured accomplices in her scheme. She took up her abode at a spot within a short distance of Anandpur, and her satellites soon let it be known through the countryside that a most holy and learned *Sanyasi* had favoured the neighbourhood with his presence. It was also given out that this most saintly *Mahatma* had a special key to open the heart of the goddess Devi. The important news, of course, reached Govind, for whom it had been specially prepared, and he forthwith instructed a confidential servant to arrange an early interview with the new-comer. The youthful *sadhu*, however, betrayed no eagerness to meet the *guru*, and merely sent word to the effect that if Govind wished to come he might do so, but on condition that he came without any pomp or following, in an ascetic garb, at midnight and alone.

These conditions excited the imagination of Govind Singh, and enhanced the importance of the *sadhu* in his eyes. So, having donned the orange-coloured vestments of an ascetic, he sought the saintly *Mahatma* in the stillness of the night at the appointed hour.

He was graciously received, and the usual exchange of compliments and ideas took place. After a little while, on some pretext or other the *sadhu* retired, and then re-appeared before the astonished *guru* decked in silks and jewellery, a young and fascinating woman, with every attraction that could lure an ordinary mortal to her embraces. But Govind, like Joseph under somewhat similar circumstances, kept his virtue, and, after rebuking Anup Kaur, made good his escape; not, however, before the disappointed temptress had raised the cry of "Thief!" Govind, who was never at any time deficient in artfulness, joined in the cry, and, seizing Anup Kaur's brother in the darkness, added greatly to the confusion, in which he managed to slip away safely.

When Govind Singh returned home he gave the ascetic garb he had assumed for the memorable occasion to one of his followers, Bir Singh, a very holy personage, and authorised him to found a new sect of *sadhus*, to be called *Nirmalis*, or *the pure*, in commemoration of the event.

This adventure of Govind's bore fruit of another kind also. The wiles of Anup Kaur had made a deep impression on him, and he wrote, or more likely collected, no less than four hundred and four stories on the wiles of women, for the timely warning, it is said, of his simple followers.

The *Nirmalis* are, on the whole, a learned order much given to Sanskrit studies, and are followers of the Vedanta philosophy. There is a tradition amongst them that five original members of the order went to study Sanskrit theology at Benares, but were denied the privilege of such studies by the Brahmans, because they happened to be *Sudras* by caste. However, Guru Govind Singh cheered the disappointed students by the prediction that their order would be famous for its learned men, from whom the Brahmans themselves would be glad to receive instruction.

Nirmalis wear their hair long, and dress themselves in reddish-yellow garments.

The *Nihangs* or *Akalis*.[1]—The circumstances which gave rise to this sect are connected with the flight of Govind Singh from Cham Kor, famous in *Sikh* annals. At this place, in a little fortified enclosure, some forty *Sikhs* defended themselves against a large number of the Mogul soldiers sent against them by the Muhammadan governor of Lahore. When hard pressed by the Imperial troops, Govind Singh dressed up one of his men in his own clothes, and, leaving him in charge of the defence, escaped secretly and alone from the beleaguered post. The place, though stoutly defended, was eventually captured by the Moguls, but a few of the brave defenders managed to get away, and went at once in search of their revered *guru*. They found him not far from the village of Machiwara, asleep near a well, quite overcome with fatigue.

In this village Govind had some Muslim friends, to whom he appealed for help in order to conceal himself from the pursuit of the Mogul soldiery, who would no doubt be scouring the country in search of him. These good friends helped him to disguise himself in the blue dress of a Muslim *faquir*, known about those parts as an

[1] *Nihang*=humble. *Akali*=immortal.

Uch ka pir (a saint of Uch), so named from the village of Uch near Multan, where lived numerous *Sayads* or descendants of the prophet Muhammad. To make the disguise more effective, Govind Singh was placed on a light bed, known as a *chárpái*, and carried along the road as an *Uch ka pir* would ordinarily be carried. Of the men who shouldered his *chárpái* two were *Sikhs*, and two, whose names are remembered to this day,—Nabi Khan and Ghani Khan,—were Muhammadans. A third *Sikh* was in attendance, fanning the pseudo-*pir*. They had not gone far when they were overtaken by the Muhammadan troops, who looked upon Pir-ji with some suspicion. To test the case, the soldiers requested the *pir* to prove that he was what he professed to be, by eating with them. In reply, the attendants said that the holy man never ate anything at all, except perhaps *one* grain of barley in the month, but that they themselves would willingly eat with the Moguls; and they did so, the three *Sikhs* along with their two Muslim friends.

When the party reached a village inhabited by Govind's own people, he burnt a portion of the blue clothes he had assumed by way of disguise, and the remainder he presented to one Man Singh, a favouite follower of his, to be worn by him as the distinctive garb of a new order—*Nihangs* or *Akalis*—which he was authorised to found.

The *Akalis*, in consequence, wear blue garments, but the dress they have adopted, in which their veneration of warlike weapons finds exaggerated expression, is grotesque. At the commencement of the section is the likeness of a present-day *Akali*, in all his war paint, which speaks for itself. During the *Sikh raj*, the *Akalis* were the most fanatical followers of the cult of Guru Govind Singh, and their weapons were steeped in blood on many a fierce battlefield; but, redoubtable though they were, their reckless fanaticism was hardly a match for the steady courage of the Purbia sepoys, who taught them and their Maharajah Ranjit Singh the supreme importance of training and discipline, a lesson which the astute Maharajah laid to heart, and turned to good account in the later years of his strenuous life.[1]

The manners and customs of these sectaries are as peculiar as their personal appearance. When an *Akali* is going to eat, he is required to shout with a loud voice, "Is anyone in want of a meal ?" and, in the unlikely event of anybody coming forward in response to this inquiry, he is to satisfy the hungry stranger before touching food himself.

At *Sikh dharmsalas*, which are chapels and rest-houses combined, it is the common practice of the *Akalis* to gather idly and expectantly round a large stone mortar, in which one of the party busies himself in bruising bhang (hemp leaves) with a stout wooden pestle. When the leaves are reduced to a green pulp, this is mixed with water and sugar and drunk with great appreciation by these fantastically clad *immortals*.

Many *Akalis*, wandering about the country in comfort with horses and camels, do not hesitate to ask for pecuniary assistance. The leader of one of these bands once paid me a visit, sending in the following visiting-card :—

PREM SINGH

(NIHANG SINGH)

VAHIRIYA.

(Of the party of Nihangs that travel about and have no fixed abode.)

I began this sketch of the mendicant orders with an account of the harmless, unobtrusive Jains wandering over the country on foot, carrying merely a besom, not of destruction, but of ultra-tenderness for the lowly life of insects and lower organisms. I have concluded my account by introducing to the reader the truculent bhang-drinking *Akali* roving about, often on horseback or camel-back, bristling all over with weapons of war.

Although the armed *Akali* may, by an obvious association of ideas, recall to mind the famous military

[1] *Memoirs of Colonel Alexander Gardner*, chap. xi.

orders of the West,—the Templars, Hospitallers, and Teutonic knights of the Middle Ages,—the resemblance is too slight and trifling for even a moment's consideration. However, the immense interval, both chronological and pyschological, between the Jains of the fifth century B.C. and the *Akalis* of the seventeenth century of our era, may well serve as an emphatic illustration of the wonderful dissimilitude of some of the ideals which underlie the practice of asceticism and mendicancy in India.

CHAPTER IX

PERSONAL EXPERIENCES WITH SADHUS, GOOD AND BAD

1. The Swinging Bairagi. 2. The Sanyasi Swami Bhaskarananda of Benares. 3. Gareeb Das, an Urdhabahu Bairagi. 4. A Yogi who protected Amritsar from the Plague. 5. A Brahmachari from the Tamil Country. 6. A Sadhu of European Descent at Simla. 7. A Naked Sanyasi and his Companion, a Princess of B——. 8. A Sadhu of Royal Lineage, Prince Bir Bhanu Singh. 9. A Sadhu who had found God. 10. A Sun-worshipping Bairagi. 11. Yogis and Pious Women. 12. A pseudo-Sadhu and his Adventures. 13. Yogi Guests. 14. A Sadhu as Restaurateur. 15. A Saint in Chains.

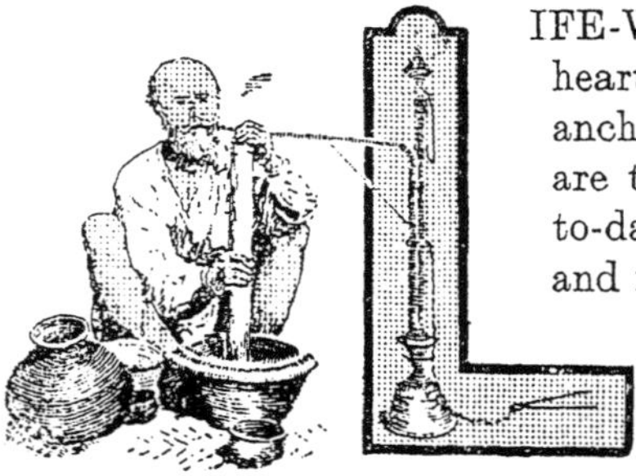

LIFE-WEARY as well as light-hearted *sadhus*, professional anchorites both good and bad, are to be found all over India to-day just as in times past; and if in the previous chapters I have succeeded at all in awakening the reader's interest in Indian *sadhus*, he will not object to a closer and, as it were, more personal acquaintance with these ascetics, such as is afforded by the following narratives of actual interviews with them, and of trustworthy accounts of their doings carefully sifted and punctually noted down by me as soon as the facts were placed in my possession.

1. The Swinging Bairagi.

Near a large tank known as *Ratan Chand's talao*, in the neighbourhood of a group of Hindu temples in Lahore, and under some fine old peepul trees, two or three hundred people, mostly Hindus of both sexes, were assembled one fine evening in November, most of them attentively watching a palanquin which had been placed on the high platform of a *samadh* or cenotaph erected to the memory of a Hindu lady by her wealthy son. The screens of the palanquin were drawn back, but I could see nothing within until I approached quite near, when I discovered the emaciated figure of an almost naked man sitting with his knees drawn up against his chin in an attitude common enough in India, but one which the European would find it rather difficult to imitate.

Down the length of the palanquin was a board, closely studded with blunt iron nails, and it was upon a portion of this most uncomfortable bed of spikes that the *Bairagi* was seated, and was supposed, perhaps quite correctly, to sleep at night. Above the bony shins and exaggerated knot-like knees of this seated figure appeared a human head with an immense shock of hair like a chignon hanging heavily behind it. Its hollow eyes, peering over a pair of green glass-and-wire goggles, had a queer hunted look about them, and its nostrils seemed strangely misshapen, one being apparently distended with some sort of plug or other. From this repulsive figure there proceeded, from time to time, sundry guttural sounds and hollow coughs.

A faithful disciple, conveniently at hand, explained to me that his master in the palanquin was more than one hundred and thirty years of age, and had resolved to undergo certain penances until he should succeed in collecting enough money to feast one hundred thousand Brahmans and to give each one of his guests the present of at least one rupee, apparently for being good enough to partake of the banquet provided for him.

As I stood near the palanquin a succession of men and women, mostly the latter, mounted the platform, approached the ascetic, and, bowing down before him so that their heads touched the very floor, placed their offerings, consisting for the most part of pice or of small silver coins, before the holy man. This done, they passed on without an audible word, though some silent wish or prayer was no doubt in each one's heart. The saint did not condescend to notice anyone, but merely looked absently, with those queer hunted eyes of his, at his admirers as they approached his presence and added their contributions towards the considerable sum necessary for the fulfilment of his vow.

Presently a stir took place amongst the ascetic's attendants. The usual time for him to perform his ablutions had arrived. A pair of wooden-soled sandals studded with spikes were placed beside the palanquin, and upon their prickly surface the poor fellow was helped to place his bare feet. With the assistance of his men, the emaciated *Bairagi* was brought forward and allowed to subside on to a low wooden stool about four or five inches high. When he emerged from his palanquin the onlookers took up what, according to Indian ideas, is a most respectful attitude, all present facing the ascetic with slightly bowed heads and palms joined together before their breasts. Anyone who may have seen a picture of a Rajah's *durbar*, painted by an Indian artist, will at once comprehend what I mean. All faces turned in one direction,—the direction of the Rajah,—each man's feet set close together side by side, his palms accurately joined one against the other and the fingers slanting upwards at an angle of about forty-five degrees—all beautifully regular, all uniformly respectful.

The saint reputed to be one hundred and thirty years old, though certainly very rickety and worn, was probably not more than half that age. He coughed a good deal and seemed very weak.

When about to perform his ablutions in public, he requested the people nearest him to stand back a little, lest the water should reach and inconvenience them. A slight backward movement was the result, and, when an attendant poured some water on the *Bairagi's* hands, it was seen that his wrists were united by an iron chain not more than six or seven inches long. Now came the important operation of dislodging the huge plug from his right nostril. As the *sadhu* removed it, not without a little effort, it was followed by a loosely twisted cord of unspun cotton about eight or nine inches long, which had apparently been hanging in the pharynx at the back of the nose. No wonder the poor fellow coughed so frequently and so painfully. Two cotton cords, similar to the one described but somewhat longer, were handed to the *Bairagi*. Their ends were pointed and perhaps a little stiffened with wax. With an unpleasant, almost painful, grunt or moan, he passed them both up his nostrils, and then, opening his mouth as wide as possible, fished up with his long skinny fingers the pendent ends of the two cords. All four extremities were now in his hands, and he proceeded to draw the strings to and fro through his nose and mouth five or six times. When Maharaj, as they called him, had thus cleansed his nostrils and throat, two narrow bamboo tubes, each about eighteen inches long, were brought to him. One had a small funnel at its extremity. The *Bairagi* having held his head aslant, the small end of the funnel tube was applied to his right nostril and one end of the other tube to his left nostril, the latter being lower than the former. Water was now poured, from a vessel with a spout, into the funnel, and came off in a continuous stream at the end of the other and lower tube—a rather difficult performance this, I should fancy. It remained to plug the *left* nostril for the night as the other had previously been, for they were stopped turn about. This operation was accomplished by passing a long wick, or cotton cord, up the nose, and finally introducing its other and knotted end with a little force into the much distended nostril. As the stiffened end of the cord disappeared up the ascetic's nose, a veracious disciple assured us that it had gone straight up into the brain. He repeated this statement many times, and the *Bairagi*, who heard it, and knew it was not true, did not contradict it.

These operations duly accomplished in the public gaze, the holy man was helped back once more into his uncomfortable lodging in the palanquin. I learnt that twice a day, morning and evening, Maharaj repeated this disgusting and unedifying performance, and that twice a day people assembled to see and admire it, although it is neither original in its conception,—for other *Bairagis* do the like,—nor, I should think, specially agreeable for any-one to behold.

Had this worn-out ascetic so assiduously devoted to the regular cleansing of his nostrils and throat ever had a romance in his life? Had he been deceived, disillusioned, driven to despair? Had that uncouth figure ever been acceptable to the fair sex? Had those strange hunted eyes ever gleamed with rage or melted with passion? Possibly; but these are questions more easily asked than answered. The *Bairagi* himself did not speak; and the motive assigned for all his severe penance, the desire to feed a hundred thousand Brahmans, could be accounted rational only on the supposition that he desired to expiate some sin, or more likely to acquire merit and power through his austerities, the feeding of one hundred thousand Brahmans being set before himself as a definite object to limit the duration of his self-imposed hardships.

I had leisure now to study my company and surroundings. At the foot of one of the peepul trees I found three *sadhus* sitting round a small fire, all of them young and healthy. They had no connection with the *Bairagi* who was attracting so much attention, and rather affected to turn their backs upon him. Two of these men were so scantily clothed that their united garments would have hardly made a decent-sized pocket-handkerchief; the third was absolutely naked, sky-clothed (*digambara*) he would himself have said, under broad daylight, in a public place, and amidst a mixed crowd of both sexes. The *sky-clothed* one was, I have no doubt, an abandoned scamp. He looked it. A grave and well-dressed man ventured to suggest, in my hearing, the desirability of a rag in the interests of decency, to which the religious man made some flippant observation about the trouble of keeping it tied.

Before I left the spot I learned that the *sadhu* of the spiky bed had yet another mode of drawing the wondering multitude to visit him and to contribute their portion towards the accomplishment of his vow. Once a day, in the afternoon, he used to have himself suspended, head downwards, from a sturdy branch of a great tree, before the admiring gaze of a large concourse of people. On the first suitable opportunity I came to see this part of his performance.

It was a lovely day. A crowd of about five hundred men and women had assembled, and, in Oriental fashion, were meekly and quietly sitting down on the ground awaiting the great man's convenience. A few persons, mostly women, pressed on to the platform, and I noticed a girl of about sixteen in bright red clothes sit down and peer into the palanquin with wondering curiosity. Most likely she was from the country, and had come to Lahore from some neighbouring village on purpose to see Maharaj. A female companion pulled her roughly away, but disengaging herself she came back again to stare with wide-open eyes at the wonderful *sadhu*, until she was pushed aside by others who did not approve of her monopolising the best position for viewing his saintship.

At about one o'clock an attendant came forward and set to work preparing a space about ten feet square, under a large peepul tree, by smearing it over with a mixture of clay, cow-dung, and water. This done, he placed a pile of dried cow-dung cakes upon it and applied a light. A cloud of white smoke was quickly diffused all around. When the fuel happened to blaze up the attendant moderated its energy by sprinkling a little water on it, thus bringing it back to the desired smoky condition. The *Bairagi* now came forth, helped as before, and, after washing his hands, had his hair firmly tied up in a cloth which also covered his face. He next put one foot into a loop of thick cotton rope depending from a branch of the tree, and was hauled up, head downwards, till he hung suspended about three feet above the smouldering fire. With one hand he grasped the free foot, and with the other he manipulated a rosary concealed in a bag called a *gomukhi*. By a slender string passed round his body one of his disciples kept him swaying over the smoky fire, into which a Brahman was throwing grain, ghee, and other things. For seven-and-twenty minutes by my watch the *Bairagi* was swung head downwards over that smouldering fire. When he had counted his beads he dropped the bag and was then immediately taken down, looking perhaps a slight degree more exhausted for his half-hour's constant fumigation feet upwards.

Never a word was spoken throughout the entire performance about right or wrong, not one syllable about duty or worship. There was the dumb show, and nothing more.

As the emaciated figure, resembling a skeleton rather than a man, swayed to and fro like the pendulum of some strange old-world clock—the clock of Indian ideas—I tried to read on the living dial before me what time of day it was. The circle of onlookers was a large one, composed of Orientals, whose thoughts and ideas are very inscrutable, yet it seemed to me that the face of the very complicated, but interesting, dial I was studying indicated that dawn was approaching, though the daybreak had not yet appeared.

A few generations hence the *Bairagi* clock I have described will be unknown, at least in the great cities of India.

2. The Sanyasi Swami Bhaskarananda of Benares.

In the holy city of Benares there lived for many years a famous *Sanyasi*, Swami Bhaskarananda Saraswati, who died in 1899, being then sixty-six years of age.

This interesting old gentleman, who was more than a local celebrity, resided in excellent quarters in a fine garden placed at his disposal, known as Anundabagh, belonging to the Rajah of Amity. There, at the end of 1895, I paid him a visit, having been informed that he was always pleased to receive strangers who cared to make his acquaintance. When I was announced, the *Sanyasi*, who had been sitting stark naked, wrapped a loin cloth about him as a polite concession to my narrow conventional prejudices, and stepped forward to welcome me with a most engaging smile. Strange as it may seem, there was undeniably something refined and attractive about the personality of this naked ascetic with his transparently benevolent countenance, rather light brown complexion, clean-shaven head and face, toothless mouth, and keen, bright, impressive eyes.

A very learned Sanskrit scholar, and deeply versed in the Vedanta philosophy, this *sadhu* was well known to and venerated by his Hindu countrymen throughout Northern India.

The old man asked me many questions about my occupation and the object of my visit to Benares, and in my turn I ventured to inquire whether his practice of going entirely naked at all times was not rather trying in the winter. "No," he said, smiling pleasantly; "by long habit my entire person has become accustomed to being exposed, just as your face and hands are. I really feel no inconvenience."

Though a recluse, Swami Bhaskarananda, for whom the world, which after all is only an illusion, had no attraction whatever, kept a visitors' book, and, having directed an attendant to produce it, turned over the pages, pointing out in it with evident pride the signatures of two or three British M.P.'s. After we had conversed for some time on various subjects, he courteously gave me some Sanskrit pamphlets, written by himself, on religious and philosophical matters. I told Swami-ji that I had some idea of publishing a book about Indian ascetics. He expressed his pleasure at this, and was almost childishly delighted when I said that I should probably mention him in my book. Apparently to help me in this matter, he presented me with a short biography of himself, written in English by one Gopal Chander Chatterjee, to which was prefixed a lithographed likeness of Swami-ji. After a pleasant hour with the ascetic I took leave of him, but had barely left the premises when an attendant came after me to call me back.[1] I retraced my steps, and Swami-ji most courteously

[1] Prince Bojidar Karageorgevitch visited a *sadhu* at Benares, who, though he does not name him, was no doubt Swami Bhaskarananda. The prince says with reference to this event: "As I was leaving, the *faquir* called me back, asked me to think of him sometimes, and gave me one of the splendid yellow roses that hung about him like a glory."—*Enchanted India*, p. 163. I wonder if Swami-ji had a well-thought-out habit of thus courteously recalling his visitors with the object of impressing himself more strongly upon their memories.

said he felt he must have at least one more word with me before we parted, perhaps for ever; and he then, with many good wishes for my welfare, kindly handed me a photograph of himself *for my book*, as he said, and I have much pleasure in reproducing it now (Fig. 11), as I have also in calling to mind the serenity, cheerfulness, and urbanity of this famous and highly venerated Hindu ascetic.

In a little lodge or chapel near the gate, and within the walls of the *bagh* where he resided, I noticed a life-size marble statue of the saint. It was a good likeness. Later on I saw for sale in the idol-shops in the bazaars of the city many stone and brass statuettes, which appeared to be faithful copies of the statue I have just referred to.

From the biographical sketch which he gave me I derived the following characteristic particulars regarding the *Sanyasi's* past history :—

His real name was Matiram Misra. He was born in 1833 of a good Brahman family, was invested with the sacred thread at the age of eight, and married four years later. From his eighth to his seventeenth year he was a diligent and most successful student of the Sanskrit language and of the Vedanta philosophy. A son was born to him when he was but eighteen years old. By this event he was, in his own opinion, freed from any further social obligations, "he realised the unreality of this world and its pleasures," and resolved, contrary to the wishes of his parents, to renounce the world and become a wandering ascetic.

So one day he disappeared from his father's house and went on foot to Ujjaini, where he put up in a temple of Siva. Here he continued his Vedantic studies and *began to practise yoga.* But the spirit of unrest, which in India drives so many to embrace the calling of the ascetic, took imperious possession of him. He accordingly left his temporary abode and visited the various sacred places of Malwa and Gujrat. At the latter city, however, he settled down for a period of seven years, which he devoted to a further study of the Vedanta philosophy.

When Matiram had reached the age of twenty-seven,

THE SANYASI BHASKARANANDA OF BENARES.

FIG. 11.

To face page 210.

"he resolved," says his Bengali biographer, "to enter the austere Asram of *Sanyas*. The true knowledge of *gnan* had dawned in his mind. He saw through the unreal nature of the world, and felt the existence of one Supreme Soul all through the universe. . . .

"The world," continues the philosophical biographer, "is not real. It never existed, it does not exist, and it will not come into existence in future. We all dream, and, while sleeping, we think that the things we see in the dream are real, but as soon as we wake up we perceive the mistake. In the same way we are sleeping in the lap of ignorance, and as soon as true knowledge will dawn on us we shall be able to know that the world is but a dream, a shadow and not a substance."

On the occasion of his admission to the sect of the *Sanyasis*, Matiram Misra received the new name by which he was to be known in after-years, and, according to the custom of the sect he had joined, discontinued wearing the sacred thread, which was the proud symbol of his Brahmanhood.

After some time spent "in the contemplation of the Jibatma (or the human soul) as being one with the Paratma or the Supreme Essence," he started upon a round of travels, in the course of which he visited his native village once more.

There he saw his parents, his long-neglected wife, and the associates of his youth, but the ties which had once bound him to his relatives and friends had been dissolved for ever. To such as would listen to him he explained the utter worthlessness of the world and its hollow pleasures, and then, the spirit of unrest having again seized upon him, he took his departure to make an extensive tour of the *tirthas*, or holy places, of a land of shrines. Alone, without any money, clad in a single garment, did the *Sanyasi* roam from end to end of India, visiting Bengal, Behar, Orissa, Madras, Bombay, Central India, and the Himalayas, experiencing on the long and weary way many dangers and hardships, such as floods, snow-storms, and starvation. While on his round of travels, he received unmoved the news of the death of his only son.

For thirteen years Swami Bhaskarananda travelled about India, always practising *tapasya* (penance), and then feeling, after his long probation and constant striving, that he had obtained the ineffable *knowledge* he had desired, he settled down for the remainder of his life in the sacred city of Benares.

Here he enjoyed the greatest consideration and distinction. Pilgrims crowded to adore him. Princes from afar came to consult him, and bowed their royal heads down to his holy feet. Miracles, particularly of healing, were attributed to him, and temples were, even during his lifetime, built in his honour, and his effigy worshipped in them. Images of the saint were also set up for private worship by the Rani of Barhar, the Maharajah of Ajodia, the Maharajah of Nagadh, and other important personages, and no doubt in many humble Hindu households also, since, as I have already mentioned, likenesses made of stone and metal of Swami-ji were plentiful in the idol-shops of Benares.

In recording the above particulars of what is indeed a typical case, I have stated enough to show the honoured position and unstinted veneration with which the ascetic life in India may, even in this materialistic age, reward the successful *sadhu*.

I will conclude with the following extract from a newspaper conducted entirely by Indians :—

"DEATH OF SWAMI BHASKARANAND SARASWATI.

"The death is announced from cholera, on last Sunday night at Benares, of Swami Bhaskaranand Saraswati, the celebrated recluse and devotee of the holy city. He was buried in a sitting posture in his garden at Durga Kund, and a monument will be raised over his grave. The funeral was attended by a large concourse of people, among whom were the Maharajas of Benares and Ajodhya, the Rajas of Mainpuri and Nagod, and a large number of Indian gentlemen. The last time that we wrote about the Swami-ji was when the Hon. Mr. La Touche, then officiating Lieutenant-Governor of the North-West Provinces, paid a visit to the venerable recluse and had some conversation with him Mr. La Touche presented the Swami a *nazar* of a gold mohur, which was at once handed over to the Swami's depemdants. Swami Bhaskaranand was a most remarkable and attractive personality, and every distinguished visitor to Benares paid him his respects. Tourists from America and Europe always tried to see the Swami, who was frequently accessible, and all who saw him were struck by his wisdom and holiness. The *Pioneer* writes: 'The personality of the venerable Swami-ji Bhaskaranand Saraswati, who died at Benares shortly after midnight on Sunday, was one which interested Englishmen no less than it dominated the Swami's own countrymen. This ascetic of ascetics, who had long ago passed so far on the way to Nirvana that no human contamination could any longer touch him, who was as far above considerations of caste as the pariah is below, and who has sat for years at Benares squat, hands crossed and clotheless, waiting for his deliverance from mortality, was a man of high intellectual powers, who took a keen interest not only in the affairs of India, but in the politics of Europe, and from whom an English visitor always received a cordial welcome. Among the higher classes of the native community the Swami was regarded with the utmost respect and veneration, his advice on all matters mundane and supramundane being eagerly sought, while among the lower classes he was already looked upon as a divine being, and would have been worshipped as such had he not always sternly forbade any manifestation of the kind.'

"Swami Bhaskaranand was greatly appreciated and respected by a large number of Englishmen, and this was his special advantage. Before his appearance in Benares the most revered name in the sacred city was that of Trailangya Swami, who also sat clotheless for years on the bank of the Ganges. He was profoundly learned and a *Paramahansa* of the highest order; but, as he had imposed upon himself a vow of silence, he was not much known among Englishmen. But so long as holy men of this type appear in India—and it is in this country alone that the race has never become extinct—we need not despair of the future."—The *Tribune*, 15th July 1899 (Lahore).

3. Gareeb Das, an Urdhabahu Bairagi.

Adjoining the famous Golden Temple at Amritsar is a grove known as Guru Bagh; and here a *sadhu*, conspicuous on account of having both arms rigidly uplifted above his head, took up his temporary abode attended by a few disciples. This was in the month of October, at the time of the Divali festival, which annually attracts a large multitude of people to the holy city of the *Sikhs*.

When I saw the *sadhu*, his emaciated arms were apparently quite rigid, and the clenched hands, which were about six inches apart, were particularly painful to look at —wasted and shrunken, with great curved nails growing like bird's claws out of the thin fingers.

He had his person rubbed all over with white ashes, and he wore a small loin cloth and a neatly tied turban. His features were long, and the expression of his face agreeable. What he looked like, and his utter helplessness, the portrait of him in the frontispiece will, I think, make quite clear.

In conversation with him I ascertained that he was a *Bairagi*, that he came from Ajudya, and had been the *chela* of a famous *guru* formerly attached to the Hunaman Gari monastery in that city, but now deceased. I had visited Ajudya, and could talk about it and the sacred Surayu (Gogra), which flows by that ancient town; and so the *sadhu*, touched by old associations, became communicative. His native place, he told me, was Bas Bareilli in Oudh, and his name Gareeb Das.

What I wished particularly to ascertain from the *Bairagi* was what motive could possibly have induced him to subject himself voluntarily to such terrible, such almost inconceivable personal hardships as were plainly involved in the penance he had adopted. Not only had he deprived himself of the use of both his arms, but by the awkward unnatural position which he had forced them to assume he had made them a source of constant trouble, weariness, and inconvenience to himself, both waking and sleeping. His replies to my inquiries were evasive and unsatisfactory, probably because he was an illiterate man. At first he said that from the Scriptures he had received his mandate to perform this penance—which cryptic statement he subsequently elucidated by saying that from several penances recommended in religious books he had selected this one, as it had been adopted by several members of his own sect and monastery. His object in thus afflicting himself was to have communication with Permāshwar (God), or, as he also said, to obtain *mukti* (salvation). An unsympathetic and ill-mannered bystander, on hearing the *sadhu's* statement of his spiritual aspirations, contemptuously cited a Sanskrit distich which meant, "From penance comes a kingdom, and from the kingdom comes hell"—in allusion to a common belief that, by such mortifications of the flesh, *sadhus* really strive for *raj* or power and position in the next mundane life, that they gain their end,[1] and then fall into the hell whither power and dominion inevitably lead one.

Gareeb Das the ascetic, when I saw him, had had his arms up above his head for eight long years, and desired to make no change for a further period of four years, at the end of which time he hoped to restore them to their former state, firstly by presents and feasts to the Brahmans, whose intercession would thus be secured, and secondly by the application of certain emollients with peculiar stimulating properties known to the *sadhus*. "If it be the will of God," added Gareeb Das, speaking on this subject, "then my arms will be restored to their proper use when the appointed time comes."

Referring to such cases, the missionary Ward says: "When a person wishes to bring the arm to its former position, he anoints the joints with clarified butter; and in about two months, by degrees, the arm obtains its

[1] As indeed did the Brahman Muconda, who, by undergoing the severest austerities and a voluntary death by fire, with the view of being reborn in the purple, actually succeeded in coming back to this world as no less a personage than the famous Mogul Emperor Akbar.—Wilford's Essays, cited in Forbes's *Oriental Memoirs*, vol. iii. pp. 149, 150.

former position, and in time becomes as strong as before."[1]

As there are European thieves who do not hesitate to rob a church, so there are, it would seem, Indian representatives of the same ancient, if disreputable, fraternity, who have no scruples about appropriating the property of even a helpless *sadhu*. This was illustrated when Gareeb Das was deprived by impudent thieves of all his portable property, including a *book*, which rumour declared was actually a bank pass-book, testifying to cash deposits mounting up to as much as a *lakh* of rupees. The disgusted *sadhu* promptly removed himself from the Guru Bagh where he had been robbed, and some of my servants met and conversed with him near the railway station, waiting for the train which was to take him away to Jeypore on his homeward journey. Such was the tale which was current in Amritsar, and which I noted down on the 26th of October. What was my surprise on the 7th of November to find my friend Gareeb Das once again established in the Guru Bagh, the story of the robbery having been in all probability a mere invention got up to stimulate public interest in *sadhuji*. On this occasion the ascetic had a small private enclosure of his own, made up of bamboos and cloth screens. People were crowding in and out of this enclosure in goodly numbers. When I went in I noticed great heaps, literally *heaps*, of flour, salt, sugar, and such things—in fact, sacks and sacks full. It appeared that a few days previously the *sadhu* had given notice in the city that he would not *eat* anything until he had entertained five hundred unmarried girls at a feast. He hoped to accomplish this before the end of December, but contributions had come in so quickly that the feast-day had been fixed for the 9th of November. While I was learning these particulars the *sadhu* rose and walked a few paces with his arms above his head, and as he did so the poor fellow looked so utterly and painfully helpless that I could not but experience a feeling of the greatest compassion for him, not unmingled with a

[1] *A View of the History, Literature, and Religion of the Hindus*, p. 297 (Madras Edition, 1863).

certain admiration of his steadfastness and prolonged endurance.

Before I took my leave of the ascetic, an attendant, making a very polite speech, offered me a couple of handfuls of raisins and almonds. I took just two raisins and dropped a rupee on the remainder. The money was removed and the raisins and almonds given to the policeman who was in attendance upon me, in accordance with the rule which prevails at the Golden Temple. The Punjabi policeman willingly accepted the gift, carefully tying up the dried fruits and nuts in a very dirty handkerchief.

The *sadhu's* feast to the unmarried girls came off in proper time, and was a complete success, for a great many Hindu ladies of good position came on the appointed day and helped to cook and distribute the food amongst the invited guests. In this way Gareeb Das, without spending a single rupee out of his own pocket, and himself a cripple, was enabled, through the liberal contributions and helpful courtesy of his admirers, to play the host munificently to five hundred youthful maidens of Amritsar.

4. A Yogi who protected Amritsar from the Plague.

Evil days had come upon the land. The plague had made its appearance in the Punjab, and with it stringent orders for the compulsory segregation of all real and suspected cases—a measure dreaded by the people far more than the fell disease itself. Rather than have the privacy of their homes invaded, rather than have their loved ones forcibly separated from them in the hour of their dire need and committed to the unsympathetic care of hirelings, the people had risen in armed opposition to the authorities, and several lives had been sacrificed in the conflict.

"If it be the will of God that we should die, let us die together as we have lived together," was the feeling which animated the hearts of a people not yet *civilised* enough to appreciate the highly prudent sentiments which elsewhere enable men to unmurmuringly give up their dearest to the hospitals for infectious diseases, and save their precious selves from danger *for the public good.*

Well, in the evil days I refer to, a *Yogi* visited Amritsar, and it was rumoured that his object was to avert from the city certain impending calamities.

I found him near the fine tank known as Durgiana, in a large space enclosed by canvas walls. He was seated on a slightly raised platform of beaten earth, over which a cloth had been spread. He was enveloped in a clean white cotton sheet of good quality. Only a portion of his face was visible, one eye and cheek being concealed by his matted locks. His nose was bold and prominent, but the eye on the visible side of his face was half closed. Although supposed to be practising *yoga*, he kept his ears and half-closed eyes about him. By the *Yogi's* side there were within easy reach two plates, one containing rose-petals and the other cardamums; there were also a brass *lotah* and another brass water-pot shaped to resemble a gourd. A woman with a young child was prostrating herself in adoration before the saint when I first approached him, but seeing me she timidly withdrew to some little distance, and then, spell-bound by curiosity, kept her eyes fixed upon me. While still in apparent meditation, the *sadhu* was good enough to give me a handful of rose-petals and some cardamums, and in return I put a rupee into a brass salver just in front of him, where already lay some eight or ten rupees, together with a lot of small silver and copper coins.

My companion, a pandit who could speak Sanskrit, asked the *Yogi* in most respectful terms to tell me something about *yoga*, as I was much interested in the matter; but all the saint vouchsafed was some Sanskrit verses on the importance of *truth.* I inquired how long he intended to stay at Amritsar.

"Who knows?" was the reply. "I am a bird (*perind*): here to-day, gone to-morrow."

However, his Brahman attendants were more communicative. The *Yogi's* mission, they explained, was to avert a threatened calamity, and with this end in view he proposed to feast—

(1) The unmarried girls of Amritsar.
(2) The *sadhus* who might be there.
(3) Muslim *faquirs.*

Why these last I could not understand. Of course the feasts were to be given at the expense of the inhabitants of the endangered city; that is, out of their contributions.

As a preliminary step, the *Yogi* determined to carry out daily the bloodless *havan* or *hom* sacrifice in the orthodox style, and in this was, of course, willingly assisted by a number of Brahmans. When I visited the *Yogi*, preparations for the day's *havan* were going on under a fine peepul tree a few yards away. A canopy raised about nine feet above the ground was stretched over the spot where some fuel, kindled but not suffered to blaze up, was quietly smouldering. Two huge iron tongs stuck upright in the ground gave a ceremonial appearance to the place. The chief officiating Brahmans were away in the town investing many *twice-born* youths with the sacred thread, as it was the festival of Baisakhi, and their services much in demand for this purpose. For several days the *havan* had been performed regularly, and presents of food-stuffs for the proposed feasts had been gradually accumulating. However, the results had not been as satisfactory as the Brahmans had hoped, so proceedings on a larger and more attractive scale were to be undertaken, and for this purpose a big trough-like receptacle lined with bricks some six or eight feet square was being constructed, where the flames of a really imposing *havan* might attract the attention and liberality of the public.

My visit was a matter of gratification to the *Yogi*, even though he had turned his back upon the world and its foolish vanities, for the following day he mentioned, with ill-concealed pride, to some college students that a *sahib* had been to see him. He also informed them incidentally that he had inflicted certain burns upon his own arm as a *qurbani*, or sacrifice, for the safety of the city, which was threatened with serious trouble.

The *Yogi's* feasts, I believe, came off satisfactorily, and it is worth mentioning that the plague did not invade Amritsar that year. To a majority of the ignorant populace these two facts were plainly cause and effect, and the claims of *sadhuism* justified once more by irrefragable results.

All *Yogis* are not as public-spirited as this self-constituted tutelary saint of Amritsar. I knew one man who sojourned in a big shed usually occupied by members of the sect, and there he passed his time pretty contentedly, toping. He was always pleased to see me was this thirsty soul, for my visits flattered his vanity and brought a rupee or two to his scanty exchequer. Once I saw a *Sanyasi* with him, apparently on the best of terms, and learnt that the two lived together and *ate together*. Whether this was quite warranted by custom I do not know, but I think not. There was also a boy-*Yogi* in the company, of about twelve years of age, with the usual *yogi* emblems, including the large ear-rings. I ascertained that he had been dedicated to the order by his parents. While I talked with them, the *guru*, to refresh himself, poured out a small cup of ardent country spirits and tossed it off with evident relish. I was afterwards told that the old fellow drank pretty freely, but never became quarrelsome. Of food he partook very sparingly. In the shed which they inhabited temporarily, the *Yogis*, wild-looking fellows, were grouped in small parties round two or three fires. Many lay visitors were there too, squatted about and respectfully watching the saints. Sunset being the hour for the adoration of the *guru*, his own three or four *chelas* gathered round my inebriate friend, just as the solar orb was on the horizon, and bowed their heads down to their *guru's* feet. They blew their little whistles as if they were sounding trumpets in the presence of a king, and then, placing their open hands side by side to form a sort of bowl, waved them before him in small circles as if performing the Hindu rite of *artee* in honour of a god. There were no lights, it is true, but the ceremony, in its artless imitation, was quite unmistakable.

PERSONAL EXPERIENCES WITH SADHUS

5. A Wandering Brahmachari from the Tamil Country.

A young *sadhu*, about twenty-five years of age, good-looking, well clad, and in robust health, who said he was a *Brahmachari* and a bachelor, visited me at Amritsar. He spoke broken English, but could make himself understood fairly well. On his forehead, just above the nose, a bright red spot was painted. Round his neck he wore a necklet of rudraksha berries, and in his hand he carried a thin book or pamphlet in the Tamil language. It was illustrated with the quaintest woodcuts imaginable—showing the difficulties awaiting and the punishments inflicted upon the wicked after death. The last picture in the book was a by no means inviting representation of Swarga, or the regions of delight, which looked very like a bad imitation of some portions of Benares.

With his little book to remind him, both by text and picture, of the evils attendant upon misconduct in this world, and to guide his footsteps to the joys of heaven, the young *sadhu* was cheerfully earning the merit to be derived from a pilgrimage to the holy places of India, depending upon such knowledge of English as he could command to carry him successfully on his way. This appeared to me a most interesting and noteworthy fact—a *sadhu* wandering over India with the aid of the *English* language. He told me he was from the extreme south of India, "near Cape Comorin," and that Tamil was his native tongue. However, his appearance showed me he was no Dravidian, and, on my questioning him a little, he admitted that he was a Guzrati by race, but was born and reared in the extreme south of India. Our *sadhu* felt the importance of his little book so much, that, uninvited, he exhibited and explained some of the quaint illustrations to me. One represented a curious river, the *Vitarni* (difficult to be crossed), barring the way to Swarga, through which, however, a passage could be successfully made by the spirits of such men as during their earthly life had prudently made gifts of cows to the Brahmans, this meritorious act entitling the generous donor to take hold of the tail of one of the sacred cows in the river and to be towed across to the other bank of this terrible Hindu Styx. On my suggesting that under these circumstances he should not fail to present cows to the Brahmans, the *sadhu* laughed pleasantly and said, "You will give to me, and I will give to them," a view of the case with which, needless to say, I did not quite fall in. The Vitarni river is a favourite subject with the Hindu artist, who loves to impress upon the worldly-minded the dangers of its swollen flood, and the best, perhaps the only, way of reaching its farther side.

Another picture in the *sadhu's* precious book made evident how *pindas* offered to the souls of the dead supply materials for the gradual reconstruction of the body in *nine* consecutive months, the head being the first part to be re-created. The nine stages of reconstruction were all separately and successively depicted upon the same page.

The *Brahmachari* said he had come from the south especially to see the far-famed Devali festival at Amritsar, and intended going on to Hardwar in order to be present there at the eclipse of the moon on the 27th of December. He dreaded nothing in his pleasant wanderings except the officers on plague duty, who, he said, gave a great deal of trouble to innocent travellers.

Sanyasis were not held in much esteem by this young *Brahmachari*. He considered them "bad men," because they did not perform the prescribed ceremonies for the dead, and practised interment instead of cremation. An Indian gentleman who was present during the interview said that he had seen *Sanyasis'* bodies disposed of by simply sinking them, with stones or bags of sand, in a flowing stream. He laughed, and so did the *Brahmachari*, when I remarked that in this way the rivers were polluted and rendered insalubrious. They deprecated this notion, holding that, as the sacred water *purified* all things, it could not itself be polluted by anything.

6. A Sadhu of European Descent at Simla.

Exceedingly rare indeed, as one may well imagine, are *non-Indian sadhus*, yet such are not quite unknown.

A SADHU OF EUROPEAN DESCENT.

FIG. 12. *To face page 222.*

Some years ago at Simla, the summer capital of the Indian Government, I interviewed one Charles de Russette, a young man of French descent, who, although brought up as a Christian and properly educated in Bishop Cotton's school in that town, had, while a mere boy, embraced the life of a *sadhu*. I understood that he had inherited some property, which he made over to his sisters, reserving nothing for himself. Why he abandoned Christianity for Hinduism I did not find out, as he was disinclined to talk about the matter; but, whatever the cause which severed him from European life and thought, it was evident that he did not regret the step he had taken, and that he was well satisfied with his condition and mode of life as a Hindu devotee—a *Sanyasi*, I think.

Judging from outward appearances, the man had not suffered any such physical inconveniences as would affect his health, and he was particularly well clothed, though not in any *sadhu* style that I have ever seen. He informed me that he lived his solitary life in the neighbourhood of Simla throughout the year, even in winter, when the snow lay deep upon the mountains. Of his fellow *sadhus* he spoke in terms of high praise, and assured me that he had seen *Yogi* adepts perform many most wonderful acts. Of virtue and vice he discoursed in the usual way, maintaining that it was not necessary to be a Christian in order to lead a virtuous life. De Russette's intellectual capacity seemed of a very ordinary kind, but I have no doubt he commands the highest respect from the natives, and lives idly, happy and contented, without any anxiety about the morrow.

The photograph reproduced here (Fig. 12) is an excellent likeness of the man as I saw him at Simla in 1894.

7. A Naked Sanyasi and his Companion, a Princess of B——.

Information that an interesting group of *sadhus* was encamped on the *maidan* (open plain) near the Lahore Fort having reached me, I went there one morning to make the acquaintance of the visitors and increase my stock of knowledge about *sadhuism*.

The leaders of the party were a naked *Sanyasi*, and an almost naked *Sanyasin* who let people understand that she was a widowed and childless daughter of the Rajah of B——. Not many minutes' conversation with the *sadhu* were needed to satisfy me that he was at best a shameless reprobate, but, as I thought his portrait would enrich my collection, I expressed a wish to take a photograph of him and his followers. This suggestion tickled his vanity, and he had the effrontery, though I am sure he did not wish to be impertinent, to offer to have himself taken in a most objectionable and unseemly attitude, which would demonstrate his virility to the greatest advantage. His female companion was, I should say, under twenty-five years of age, and not particularly attractive. She wore her hair cut short and bleached a sort of yellow-brown, while the *Sanyasi* wore a respectable beard, and had his long, neatly plaited hair wound round his head, and kept in place by a bit of a turban of dark-coloured cotton cloth. Both of them had ashes rubbed over their persons. Three or four *sadhus*, one of them a *Kanphata Yogi*, had joined these worthies as travelling companions. A boy devotee of about twelve years of age also belonged to the company, and seemed devoted to the *Sanyasin*.

While I conversed with the *sadhus* under a group of trees, there was a small and ever-changing gathering of about two hundred persons round these queer, though evidently much respected, wanderers. Most of the visitors had dropped in, as it were, to pay their respects to the *sadhus* after having had their morning bath in the river. The naked mendicant and his companion, the almost nude *Sanyasin*, were not edifying sights; yet women, girls, and children of respectable families were all gazing at them reverentially, without any sign of shame or bashfulness. They were holy privileged people these *sadhus*, and not to be regarded with ordinary eyes or judged by customary standards. Yet, whilst I was present, a protest was raised by some *Aryas*—sectarians of a new school—against the *Sanyasi's* nudeness. Angry accusations and bitter retorts were exchanged, and in the course of the altercation the *Sanyasi* tried to turn the tables upon his censors by asking them significantly what they gained by deserting the religion of their ancestors.[1]

Meanwhile, as a sort of practical reply to the *Arya* objectors, offerings were accumulating near the *sadhus*—wheat, flour, rice, lentils, ghee, and also copper and silver coins. It was plain that the *Sanyasi* and his companions were in favour and not faring badly. As we conversed, the leader of the party, followed by the woman and then by the others, indulged in the luxury of pipes of charas, exhaling wonderful volumes of dense white smoke from their lungs. Just a pull or two was quite enough for each one, for the smoke was so pungent that it had to be drawn through a wet cloth applied to the bottom of the tall *chillum* or pipe which is used in charas-smoking.

At this visit it was arranged that the group should be photographed by me the next morning. When, at the appointed time, I came to the camping-ground with my camera, I found to my surprise that the *sadhus* had all disappeared, leaving not a trace behind them. However, I was bent on having their portraits if possible, and, after patient inquiries and no little discouragement, followed them up to a little temple of Siva near one of the city gates. They were dismayed when they saw me, for they had been artfully told I was a police officer and wished to have their photographs in order to get them into trouble. I learned also that the principal *sadhu* had been forced by the *Aryas* to put on a rag about his loins. He and a number of Hindu men who were present at the temple—*no* women visitors were there—informed me that the ascetics had been very badly used by the *Aryas*, who had scattered and spoiled all the offerings which had been made to them, and even caused their plates and utensils to be looted. How much truth there was in these allegations I cannot say, but the *Aryas* knew me very well, and no doubt surmised that I was in quest of materials for a book, and, possibly, it did not suit these sectarians to have the naked

[1] An account of the rise and progress of the *Aryas* will be found in my *Indian Life, Religious and Social.*

sadhu described for European readers, hence their opposition and interference. However, the soothing influence of two or three rupees enabled me to dispel the suspicions aroused in the minds of the *Sanyasi* and his supporters and to secure the photograph I wanted. This I have now much pleasure in reproducing (Fig. 13), as it is, I am inclined to think, unique in its character.

8. A Sadhu of Royal Lineage—"Prince Bir Bhanu Singh."

On the 21st of May 1899, at the Sankalwalla monastery, alongside the Golden Temple of Amritsar, I interviewed a young *sadhu* of about thirty years of age, who had aroused my interest by claiming to be a son of Maharajah Duleep Singh. Now, Duleep Singh was the infant King of the Punjab when that country was annexed by the British in 1849. He was removed to England, embraced Christianity there, lived the life of an English gentleman, and, in his old age, offended by what he considered the parsimony of the Government towards him, tried to foment sedition in the Punjab with a view to his own restoration to the throne of his father, the famous Ranjit Singh.

The *sadhu* who claimed to be Ranjit's grandson said he was born in England, and stated that, a few months before his arrival at Amritsar, he had met another son of the late Maharajah Duleep Singh. The young man, who had a weak face, mild grey eyes, and did not look particularly robust, was under the surveillance of two policemen not in uniform. My advent was the excuse for a number of idlers to congregate. A chair was brought for me. Two men who accompanied me squatted with the *sadhu* on his mat under the roof of a long vaulted arcade—a cloister, in fact.

My host, if I may so designate him, informed me that he had been brought to India when very young, and had been educated at Benares. Who his mother was I did not like to inquire. I had a pandit with me who conversed with the *sadhu*, and afterwards assured me

A SANYASI AND A SANYASIN, WITH THEIR COMPANIONS.

FIG. 13.

To face page 226.

that he had some tincture of Sanskrit learning, and that his pronunciation was that of a native of Bengal. I ascertained for myself that he had a very imperfect, or perhaps I should rather say a very elementary, knowledge of English. He affirmed that he was in faith a *Sikh* (pronouncing the word *seek* as the Bengalis do), though he had not adopted *Sikh* customs and outward symbols. As to philosophy, he was a Vedantist of very liberal opinions, but belonged to no sect; that is, he had not been initiated into any particular order or brotherhood. He read to us in Sanskrit from a sheet of ordinary letter-paper the religious views he had formed, and these were expounded to me, bit by bit, in Hindi by the pandit who was my companion.

All the while the *sadhu* was clearly very nervous, his hands trembling visibly as he stated and explained his ideas. Lying on the mat near him was a portion of a copy of the New Testament in English, and when I made some reference to it the *sadhu* spoke of Nanak and Christ with equal reverence; but, a minute after, he somewhat discounted his admiration by adding that there were thousands of Nanaks and Christs. According to his opinion, *everyone* should have a *guru*; but he admitted that it was not necessary for Christ to have had one.

The princely ascetic hinted, somewhat darkly, that he too had a *message* to deliver to the world, and that it was connected with the Bible; but apparently the time for proclaiming it had not arrived.

As I was leaving he mentioned to me that he practised *yoga*. "Do you?" I said. "Yes," was the smiling reply; "that is the only way to love God with all your heart."

The well-dressed *sadhu* and his official escort are depicted in the annexed photograph (Fig. 14).

A young graduate of the Punjab University who had accompanied me in my visit to the *sadhu* entertained a strange suspicion (they are wonderfully suspicious these educated Indians) that this man was really a Government spy, playing a character and employed as a sort of decoy to *test the loyalty of the Sikh community*. For my part,

I could not help expressing a hope that the poor fellow was not a wretched tool in the hands of unscrupulous agitators.

I subjoin without verbal alteration a curious printed leaflet in strange English which the *sadhu* "Prince Bir Bhanu Singh" was good enough to hand to me as we parted.

"GOOD COMMENDMENTS OF HOLY BIBLE.

"O carnel minded man! thou better clean thy own flesh and teach other the same salvation said by Lord Christ. Who has not enjoyed this; he is not of him. To whom he hath said to be child to keep his sayings.

"O carnel minded man! not fail, to keep his sayings; believe him early. Be sure, he came from Almighty power. Heaven is witness of this, therefore every Pall, want to oblige both king to people with this God comendments if they are without this.

"O carnel minded man! of this world! believe my pen that he is above because the heaven can't entice him, who hath come to know the best work of Lord Christ.

"O carnel minded man! Christ hath Bent closely well all his hearts unto God. And hath fought best against all world. He is found only teacher of open heart, who is not of him; therefore he can oblige them both king to people with good comendments said by him.

"O carnel minded man! beseech you! that you have done wrong all without the best knowledge teached by glorified son of Almighty father. He has nothing with you but only the same salvation as he taught to his Pall to purify first his own flesh and then love God with all hearts; because without this, none can caught the same light as they did thyself before their advocate Lord Christ.

"O carnel mind! you are blind to find out the same light told by the holy tongue because you are not cleaned after the same manner as Pall learned with Christ, therefore you are bound to follow the best work of him. If you fail to do so, you are obliged to keep his sayings as child.

A SADHU OF PRINCELY LINEAGE.

FIG. 14.

To face page 228.

"O carnel minded man! I believe now that you in net, as the sun light the day, and the moon light the night, but God is only perfect to enlight the heart of prayer, therefore thou better taste of this enjoyment.

"O carnel minded man! he enjoy the same salvation as the holy work of Almighty father and glorified son Lord's Lord Christ. Who spoked very boldly that I know none. O my beloved father give them knowledge to be well wisher unto you.

"O carnel minded man! his father and he both are of one mind and his Pall enjoy the same salvation as they did themselves, therefore ye be follower after them; you shall see no death.

"O carnel minded man! without this enjoyment you better be child to keep his sayings without discussion. He can then take you out from the room of death and can give you a seat in the house of Almighty father.

"O carnel minded man! you fear by every step, because God is creator of all things. Do best for thyself. Be sure, that a blind man can trouble other's face with a burn torch but can not give road exactly, therefore you are bound to follow the best work of him."

PRINCE
BIR BHANU SINGH.
An Advocate of Holy
English Bible.
Songola Akhara
Amritsar
Punjab."

4. 6. 99.
Bearer.
Hor Doyal Agni Hotri
of Kanoos.

9. A SADHU WHO HAD FOUND GOD.

He had never had occasion to do a day's work in his life, explained a *sadhu* who, in order to make my acquaintance, paid me a visit in 1895. He had inherited sufficient property in his native village to render any labour for a livelihood quite unnecessary in his case. He had faithfully done his duty to his family and to society, having had sons and grandsons born unto him, and for *two-and-twenty years* he had very strictly performed the ceremonies prescribed by his religion, down to the minutest and most trying details.

At length one day his steady and prolonged devotion to duty met with recognition. A voice came to him saying, "I am with thee, thou art clean, refrain henceforth from all these observances." The voice was a clear and *audible* voice, like that of one man speaking to another, not a voice in the heart or the inner consciousness.

Convinced that it was the voice of God which spoke thus unto him, he obeyed its command unhesitatingly. Some months later the same voice said to him, "Thou hast nothing to do with property, or with family ties. Go forth from thy home. I am with thee always." He resigned all his property forthwith to his children, distributed five hundred and twenty-five rupees in cash amongst the poor, cancelled all debts due to him, and wandered forth alone.

"I don't believe in *Shastras* or *Vedas* or *Mantras*," said the *sadhu* to me, "I have God!" Catechised on this point, my visitor admitted that such things as Vedas and the like were useful for worldlings, but not for one who *had found God.* To whom was he to pray when God was *always with him*, guiding and instructing him?

However, with all his emancipation from theological and ceremonial restraints, the *sadhu*, I found out, was not prepared to eat food which had been handled or even touched by me. He had not, as yet, received God's permission to do so much as *that.* The hereditary caste prejudice was too strongly ingrained in him, too essential a portion of his very nature, to be lightly set aside even by this enfranchised Hindu.

My visitor boasted that he took no medicine when he got sick, and that he recovered his health without the aid of any physician. "When my appointed time comes, who can save my life?" said he. "And, till the predestined moment has arrived, how can I possibly die?"

The ascetic was comfortably and cleanly dressed in an orange-coloured *dhoty* or loin cloth and a long *kurta* or tunic of the same tint, and wore a small, neatly tied turban. But for the colour of his clothes, it would not have been possible to recognise in this man a professed *sadhu*.

He had discarded the sacred thread although entitled to wear it, being a *Kshatriya* by birth; but he had not been initiated into any of the existing sects or orders of Hindu ascetics.

He did not speak of Siva or Vishnu, but only of *God*.

A few days after the *sadhu's* visit to me, I learned, without surprise, that he had not been quite disinterested in seeking my acquaintance. What he really wanted, and applied for, was pecuniary help to print and circulate a pamphlet or booklet of a religious character of which he was himself the author.

10. A Sun-Worshipping Bairagi.

Not far from the Shahalmi gate of Lahore city, outside the walls, are some fine peepul trees. About the foot of one of these a circular earthen platform had been constructed about three feet above the ground-level, with rude steps leading up to it. Passing this spot, I noticed three or four women seated on the platform conversing with a *sadhu*, a handsome dark fellow, not over-clothed, with his hair in a great coil upon his head. Another ascetic was standing on one leg facing the trunk of the tree, his head enveloped in a loose cloth resembling a napkin, and his face uplifted towards the sun, which was shining through the branches of the tree. Well worth closer study was this group; and so I paused to regard it, and to learn, if possible, something about the *sadhus*. The man standing on one leg was going through certain devotions. In his left hand he held a bag containing a rosary, and, with his right inserted in the bag, he counted his beads while he muttered certain prayers or prescribed religious formulas. I photographed him in this position (Fig. 15). When he had finished his prayers, he stood, still on one leg, before a tiny brass idol of Ramachandra which had been placed against the tree, almost smothered under a profusion of marigold flowers. The *sadhu* now poured out three shells full of water before the idol, made certain obeisances, and went to the other side of the tree. There, again on one leg, and facing the bright unclouded sun, he muttered his prayers to the great luminary. At first he held one hand outstretched towards Surya; then he entwined the fingers of the two hands together in strange ways; next held his hands, with palms opposed, towards the sun-god; and, lastly, extended both his hands appealingly towards the grand object of his worship. Uttering some Sanskrit words in a loud voice, he brought his devotions to an end by a libation of a conch full of water to the sun. After turning round three times, he went back to the other side of the tree and sat down. He was now free to converse with visitors, so I addressed him, and learned that he was a *Bairagi* whose native place was Benares. He said he had been to Kashmir to visit Amar Nath, that he had been favoured by the Maharajah of Jummu, and was in the receipt of a subsistence allowance granted him by that chief. He also spoke of the favours he had received from the Rajah of Baroda. All this, of course, to raise him in my estimation.

The *Bairagi* had been a year in Lahore, living under the peepul tree where I found him. His place of abode—the raised earthen platform—was smooth, clean, and well swept. On it were piled in one place a lot of wood fuel, both dry and green. A smouldering fire declared its presence by the white smoke it gave off into the breezy atmosphere. There were three or four garments lying in a heap together, which I presume were the *Bairagi's* bedding and covering during the night. Near the diminutive idol stood a gourd-shaped brass vessel, which seemed to be quite new, and a huge peculiar serpentine trumpet.

When I opened conversation with the *Bairagi*, my attendant, well versed in such matters, offered him, very respectfully, a couple of rupees, which, no doubt, helped to place us at once on a friendly footing. It is true the *sadhu* did not touch the money, but indicated by a gesture that it might be placed on a mat near him. I could see that he kept a watchful eye on it for a few minutes; he

A SUN-WORSHIPPING BAIRAGI.

Fig. 15.

To face page 232.

then quietly signed to one of his *chelas* to remove the silver coins. As to his habits, the *Bairagi* assured me that he did not smoke charas nor drink bhang. Tobacco was the only luxury in which he indulged, and while I was with him he disposed of a *chillum* (pipe) of it to his own enjoyment.

When I first arrived at the *Bairagi's* platform there were very few people about—only the three or four women to whom I have already referred, and a small party of children playing under the trees; but my presence soon brought a crowd round us, for we were close to a public thoroughfare. Near by was a women's bathing-place in the canal, concealed from public view by a sheet-iron screen. From behind this enclosure, as I conversed with the *Bairagi*, emerged a woman in dripping garments, exposing a good deal of her shapely person. Two elderly attendants waited upon her as she changed her wet clothes without much affectation or ceremony, and seated herself on a stool in the sunshine to have her long black tresses dried and otherwise attended to. The woman was certainly fair to look upon, and the thought struck me that the spot was well chosen by the *Bairagis* for their sojourn, if they wished to conquer, and not flee ignominiously from, certain temptations against which frail humanity is not usually very strong. Perhaps, however, the saints were not quite so heroic, or so foolish, as I have imagined, and were guided to the selection of that particular place for their camping-ground merely by a keen eye to pecuniary results; since, after all, it is the women-folk who are the best supporters of *sadhuism* in India or elsewhere.

11. Yogis and Pious Women.

A party of half a dozen or more *Yogis* came to Lahore and made themselves somewhat conspicuous by occupying favourable positions alongside some of the main thoroughfares. One of these *sadhus* used to sit at the meeting of three roads, and was the object of a great deal of attention, especially from the women, who paid their respects to Maharaj as they went by him on their homeward journey after the daily matutinal bath in the river Ravi.

These good creatures were much exercised in mind at seeing the holy ascetics eating pinches of wood ashes from time to time, and some, more devout or more impulsive than the others, begged one of the *Yogis* to permit them to minister to his wants. He haughtily declined their assistance; but to one pious lady, more pressing than the rest in her offers of service, he condescended to explain that he had taken a vow never to lift a morsel of food (or anything but ashes) to his mouth with his own hand. "Permit me, Maharaj," said the ministrant fair one, "to feed you with my own hands. It will be an honour to me and mine."

The saint good-naturedly, but still reluctantly, yielded the point. Henceforth the favoured one fed his saintship daily, and so did one or two other women—amongst them a beautiful girl of about sixteen years of age. Every day, when the *Yogi* had partaken of as much food as he cared for, he would bless the remainder, bidding his kind friends to partake of it themselves.

The regular meal-time of the lucky *Yogi* became an event of interest to the passers-by, and a certain man, who probably lived or had his place of business in the immediate neighbourhood, was in the habit of coming to watch the proceedings. Observing, perhaps with a pang of jealousy, the beautiful young girl I have alluded to feeding the almost naked *Yogi* with her own delicate fingers, this discontented spectator ventured to wonder in audible terms whether she was as attentive to her husband as she was to the saint. Of course the young wife, drawing her veil over her face bashfully, suggested that the rude fellow might mind his own business; but the *Yogi*, irritated by his impertinence, showered a volley of abuse upon him, desiring him at the same time to take himself off and not stand there staring at his betters. Uncomplimentary epithets were freely exchanged, till the ascetic, losing his temper, threw his stick at the intruder, but without effect. He next hurled a piece of lighted firewood at the man, and, more successful this time, struck his adversary on the arm, with the result that he was slightly burnt.

In a rage—literally a burning rage now—the meddlesome fellow flew at the *sadhu* and beat him soundly with a stick. Bystanders in horror hastened to interfere, when a new arrival, pressing forward to see what the excitement was about, grasped the situation and laughingly exclaimed, " Oh, ——, so you have come here, have you ? "

Noticing his familiar mode of address, several present queried with surprise, " Do you know the Maharaj ? Whence does he come ? " and so on.

" Who is he ? Why ——, the son of ——, a *choorah* (sweeper) by caste, and I see that there are several of his caste-mates not far off."

" A *choorah* ? Are you sure ? " came from many voices.

" I should rather think I am sure—he is one of my own *beraderi*. Have I not known him since he was a child ? "

This disclosure was like a bolt out of the blue!

" *Toba! toba!* " said the horrified bystanders. " And these respectable ladies have been feeding *choorahs* with their own hands and eating their contaminated leavings."

The pious women victimised by the *Yogi* veiled their faces closely and fled without a word, overwhelmed with shame and anxiety. " *Toba! toba!* " passed from mouth to mouth, and the crowd was moved by mingled feelings of merriment, indignation, and disgust at the discomfiture and punishment of the low-caste *Yogi*,[1] and at the terrible —how terrible only the Hindu knows—predicament in which the women zealous of good works had quite innocently placed themselves and their families.

12. A PSEUDO-SADHU AND HIS ADVENTURES.

At a public meeting I heard a well-dressed man, evidently a *Sikh*, referring, not without sly humour and a touch of conscious pride, to the days when, as a

[1] I did not learn whether these men were real *Yogis*, or only pretenders.

pseudo-*sadhu*, he had successfully eluded the vigilance of the police, living unrecognised amongst many real *sadhus*, men of true piety and estimable character.

Naturally, I wished to know something more about this man and his experiences. My inquiries eventually led to my learning the following story of his adventures from a *Sikh* gentleman, who assured me that he had heard it from the quondam-*sadhu* himself. The details may or may not be accurate—most likely the latter; but the main features of the narrative are probably those accepted by the public and known in the bazaars.

Being implicated in some way in certain seditious movements in connection with political designs of the late Maharajah Duleep Singh which caused a flutter in the Punjab a few years ago, the *Sikh* in question was arrested by order of the Government, and detained as a prisoner in the fort of Lahore in charge of the military authorities.

The cell in which he was confined was in an upper storey, and opened upon the flat terrace roof of one of the buildings. It was guarded by British soldiers; but nevertheless the hope of effecting an escape from his jailers did not desert the captive. It was the custom for the relieving sentry to open the door of the cell and satisfy himself of the actual presence of the prisoner there, before he commenced his watch upon the roof-top.

Day followed day, and the hope of escape became less and less, when one night the soldier who came to take over charge, being slightly the worse for liquor, carelessly omitted to lock the cell door securely. The long-wished-for hour had come. Listening breathlessly to the monotonous tramp, tramp of the sentry as he walked to and fro, the prisoner seized the most favourable moment to effect his escape, and, moving rapidly and silently with bare feet across an open space, crept up to the parapet. The night was clear enough to show him that a jump down from that position was not to be thought of, but the flat roof of a less lofty building was much nearer than the surface of the country outside, and seemed to afford a gleam of hope to one prepared to take no ordinary risks. The fine old fort of the Mogul emperors had long since seen its best days, and was in many places crumbling away. The *Sikh* cautiously dislodged a brick or two; he then unwound his long turban, and, tying a brick to one end of it, flung it over the projecting branch of a tree which most opportunely was growing in a very convenient position. By the aid of the bough and the long turban cloth the prisoner reached the roof below. The rest was comparatively easy work. From the lower roof which he had gained he dropped into the courtyard of a small temple, scaled its comparatively low walls, and found himself on the roadway outside the fortifications

Already the prisoner was missed, and the hue-and-cry had been raised in the fort, while the earliest indications of approaching dawn showing upon the eastern sky warned him that there was not a moment to be lost.

With all the speed he could command, the escaped prisoner made for the river side, and concealed himself in the almost impenetrable forest of tall reeds and bulrushes which skirts the margin of the Ravi. All day he lay low, and, when night came on, made his way to a small village somewhat off the beaten track. There was no *serai* or recognised rest-house for travellers here, so, in accordance with the usual custom in the Punjab, our *Sikh* malcontent sought the hospitality of the village barber, who gave him shelter and some food. The *Sikh* took especial note of the place where the barber kept the instruments of his craft, and during the night quietly abstracted a razor and a pair of scissors. Provided with these, he retired to a lonely place, cut off his long hair and beard as well as he could, and then shaved his head and face quite clean. No longer was he a *Sikh*, no longer a rebel, but only a poor *sadhu* bound on a pilgrimage to Hardwar on the holy Ganges. The good folks he met helped him along, and he at last reached the sacred river and fell in with many *sadhus* there. With some of these he fraternised, and in their company wandered about from place to place for some months.

In the course of his rovings he came to Meerut, and at this important town, by putting apparently casual questions to various visitors who came to pay their respects to Sadhu-ji, he learned, to his great delight, that Government had granted a free pardon to all who had been concerned in the Duleep Singh affair. Nothing could restrain his joy. He repudiated his *sadhuism* forthwith, bade his kind companions farewell, and hastened home to learn all that had occurred amongst his kinsfolk and friends during his concealment under disguise as a religious mendicant.

13. Yogi Guests.

A pious Hindu, desirous of securing the blessing of Heaven, went to an encampment of *Yogis* outside the city and humbly invited their reverences to partake of a meal at his poor house. They graciously accepted the invitation, and preparations were duly made for their entertainment. When the time for their arrival was at hand, the host bid his wife retire to the upper chambers of the house, as he did not desire her presence in an assembly of men, even of *Yogis*. She went upstairs and sat at a window, to watch the arrival of the guests. She counted them as they entered, in her anxiety that there should be enough food for them all. There were twenty arrivals.

The feast being over, and the guests about to depart, the hostess took her seat at the same window once more, so that she might know when they were all gone, as she wished to come down as soon as possible to learn how my lords had fared. Only nineteen, as she told them off on her fingers, left the house, and so she remained upstairs, wondering impatiently what the twentieth man could be doing.

Her husband called her down; but, remembering how curtly he had dismissed her when the holy men were about to arrive at the house, she replied that she would descend when *all* the guests had gone. Her husband assured her that all had departed, and desired her to come at once and look after things, as he wished to show his respect to the *Yogis* by attending them back to their encampment. She came down, explained the cause of her hesitation, and, as became a good housewife, commenced at once attending to the pots and pans and the brass plates which had been used by the guests. Her husband then went out in a hurry to catch up the holy *sadhus* on their homeward journey.

Female neighbours, who, curious to hear all about the feast, had been waiting to visit the hostess as early as the proprieties would allow, were surprised on approaching the house to notice a young *Yogi* coming out of it *after* the master had gone away. He had a pretty big bundle tucked away under his arm, and was making off hurriedly. Some women who were intimate friends of the family, not disinclined for a bit of gossip, ventured to ask him as he passed along how he happened to stay back after all his companions had departed followed by the master of the house.

He explained that two or three men of his party, though invited, had not been able to attend the feast, and that his good hostess had kindly cooked a special supply of food for them, which he was taking with him. Hence the delay. "But, Maharaj," remarked the women, still willing to have a chat, "food is never carried in a bundle like that, but in plates or baskets. Your hostess should have thought of that."

While some were thus interviewing the holy man, who seemed to be pressed for time and anxious to move on, others had entered the house, and there, to their horror, came upon a ghastly scene—the unfortunate hostess lying dead, in a pool of her own blood, despoiled of the better part of her clothing and all the valuable gold and silver ornaments she was in the habit of wearing.

The visitors, shocked and terrified, ran after the *Yogi*, raising an alarm, and it was not long before he was apprehended. The cruel murderer had apparently managed to cleverly conceal himself somewhere in the house, till his host's departure afforded him the opportunity of carrying out his nefarious design.

14. A Sadhu as Restaurateur.

Sadhus toil not, neither do they spin, and yet they are fed, and not scantily either, even when they assemble in large numbers, sometimes in their thousands, at the religious fairs, held periodically at sacred places throughout India.

Entering a much visited enclosure at one of these *melas*, I found a *sadhu*, with his *chelas* and some huge iron cauldrons. The *sadhu*, I was informed, fed his ascetic brethren, and whoever else came to him, twice a day.

My visit was not made at meal-time, but there were in one of the immense cauldrons some fifteen gallons of milk being gently warmed. Thinking that the *sadhu* might have pecuniary resources of his own, or that the extemporised kitchen was carried on at the expense of some moneyed persons, I inquired where the needful funds came from, and was informed pointedly that *everybody* contributed towards it ; and so, after my inquisitiveness, I felt constrained to do likewise. It would seem that the *sadhu*, having secured the use of some huge cauldrons and other necessary cooking-pots of proportionately large dimensions, together with the services of a few willing helps, set up, advertised, and opened, without hesitation or misgiving, his restaurant for the free supply of food to ascetics and other hungry souls, for he knew the generous public would do the rest for him.

His confident expectations were fully realised, and his kitchen was a great success.

15. A Saint in Chains.

The ascetic whose portrait is given in an earlier portion of this volume, p. 48, although a Muslim, deserves a passing notice here, not only on account of the unusual nature of his self-inflicted torture, but more particularly for the motive which prompted it.

Some Indian newspapers in 1891 drew attention to a *faquir* who was moving about the country under a heavy self-imposed burden of massive iron chains. This ascetic happening to come my way, I found an opportunity of interviewing him in his temporary abode in the native quarter of Lahore. He was a tall, large-boned man, under fifty years of age, and, though much emaciated by his austerities, retained ample evidence of a naturally vigorous physique.

Accompanied by my son, I ascended to the upper room where Sabit Alli Shah, surnamed Sankal-Walah, or *the man of chains*, was putting up, and where he was expecting our visit. We found him stretched upon a mat, heavily weighted with iron chains.

According to the hasty judgments of some Europeans who had referred to Sankal-Walah in the public prints, the ascetic, conscience-stricken, was expiating his sins by the torture of his body; but I ascertained, in conversation with him, that the object and motive of his austerities were something very different indeed. He had, it appeared, suffered grave injustice at the hands of certain influential persons, and, unable or unwilling to take vengeance upon them personally, he imposed this heavy burden upon himself, in the hope that God would pity his misery and mete out just punishment to his enemies.

After some persuasion, I was able to get the *faquir* to stand to us for his photograph. He was so weak, and his chains so heavy, that it was no easy matter to get him on his feet, or to keep him standing for even a few moments. However, my son was able to secure a satisfactory photograph of the ascetic, as the reproduction in Chapter III. will show.

The *faquir* subsequently informed me by letter that he was raising a subscription for the performance of a ceremony at which he would formally lay aside his chains. These, I understood, would be deposited at the shrine of the famous saint, Data Ganj Bakhsh. Whether the wished-for vengeance had overtaken Sabit Alli Shah's enemies, or the time limit fixed by him self for carrying the chains had expired, I cannot tell; but this I know, that the money required for the ceremony was not forthcoming, and that the unhappy *faquir*, still burdened with his load of iron, left Lahore in disgust and despair.

CHAPTER X

SOME SADHVIS OR FEMALE DEVOTEES

1. A public Lecturer, Srimati Pandita Mai Jivan Mukut. 2. Shri Maji, the Recluse of Annandgupha. 3. Premi, a young Sadhvi who embraced Christianity.

ONCE only have I had the pleasure of listening to an Indian woman lecturing with unveiled face to a mixed audience in public, and that woman was a professed *sadhvi* or female ascetic, who, whatever her real name may have been, was, since the adoption of the new life, known as Srimati Pandita Mai Jivan Mukut. She was, I understood, a native of Jummu in Kashmir territory, and a widow. She had studied some Sanskrit, was fairly well read in Hindi and Punjabi literature, and so great was her zeal for the spread of knowledge that she had opened a school for girls in her native town.

Her appearance before the world in the character of a lecturer was very distasteful to her people and to her late husband's family; but she, having quite emancipated herself from the prejudices of her countrymen, cared not for these things.

When I attended her lecture in the spacious courtyard of a house in Amritsar, her reputation, appreciation of her rare abilities, or perhaps merely idle curiosity, had brought together a large crowd, including a great number of Hindu ladies of the better classes, with their children, all eager to listen to the words of wisdom which might fall from the *sadhvi's* lips.

At first the ladies with their little ones occupied a place apart, but, as their numbers swelled and their interest in the proceedings increased, they gradually edged themselves into more favourable places, at the same time observing only a very nominal *purdah*.

A preliminary speech was made by the chairman in the ordinary way, and then the lecturer's *guru*, a portly middle-aged *sadhu*, who, if appearances were not deceptive, basked in Fortune's smiles, made some complimentary remarks about his very interesting pupil. Other speakers followed in the style usually adopted on such occasions.

When the event of the afternoon was at length reached, Jivan Mukut took up her position on a raised platform, and, standing up with unveiled face and a remarkable absence of self-consciousness, proceeded to expound the duties of women. To help her, she had a few notes in the form of couplets or verses composed by herself, which filled, I think, barely a sheet of note-paper, and served as the texts of the successive portions of her speech.

She read out, in its proper turn, the appropriate verse, and then, with reference to it, went on to illustrate the points she wished to explain or emphasise by frequent allusions to stories in the sacred epics and Puranas. For considerably over an hour she held the undivided attention of her audience, as with wonderful fluency of expression and apt illustrations she expounded the duties of her sex and strongly advocated the education of women. *Sadhvi* or not, unworldly or otherwise, Jivan Mukut, clever and self-possessed, undoubtedly appreciated to the full the applause which frequently interrupted her very sensible speech.

A few days after the lecture I made bold to ask for a copy of the lady's photograph, and, through some friends of hers, was fortunate enough to obtain the one reproduced on the opposite page (Fig. 16), which I was assured was taken expressly for me, and the negative destroyed to prevent any unauthorised copies being printed.

2. Shri Maji, the Recluse of Annandgupha, near Benares.

Though common amongst the Jains, female ascetics are rare amongst Hindus. There was one, however, who resided near Benares for many years, honoured and respected by the Hindu community. I regret that I did not see her myself, but the following particulars regarding her were communicated to me :—

Shri Maji, the Benares *Yogini*, was born in 1826 A.D. Her name was Hari Kuer Bai, but the love she inspired earned for her the affectionate title Maji, by which she was known to a large public. Her family came originally from Gujrat, but as her ancestors had been residents of Benares for some generations, and she herself had been brought up there, her admirers, connecting her with their sacred city, gave her the cognomen *Benarsi*. Maji, who was the youngest of six children, was but five years old when her mother died. Her father, Shri Rameshwar Dev, was a good Sanskrit scholar and a man of strong religious feelings. The youngest child, inheriting his devotional temperament and love of learning, became his favourite. To her he devoted much of his time, teaching her Sanskrit and instructing her in religious duties. She proved an apt pupil, who by her progress amply repaid the fond instructor for his labours as teacher and spiritual guide.

When ten years of age, Maji was married at Benares to a Brahman youth. Three years after her marriage she went to the house of her father-in-law ; in other words, she joined her young husband. Hardly two years after that she became a widow, and returned to her father's house, being then only fifteen years old, fully resolved to devote her life to the study of religious books and the practice of *yoga*. Within a short time Maji acquired a fair reputation amongst the learned pandits of Benares. Her father made many pilgrimages on foot, and she accompanied him,

THE SADHVI SRIMATI PANDITA MAI JIVAN MUKUT.

carrying on her head, in Indian fashion, all the simple necessaries for their journey. In these pedestrian pilgrimages, which occupied some five years, the father and daughter visited Jugganath, Hardwar, Brindaban, Badrinath, Kedarnath, and many other holy places. When they returned to Benares in 1846, Rameshwar Dev's *guru*, Swami Sri Sachda Nand, who used to live in an underground cave or cell known as *Annandgupha*, situated some twelve miles to the east of Benares, breathed his last, and the *gupha* or cave was left unoccupied. So the father of Shri Maji took up his abode there, and with him Maji also, always studying the sacred books of the Hindus and practising *yoga*. There, in the *gupha*, they lived together for fourteen years, till in 1860 the father died, and Maji was left alone. But she did not desert the spot, and continued to live her solitary life there till her death in November 1898, at the age of seventy-two.

Thus it appears that for thirty-eight years this *religieuse* had lived quite alone in the underground cell, *Annandgupha*, where indeed she had passed in calm tranquillity and religious study no less than fifty-two years of her life.

To her cave came, year after year, people from all quarters to consult the recluse whose fame had spread to distant places, and, knowing the respect in which Hindus hold such a character as Maji, we may be certain that she endured no real personal want or hardship in her old age, but passed her declining years honoured by her co-religionists, and in as much comfort as might be consistent with her ascetic professions or her self-denying simplicity would accept. A portrait of this lady, reproduced from a wood engraving, stands at the commencement of the chapter.

3. Premi, a young Sadhvi who embraced Christianity.

Both the *sadhvis* referred to in the preceding pages were widows when they adopted the ascetic profession. A Hindu widow's lot is, in accordance with the customs of the country, so supremely pathetic, so full of restrictions and of cruel *humiliations*, that it is not surprising that such a one should gladly embrace the *freedom* and *respect* which the religious calling would bring with it. But *sadhvis* are not always widows. Miss Fallon, of the Faizabad Zenana Mission, has in a little booklet of some forty-seven pages, entitled *Premi*,[1] given a simple but most valuable sketch of the life of an orphan girl who, although blessed with the world's goods and betrothed to a young Brahman, ran away from a comfortable home and an indulgent grandmother in order to *find God*, for whom her infant soul thirsted.

Ten years she spent as the *chelin* (female disciple) of a most worthy *guru*, who, having instructed her in the right way, and made her practise many austerities, duly initiated her, in the presence of other *sadhus*, into the sect or order to which he belonged, conferring upon her a new name, meaning "under the shadow of the Almighty," by which she should be known thenceforward.

In company with her spiritual guide, and other disciples of his, she visited, as a religious pilgrim, many of the sacred shrines of India and the Himalayas. Lost one day amongst the mountain forests of Nepal, the forlorn child cried out in despair, "O God, Thou knowest I have given up all for Thee—home and friends and everything; and if it be Thy will that this body should be eaten by tigers, I do not mind, only let my spirit be with Thee;" and there, in the gloomy solitude of those terrible jungles, she distinctly heard a voice utter these comforting words: "Thou art My servant, and no harm will come to thee," which effectually dispelled all her fears.

This exceedingly self-willed and highly emotional girl was at the age of eighteen attracted towards the Zenana missionaries, apparently in the first instance by the desire for knowledge. This is how Miss Fallon describes her: "Among the crowd I soon spied a wild-looking bright-eyed girl, her forehead besmeared with sandalwood, very little on in the way of clothing, a *mala* (beads) in her hand, her hair in a loose knot on the top of her head,

[1] *Premi, the Story of a Hindu Girl*, by Miss Fallon, Zenana missionary at Faizabad: with an Introduction by Sir Monier Williams (James Nisbet & Co., London).

and looking every inch a *sadhu* (Hindu devotee). One of my teachers whispered to me, 'That is the girl who came to our school the other day and said she wanted to learn to read.' Of course my interest was aroused, and at a sign from me the girl jumped up to where we were sitting, as nimbly as a deer, and, smiling all over, sat down at my feet."

This was Bindraban's first contact with the missionaries, and, after a bitter and prostrating mental struggle, this wild, impulsive, emotional child of nature embraced Christianity, and had once more a new name, this time Premi (beloved), given to her.

With what pain and sorrow her *guru* saw the Brahman girl, his favoured disciple for so many years, give up the religion of her forefathers, we may easily imagine; yet, when she elected to stay with Miss Fallon, the old *sadhu's* message to that lady was full of a dignified resignation, conveying as it did the promise of a divine blessing upon Miss Fallon for her kindness to the young *sadhvi*.

That the *guru's* teaching had at least made for righteousness may be illustrated by the following anecdote, which relates to the occasion of the first meeting between the wayward impressionable *sadhvi* and Miss Fallon:—

It was growing dark before the girl started for the convent where she was staying, and Miss Fallon asked her if she was not afraid to go alone, as there were so many bad people about who might do her harm.

"Why should I fear?" said the girl, drawing herself up. "My *guru* said, 'Child, sin can never touch you unless it is in your heart.'"

CHAPTER XI

HINDU MONASTERIES

Monasteries have existed in India since the earliest times, and are at present to be found scattered all over the Country—Religious and Worldly Motives which prompt the Foundation of Monasteries—Management of Monastic Properties—Monks not expected to labour in any way—Installation of an Abbot described—A Visit to the Udasi Akhara of Santokh Das ; the Presence of Women tolerated there—The Treasures of the place and their History—A public Entertainment at the same Monastery—Respect entertained by the Sect for Ashes—Interview with another Abbot who had not a single good word for Sadhus—Visit to a Dharmsala of the Nirmali Sect ; Sanskrit Literature read and expounded there—The great Monastery at Jogi Tilla ; Interview with the Abbot ; meet some Acquaintances—A romantic Story associated with Tilla—Particulars about certain places of Pilgrimage communicated by a talkative itinerant Yogi—Sadhus' Partiality for Nudity.

THERE existed in the Indian forests in the earliest ages communities of hermits, of the type described in Sakuntala, all the residents of the penance - grove being under one head or abbot ; and since Buddhist times there have been throughout the country regularly constituted conventual establishments. Most of these are insignificant and likely to escape the notice of Europeans, but every sacred spot or plain or mountain and every crowded city knows them.

Sectarianism, always active in India, has, as we have seen, been particularly so for at least a thousand years past. Each new sect, as a matter of course, has set up its temples, and, in connection with all the more considerable ones, monasteries also, for the accommodation of the priests and attendants, and of the wandering ascetics who carry abroad the tenets of the sect and bring recruits into the sectarian fold.

The monasteries established by the founder of each sect are held in great veneration by all his followers, and it is an object of ambition to the wandering *sadhus* to visit them periodically, especially on high ceremonial occasions.[1]

Pious Hindus have been exceedingly liberal in their bequests for religious and charitable purposes, sometimes devoting considerable property towards the establishment and maintenance of temples with their connected monasteries and rest-houses.

" *The religious merit acquired by the construction of a temple and its dedication* to the worship of particular divinities is extolled in numerous sacred texts.

" Vishnu Rahasya : 'Those who in the sports of childhood create out of dust a temple for Vasudeva, even they sojourn in the regions sacred to that divinity.'

" Agni Purana : 'Of those persons who are ever contemplating the construction of a temple for Hari, the sins of a previous hundred births are destroyed.'

" Narasinha Purana : 'Whoever conceives the idea of erecting a divine temple, that very day his carnal sins are annihilated; what then shall be said of finishing the structure according to rule! Beyond description is the wealth of religious merit acquired by the person who makes an abode for Vishnu of eight bricks. The merits

[1] " The *mat'hs, asthals,* or *akharas,* the residences of the monastic communities of Hindus, are scattered over the whole country. They vary in structure and extent, according to the property of which the proprietors are possessed, but they generally comprehend a set of huts or chambers for the *Mahant* or Superior and his permanent pupils; a temple sacred to the deity whom they worship, or the *samadh,* or shrine of the founder of the sect, or some eminent teacher; and a *dharmsala,* one or more sheds or buildings for the accommodation of the mendicants or travellers who are constantly visiting the *mat'h.* Ingress and egress is free to all; and indeed a restraint upon personal liberty seems never to have entered into the conception of any of the religious legislators of the Hindus."—Professor H. H. Wilson's *Sketch of the Religious Sects of the Hindus,* p. 33.

accruing from extensive buildings can be presumed in proportion. He who dies after making the first brick (for the construction of a temple) obtains the religious merit of a completed *Yajna.*'

"Vishnu Purana: 'A man attains the regions presided over by that deity whose temple he erects.'

"Vamana Purana: 'The establisher of a temple for Vishnu procures the salvation of himself and of eight generations above his grandfather!'

"Agni Purana: 'The man who causes a temple to be built to Hari, carries to the mansion of Vishnu ten thousand past and future generations.'

"Skanda Purana: 'On beginning the construction of a temple for Krishna, the sins committed in seven births are annihilated, and the ancestors rescued from hell.'"[1]

Very important, then, are the benefits to be acquired in other existences by the building of temples to the gods. But even worldly motives may operate in encouraging temple-founding, since in populous localities it is a really profitable business.

When a Hindu has surplus money he has rarely any desire to purchase the shares of joint-stock companies, or even to invest his funds in Government securities. If he is a man of the old school, and past the meridian of life, he probably talks the matter over with his *guru*, finds a suitable spot, and erects a temple, small or large, according to his means. By this act he reaps a double reward: he wins the favour of Heaven, and he also nets a not inconsiderable pecuniary gain for himself in the present time, and for his family in the future. The daily offerings of worshippers, together with the alms (mostly food) collected in daily begging expeditions amongst householders, soon provide sufficient means not only for the support of the resident priests, scholars, and attendants, but also for a fair dividend on his outlay to the owner of the shrine.

As time runs on, suppliants grateful to the local deity for favourable answers to their petitions make thank-

[1] *The Hindu Law of Endowments*, by Pandit Prannath Saraswati, M.A., B.L., pp. 43–45.

offerings to the temple, or endow it with funds and lands for general purposes, or perhaps for the feeding of a fixed number of poor *sadhus* or other mendicants. The offerings of timorous souls to avert calamity also add to the temple chest. Under favourable conditions or happy accidents, the revenues of the establishment assume by slow degrees respectable proportions, and its regular charities provide food, and commonly shelter of some sort, for a number of both voluntary and involuntary mendicants.[1] Thus under the stimulus of religious zeal, cupidity, charity, superstition, and a love of indolence, spring up temples and monasteries, their multiplication tending powerfully to increase the army of wandering mendicants, since they afford these religious wayfarers harbours of refuge, which they certainly appreciate, and which they make use of to the fullest extent.

The object and method of temple-founding being, as we have seen, not altogether unconnected with prospective dividends, it follows that the hereditary principle naturally plays an important part in the arrangements for the management of such property and the revenues derivable therefrom.

The equitable partition of the revenues becomes a fertile source of contention amongst the proprietors. Dishonesty and peculation are not unknown, and I have had described to me some of the ingenious methods by which on great festivals the liberal offerings deposited before the idols by the visitors to a temple or shrine are cleverly purloined by the attendants employing literally both hands and unshod feet for this dishonest purpose.

Some of the Hindu monastic institutions have, through

[1] In some of the large *mat'hs* a contribution of not less than one hundred rupees secures one full meal a day for life. Of course more than the amount just named is usually expected, and paid, for the privilege in question. But, think of it! One hundred rupees paid down, and a plentiful dinner secured for life.

Amongst the *Templars*, the *Affiliati*, "in return for a certain sum paid down, received their daily maintenance (their commons) out of the corporate fund."—King's *Gnostics and their Remains*, p. 412. And a somewhat similar custom obtains even now amongst certain lay orders in certain Roman Catholic countries, more particularly as a provision for sickness and old age.

the liberality of princes and rich benefactors, grown so wealthy that their proper management has become important enough to claim the attention of the British authorities, who, in the interests of the public, have sometimes been obliged to interfere, with a view to the revenues being properly applied in accordance with the wishes of the donors or the requirements of the case. Yet the Hindu monasteries are on the whole respectable institutions, though, as Professor H. H. Wilson said, "there are, it is true, exceptions to this innocuous character, and robberies and murders have been traced to these religious establishments."[1]

Discipline, restraint upon freedom, and serious occupation of any sort, are practically unknown in the conventual establishments of the Hindus, because the existence of rival sects, the absence of a central authority, the practice of daily alms-seeking, and the wandering habits of the monks, sanctioned by immemorial custom, have made active interference with the ascetics not only impolitic but very nearly impossible.

Where there is practically neither restraint nor discipline, systematic labour towards any end is out of the question, and, as a matter of fact, no Hindu ascetic is ever expected to *work*. He is to live by alms, and he does so.[2] It follows that the *sadhus* do not till the lands that may have become the property of a monastery, such lands being always leased out to lay agriculturists—a fact which cannot fail to recall to one's mind, by the mere force of contrast, the laborious diligence of the monks of the West, who, at any rate in the early days of Christian monkery, often, by their untiring exertions, reclaimed the wilderness and converted it into smiling corn-fields. At the same time, it should not be overlooked that the time-honoured encouragement of laborious habits on the part of the Western monks has, when stimulated by the powerful commercial spirit of

[1] *Sketch of the Religious Sects of the Hindus*, p. 35.

[2] In the Christian monasteries of the West, where the rule of St. Benedict prevailed, all the monks were required to be engaged in *manual labour* for seven hours a day, as a duty to God and man; though it must be admitted that, when these conventual establishments waxed rich, the obligation to *work with the hands* was materially modified, and often set aside altogether.

modern times, been productive of those grotesque parodies of unworldliness, the present industrial and meanly avaricious monastic institutions in France and elsewhere, with their dishonesty and their *sweating* of the weak—features which, it would seem, are unfortunately inseparable from industrialism even in a convent.[1]

In respect to the devolution of religious *trusts* in India, Mr. John D. Mayne states: "When nothing is said in the grant as to the succession, the right of management passes by inheritance to the natural heirs of the donee, according to the rule that a grant without words of limitation conveys an estate of inheritance. The property passes into the office, and neither it nor the management is divisible among the members of the family. Where no other arrangement or usage exists, the management may be held in turns by the several heirs. Sometimes the constitution of the body vests the management in several, as representing several interests, or as a check upon each other, and any act which alters such a constitution would be invalid. Where the head of a religious institution is bound to celibacy, it is frequently the usage that he nominates his successor by appointment during his own lifetime or by will. Sometimes his nomination requires confirmation by the members of the religious body. Sometimes the right of election is vested in them."[2]

The election and installation of a new *Mahant* in the case of the larger monasteries is a function of great moment, carried out with much ceremony, extending over several days, and attended by hundreds and even thousands of interested persons, particularly wandering ascetics of the order attracted to the place by the importance of the occasion.

Installation of a Mahant.—Through the kindness of some Indian friends, I received a courteous invitation to witness the installation of Pandit S. N. as *Mahant* of a

[1] I allude, of course, to the grave scandals recently brought to light, more particularly in connection with the Bon Pasteur order.

[2] *A Treatise on Hindu Law and Usage*, by John D. Mayne, chap. xii. para. 364.

small temple of Siva, and I learned that some three hundred *Yogis* who had recently celebrated the Devali festival at Amritsar had come to Lahore in order to take part in this function.

A goodly number of these ascetics had assembled under a great banian tree, and a stranger sight could hardly have been seen anywhere in the world than that group of wild-looking men. Some had but little clothing on; some covered themselves with dark-coloured blankets; a few wore their coverings as grave-clothes (*kafan*); many had their hair bedaubed with a light yellow-coloured mud; all were powdered over with fine ashes.

For all its strangeness and wildness, the assemblage was not by any means ugly or repellent. Although their bodies had been smeared with ashes, the *Yogis* did not look dirty or squalid. Many, certainly, were finely featured men; most of them were in excellent condition, and there was a certain air of lofty indifference about them that was quite noticeable, and easily raised them above the region of contempt. Evidently, if they practised any asceticism whatever, it was of a kind not inimical to health.

At the appointed hour they rose up, and in a disorderly procession followed a brass band which had been sent to escort them, with sundry silver sticks and waving *chowries*, to the temple where the installation was to take place. The brass band commenced with a Christy minstrel melody, and, after this exhibition of its superior capabilities and European training, lapsed into strains of indigenous music.

As the procession passed along the streets, the doors and windows of the houses on either side became alive with men, women, and children, who wished to see the *tamasha* (show, spectacle). They were accustomed to processions of all kinds, and looked on with their usual apathy at the crowd of *Yogis*, now swelled into a goodly multitude by the addition of a number of ordinary citizens induced by curiosity to accompany the *sadhus* on their way. I had on the dickey-box of my carriage a *Yogi* too sick to walk, and, when he was noticed, eager faces peered into the carriage to find out who the occupants might be, and, on seeing *sahibs*, could not restrain at least a facial expression of astonishment.

As the mixed procession of *Yogis* and citizens, with the noisy brass band, made rather a long, circuitous course through the streets and lanes, I took a shorter way in my carriage, and reached the temple and adjoining buildings in advance of the heterogeneous crowd.

At the door of the house Pandit S. N. himself received us with Oriental courtesy, and had us conducted to seats upon the flat roof of one of the buildings, in a position from which the ceremony could be very conveniently viewed.

When the *Yogis* arrived they crowded into the place pell-mell; they filled the small space before the door of the temple, and took up whatever positions they thought most suitable. When the available area was occupied, a number of them came swarming up to the roof where I was sitting and made themselves comfortable there.

The *Mahants* of several Siva temples were present, all well robed in white garments. Pandit S. N. was also suitably attired, and was decorated with garlands of flowers. Many well-to-do laymen also attended, and a small party of women and children had a place to themselves. The ceremony of installation was conducted with the greatest decorum. First a large brass alms-bowl encased in soft white muslin was presented to the pandit by the *Mahant* of a temple at Amritsar, who seemed to take the leading part in the ceremonies; this alms-bowl, which had belonged to the late *Mahant*, and his predecessors, being apparently the most important badge of the office of a *Mahant*, symbolising poverty and humility.

The bowl was received standing, and, when it had been placed in the pandit's hands, he was made to sit on a cushion in the window with his back to the street, and various coloured or parti-coloured clothes were presented to him. A large flat brass dish containing sweetmeats was then brought forward. The new *Mahant*, standing up, held it in his hands for a few seconds but not without assistance, for it was too large and heavy for one pair of hands. It was then passed on for future distribution of its contents. The several *Mahants* and other ecclesiastical dignitaries present made their obeisances to him, the temple bells rang out, the trumpets blared, and a shout was raised in honour of Pandit S. N. Presents in money were now made to the new *Mahant*, and, each time the rupees were received and counted by the *parohita*, or family priest, he proclaimed in a loud voice, "So many rupees have been donated by so-and-so!"

When the presents made by all the dignitaries had been received and recorded, the followers of Pandit S. N.—that is, those who regarded him as their especial *guru*—came forward one by one, and offered a rupee with profound obeisance, sometimes a complete prostration. In return, each one received in his right hand from the new *Mahant* a pinch of something which looked very much like ashes of some kind. The recipients retired very ceremoniously, but almost immediately each one put a little of the white stuff on his tongue.

A pretty boy, nicely dressed, was led up to the pandit, and received a *teeka* on his forehead. From an adjoining roof several women and girls in holiday attire bowed low to the new *Mahant*, while many of the *Yogis* about me sidled off to have a pull at the *churrus* pipe, without which these habitual smokers could not get along even for a short while.

Having received gifts from the heads of other temples, it was now the new *Mahant's* turn to repay the compliment with interest. He had also to honour the *Yogis*, to each of whom was given two pounds of the confection known as *ludoos* and one rupee in silver. They had all been feasted at his expense the day before.

I was assured that, as a result of this interchange of compliments, the new *Mahant* would, in the end, have spent three or four hundred rupees out of his own pocket.

The *akhara* of Santokh Das is the largest monastery in Amritsar, and belongs to the *Udasi* sect. Its founder was a *sadhu* who, in the troubled times attending the decline and fall of the Mogul Empire, established himself under a *jhopree*, or shed, within a small enclosure, where he harboured Hindu children whose parents had been murdered by the Muslims, or had fled before them. By degrees he rallied many followers round him, and eventually, when the *Sikhs* succeeded in emerging triumphantly out of the turmoil and disorder of the times, he obtained a *jaghir*, or free grant of land, which enabled him to found the monastery which preserves his name. This is a typical example of the circumstances under which monasteries may come into existence and attain affluence.

When I visited the monastery the resident monks were few in number, and differed greatly amongst themselves in outward appearance. The majority were wearing their hair wound about the head in a coil like a turban—these were the *jhuttadarees*; others carried loose hanging locks (*bhoureeahs*); a few had shaven heads, and were the *Paramahansas* of the order. In regard to the *jhuttadarees*, the *Mahant* informed me that their hair was never cut, and that all the combings were added to the living hair in a sort of rope or plait, which was coiled neatly round the head. He naïvely assured me that, when the hair growing on the head became white with age, the portion of dead hair added to the plait also became white.

Most of the monks wore orange-coloured clothes; one, however, had a green coat on, which had been given to him by some charitable person. Only two or three wore *malas* of any sort.

The *Mahant* was not dressed like the *sadhus*, but wore a bright pink-coloured turban, a white long-sleeved *kurta* or tunic, and a purple *loongee* round his loins. His feet rested on wooden *kharanws* or pattens. In his hand he carried a short rosary of large beads.

As far as I could see, there was free intercourse amongst the resident monks, and their bearing towards the *Mahant*, though respectful, was not servile. Yet, two or three men prostrated themselves on the ground, and put their heads with great humility on the abbot's feet; but he took no notice whatever of them.

The *building*, constructed of brick and mortar, is of considerable size, double-storeyed in some parts. It has two hypœthral courts of unequal size, and a goodly number of small rooms for the accommodation of monks. Though substantially built, the place has no architectural pretensions. Its situation is convenient, being just near the Golden Temple, which, with the great tank surrounding it, is visible from the upper storey of the monastery.

In one of the open courts was a cluster of four *samadhs*, erected in memory of four *Mahants* who had been the predecessors of the present abbot. These had all been cremated in the court itself on a spot which was pointed out to me.

The four *samadhs* occupied a pretty considerable proportion of the court, indicating a want of consideration for the claims of posterity.[1]

Near the entrance doorway, but within the precincts, there was a place where cattle might drink water, also bathing-places for outsiders—one for men, and another for women.

This toleration of women is in striking contrast with the practice of some Christian monasteries under the control of the Eastern Church. Writing about these, Mr. Curzon, in his interesting book, *Monasteries of the Levant*, states that he was informed "that no female animal of any sort or kind is admitted on any part of the peninsula of Mount Athos; and that since the days of Constantine the soil of the Holy Mountain had never been contaminated by the tread of a woman's foot."[2] The same author also mentions having met a monk thirty or thirty-five years of age, who, having been brought to one of the Athos monasteries as an infant, had no recollection of ever having seen a woman, and was anxious to know if they resembled the stiff expressionless mediæval pictures of the Virgin which adorned the walls of the cenobitic institutions of the little peninsula which formed his very restricted world.[3]

What positive terror the insidious charms of women

[1] Where, as at Buddh Gya, the deceased abbots have all been buried, the spot occupied by their graves makes quite a small cemetery.

[2] *Monasteries of the Levant*, by the Hon. Robert Curzon, Jun., p. 306.

[3] *Ibid.* p. 347.

inspired in the minds of certain Christian anchorites, who, with Chrysostom, looked upon the sex as "a necessary evil, a deadly fascination, and a painted ill," is well known; but the circumstances which have operated in India to make women there less objectionable in the eyes of the professed ascetic are not far to seek.

In the first place, in the land of Krishna and of Sakhti worshippers, the virtue of virginity or even of continence has never been regarded with the respectful awe with which it was viewed by religious men in the West, and for this, in all probability, the influence of climate is largely accountable;[1] and then, in the next place, as the monks are nearly all wanderers, subject to little if any discipline, and practically dependent upon the charity of women, it is naturally undesirable and futile to impose rules prohibiting women from entering monasteries as visitors, particularly as some of these conventual institutions serve very conveniently as caravansaries where travellers may obtain lodgings for payment.

Having inspected the more public portions of the monastery, I was conducted to the *Mahant's* sitting-room, which I found adorned with fresco paintings representing his predecessors and their doings. While seated here, the courteous abbot explained that for the maintenance of the monastery the chief source is a *jaghir* or *grant*, made in the first instance by the *Sikh* government of Maharajah Ranjit Singh, and confirmed at a later date by the British Government, though somewhat modified and curtailed. My host now had the treasures of his reliquary brought out and arranged for me to see. There were, amongst other things, a portrait of Santokh Das, a book, a picture showing the original plan of the Golden Temple, and four fine *byraguns*, or rests—two of wood very nicely carved, one made of ivory finely cut, and the fourth of brass. My particular attention was also invited to a leaf of the peepul tree, which, by a very great stretch of imagination, might be taken to resemble a hand having an exaggerated palm and dwarf fingers. It was the leaf of a tree which had been touched with his holy hand by one of the *Sikh gurus*,

[1] Montesquieu, *De l'Esprit des Lois*, livre xvi. chap. viii.

and consequently bore leaves resembling in shape a human hand. It was preserved in a picture-frame under a glass pane, and had been presented long ago to the *akhara* by a monk of the order of the *Udasis*. Another much esteemed curiosity was a little book written on a number of pieces of paper joined together like the bellows of an accordion.

A pair of *kharanws* in the collection had a story attached to them. They were made of brass instead of wood by some *infidel* or other who wished to put Santokh Das to the test. "Look here," said he to the saint. "You are a great *sadhu*; take these from me as a token of my profound respect." He had, however, just before presenting them, maliciously heated them to a high temperature, with the view of amusing himself with the enlivening effect they would have upon the sedate ascetic as soon as he put his feet upon them. But Santokh Das stepped on to the hot brass *kharanws* without betraying any sign of inconvenience, miraculously enduring the heat, or perhaps unconscious of it.

Before I left the monastery the abbot invited me to renew my visit at the time of the Devali festival. He explained that the permanent residents in the monastery were few, that at all times there were some wandering *sadhus* receiving the hospitality of the institution, but that on certain festivals, notably the Devali, the number to be entertained taxed the resources of the house to the utmost.

Upon this invitation I came again to the *akhara* in November 1898, and found the place full of *sadhus* and many other visitors, including not a few women. There were *sadhus* moving about the courts and inside the building in a more or less aimless manner; some, particularly the *nangahs*, who do not or ought not to live under a roof, were clustered round small fires in the quadrangles, attending idly to their toilets.

Presently a cry was raised, "Un ke pujah karo, Nanak nirbani" (Perform the worship of food, (in the name of) Nanak, who has left the world).

Most of those present began to arrange themselves in the smaller courtyard in long lines, seated on the floor; others took up places on the flat roof of a one-storeyed building assigned for the purpose. Women were present in both places. I was accommodated with a chair on the roof of a range of rooms, from which I could see the people in the court as well as those on the roof opposite.

All assembled in the most sober and decorous fashion, and arranged themselves in regular lines. I noticed a small boy-*sadhu* of about eight years of age trying to find a place for himself. He was, it seems, devoted to the ascetic life by his own parents. It is a common thing for childless people to vow that, if a son is born to them, he shall be devoted to a religious life. And this is *one way in which the mendicant sects are swelled and perennially recruited.*

When the guests were all quietly seated—and there was no unseemly hurry about this—the cooks went round supplying each person with a sort of cup or small basin neatly made of dry leaves. Those who had brought their own brass cups, or *katorahs*, did not of course need the more primitive leaf-vessels. After this the cooks made the round, with large baskets, distributing big flat cakes of hot unleavened bread which had been freshly baked on heated iron pans. I noticed that the bread was given liberally, and that some of the guests evidently took an additional share for an absent friend. Then the *dâl* (lentils) was brought round in a large brass vessel with two handles, carried by a couple of men. A third, armed with an iron ladle, helped the savoury yellow food into the leaf or brass cups, as the case might be. Yet no one touched a morsel. I now counted, as well as I could, the assembled guests, and found that they numbered about two hundred persons. When the requirements of all present had been met, the order was given, "Gajo-ji waha Guru," which may be freely rendered, "Assert yourselves in the name of God." Whereupon those who wished to carry away the food which had been given them, rose and withdrew; the rest fell to, and ate their morning meal.

Before leaving the monastery I inquired about the custom of worshipping ashes, which I understood the *Udasis* followed. The *Mahant* smilingly conducted me to the threshold of the room where the Granth Sahib—the sacred book of the *Sikhs*—was kept, and which might be called the chapel. At the abbot's request one of the attendants produced a great ball, or rather a cylinder with rounded edges, made of the very finest ashes. It was coloured on the outside of a reddish tint, and looked not unlike a Dutch cheese. At one end was a small depression. Into this the attendant who carried it inserted his thumb and brought out upon its surface a fine white powder, which he applied to his forehead. Several others present followed his example. The *Mahant* explained that these sacred balls of ashes were made with much care; that the ashes were well washed, and only the finest particles which eventually subsided in the water were taken and then mixed with a white clay from the hills, without which the ashes would not have sufficient coherence.

At the termination of my very pleasant visit I was conducted by the *Mahant* to my carriage, and at the moment of parting he presented me with some sugar candy, which he politely insisted upon my receiving from his monastery.

One morning I presented myself at a monastery in the Punjab, which I need not name. Though my visit was quite unexpected, the portly abbot, who was reading a vernacular newspaper when I arrived, was most gracious in his welcome, and seemed willing to discourse upon all the ordinary topics of the day.

Being informed by one of my companions that I was much interested in *sadhus*, he forthwith broke out into a tirade against the whole crew. "There might," he said, "be one in a hundred who had any pretensions to goodness or virtue, but the rest were vile scum and unmitigated scoundrels."

What more especially annoyed him was that men who one day were ploughing their fields as ordinary peasants would the very next day, in the garb of *sadhus*, claim the hospitality of an *akhara*, spend the night with loose women, and then become transformed again into cultivators of the soil as soon as it suited their convenience to do so.

I have no doubt the *Mahant's* complaint was based on

actual experience, and that it was not without cause that he grudged the pseudo-*sadhus* their board out of the moderate revenues at his disposal; but, for all that, I felt sure that my portly host was well able to take care of himself. He wished that Government would enact that each and every *sadhu* should carry a certificate to show who and what he really was—a suggestion which might be commended to the consideration of the authorities, as its adoption would certainly be convenient at seasons of general unrest or political tension.

I was subsequently informed that this abbot's claim to the headship of the monastery was disputed, and that the question of his right of possession was engaging the attention of one of the law courts.

Two monasteries of the *Nirmali* sect, both known as Thakur Dyal Singh's *dharmsalas*, were visited by me on the 6th of September 1898. Both were of considerable size though unpretentious in design, and could easily afford accommodation to a large number of inmates, for whom several rows of small rooms were provided. Both monasteries had their own oxen to draw water and to grind the corn for the household. They had their own cows also. At the time of my visits to these establishments most of the rooms were unoccupied, and only a few monks visible. These, too, were rather a puzzle to me as regards their dress and appearance, for the only external characteristic they seemed to have in common was long hair.

Most of them wore orange-coloured clothes and *malas* of little woollen balls resembling beads, and those who were going out carried *chippees* (alms-bowls made out of cocoanut-shells) in their hands. Along with the Granth, the Bible of the *Sikhs*, other books held sacred by the Hindus were read in one of these *dharmsalas* morning and evening. Indeed, the Mahabharata was being read and expounded while I was in the monastery by a Brahman pandit, who was neither a *Nirmali* nor a *sadhu*. In the other *dharmsala* an image of Ram Chandra had been set up, though I did not see it. This *thakurdwara* had been founded by a pious woman of means.

Amongst the *sadhus* I noticed a good-looking boy of

about fifteen or sixteen years of age, and asked him why he had become a *sadhu* and given up the world, of which he could hardly have seen anything. He promptly replied that one was never too young to enter upon a good path.

Somewhat different from the establishments described above is the great *math* of Jogi Tilla, situated on the top of a conspicuous hill in the Jhelum district of the Punjab. Proceeding towards this monastery in order to be there on the occasion of a certain Hindu festival, I fell in on the way with twelve or thirteen *Yogis*, all young men in the prime of life, bound for the same place. All of them had their hair hanging about their necks, but not particularly long, and bleached a yellow-brown colour. They had the least quantity of clothing on, and had their bodies smeared with ashes. All wore the characteristic *yogi* whistle depending from the neck. Some carried huge tongs, others small hoes. Two or three alms-bowls and some brass imitations of the gourd were also to be seen. One man was armed with a formidable serpent-shaped wind instrument. None of the party seemed disposed to be communicative or even to answer my questions. As I walked along very leisurely, the *Yogis* passed me by on the road; but, when I subsequently overtook them on horseback, they were sitting beside a pool smoking charras.

Farther on I met a *Yogi* trudging along alone, and soon discovered that he was not as reticent as the men I had left behind in clouds of charras-smoke near the pool.

My new acquaintance came from the military station of Jhelum, and so probably knew something about Europeans. I learned from him that he had served an apprenticeship to a famous *guru* for four years before he was permitted to have his ears pierced to receive the huge rings which the *Kanphatti Yogis* wear and to have whispered to him the sacred and secret *mantra* of the order.

As we approached the mountain—for such it really was—we passed many groups of pedestrians on pleasure bent. One party consisted of three boys, the eldest not sixteen years old, who had come from the town of Jhelum, several miles distant. They were all neatly and cleanly dressed in light garments; but, though it was winter, not a scrap of any sort of luggage did they have with them, nor even any wraps. Several groups of women and girls, some of them attended by men, were wending their way upwards from neighbouring villages. None carried extras, unless babies be reckoned as such. I ascertained that all these visitors would be provided with accommodation and coverings by the *Yogis* at Tilla, and that the Hindus who visited the fair would be fed free of expense by the abbot of the Jogi Tilla monastery.

I rested for the night in the Government rest-house at the foot of the mountain, and the next morning found that an excellent, if narrow, road led to the summit, whence from different positions extensive prospects might be enjoyed of a country rich in poetical and historical associations, amongst the latter being the invasion of India by Alexander the Great in the fourth century B.C.

The monastery on Jogi Tilla, of which I give a photograph, is a substantial group of buildings, and its *Mahant*, a handsome, well-dressed, dignified old gentleman, who gave one the impression of being a man of authority, received me with much politeness. After the usual exchange of civilities, I was shown all over the place, which was full of visitors who had come up from the villages in the plains in order to be present at the festival. I was struck by some dark subterranean chambers which were shown me, and which I understood had been tenanted by *Yogi* anchorites, whose austerities were still remembered with awe and wonder. While walking about, I came across a score of *Yogis* sitting round a great log fire, and to my pleasure was recognised by several of them, having met them the previous year at the installation of Mahant S. N. in Lahore.

I obtained comfortable quarters in the rest-house erected especially for the accommodation of the Government Civil officers of the district, for whom this elevated spot serves as a pleasant sanatorium during the hottest time of the year. I had hardly got my things in when the *Mahant* sent over to inquire what my orders were in respect to requisites for my table, as he would have much pleasure in supplying all the wants of myself and servants while I sojourned on the mountain, or at any rate as long as the festival lasted. I did not avail myself of this kind offer, having already made my arrangements, but I saw that the crowd, mostly of village folks, who had come up the hill, enjoyed themselves right pleasantly at the fair, and were well cared for by the hospitable abbot. "The shrine of Tilla," says Mr. E. D. Maclagan, "is certainly very ancient, and is possibly a relic of a previous cult; it is mentioned in the Ain-i-Akbari. There were formerly large grants of revenue attached to the monastery, but these were abolished some years ago, when the *Mahant* was accused of murdering his rival for the *gaddi*. The *Yogis* of Tilla are not an estimable body, but are held in considerable reputation, even by Mussulmans, and they have Hindu disciples away beyond the Afghan border." [1]

Roaming about the hill-top with a local guide, my attention was directed to various geological features of the mountain formation, which told of titanic battles between rival *Yogis* and other *sadhus* in the old time. There was also pointed out to me a slab of dark-coloured stone, on which some dozen cowrie shells and sundry pieces of crude brown sugar had been placed in memory of old events which are still fresh in the recollections of the village lads and maidens. It was on this stone, they told me, that Ranja sat and sounded his whistle, and on this slab he had been initiated into the secrets and received into the sect of the *Yogis*. The story, as it was told me on the spot, is worth repeating.

Ranja, hearing the praises of Heer sung by the wandering minstrels, became enamoured of her, sought her out, and artfully succeeded in obtaining service as a cowherd in her father's house. A mutual attachment sprang up between the handsome youth and the lovely girl; but the wife of Heer's brother had her suspicions aroused by the behaviour of the lovers, and secured the cowherd's dismissal. To prevent scandals and trouble, Heer was married to another man, and Ranja, disappointed and dismissed, went off to become a *Yogi*, telling Heer he would meet her yet. To Jogi Tilla he wended his way,

[1] *Punjab Census Report*, 1891, p. 117.

THE MONASTERY OF JOGI TILLA.

FIG. 17.

To face page 266

and, seating himself upon the stone already referred to, blew a whistle he had brought with him.

The *Mahant*, who was no other than the great Gorakhnâth himself, came out and said, in a loud voice, "Who is it that blows a whistle outside there? If he is a *Jogi* he is free to come in; if not, how dare he sound a whistle so near my premises?" To this Ranja made suitable answer, that although not yet a *Jogi*, he earnestly desired to become one. His fine manners and handsome person at once won for him the favour of the great *guru*, who admitted him, there and then, into his sect, piercing Ranja's ears in the most approved manner. The new *Jogi* asked as a favour that he might be reunited to Heer, and the gracious *guru* said that his wish would be gratified. Elated with the blessing of his superior, Ranja hastened away to where his beloved lived, and *lit his fire* within view of Heer's home, but on the opposite bank of the river. The fame of his exceeding beauty soon spread abroad, and the women were dying to visit him. Heer suspected it might be her lover, and winning over her husband's sister, on some pretext or other, to visit the famous *Jogi* privately, she ascertained for herself that her surmise was quite correct, and she also contrived to arrange that Ranja should come across the river in the darkness to meet her. Night after night he found his way to her arms, and never came without a small offering in the shape of some fish caught by himself and daintily cooked with his own hands. Once the river rose in a great flood, and in the turbid rushing stream no fish could be caught. To go empty-handed to his assignation seemed too dreadful, so the devoted lover cut off a piece of his own flesh and dressed it for his mistress. "What is this?" she inquired as she put a piece into her mouth. "This is not fish, nor rabbit, nor mutton that you have brought me. I cannot eat this—what is it?" He displayed the wound in his thigh. "Ah!" exclaimed the girl tenderly, quite overcome with emotion. "You have fully played your part, my love; it is for me now to do and dare. I shall come to you in future. The river shall not part us. I'll swim across it on a stout *ghurrah*[1] every night." And she did

[1] A large water-pot of baked clay.

so regularly, guided in her dangerous course by the love-light of the *Jogi's* fire. But her doings were found out by a jealous female relative, who one night spitefully replaced Heer's trusty *ghurrah* by a similar but *unbaked* vessel. All unconscious of the substitution, Heer, in the darkness of the night, entered the river, and, with the treacherous aid of the fragile *ghurrah*, swam out into the stream. But, before she had gone half-way across, the pot softened in the water and gave way. She cried aloud to her lover for help as she felt herself drowning. Ranja at once plunged into the stream to her assistance, but the lovers were carried away in the darkness and never seen again.

The above story has been reproduced as it was told to me, but it seems to be a medley of two romances well known in the Punjab, "Hir and Ranja," and "Sohni and Mahirwal."

The name "Hir and Ranja" is strikingly reminiscent of *Hero and Leander*, but, strange to say, it is not in this one, but in the Sohni and Mahirwal legend, that the lover swims the river as Leander used to brave the dangers of the Hellespont for the love of the priestess of Venus.

On my return from Jogi Tilla it was my good fortune to have, for a part of the way, the companionship of a young and very talkative *Yogi* who had travelled a good deal. He had been, he said, to Hinglaj on the mountains, and in token of his visit had been duly branded on the right forearm. This, he explained, was done because the Devi at Hinglaj used to be worshipped by Muhammadans, and they enjoyed her special favour; so Siva directed that Hindus who went there should be branded with *his* symbol as a mark of his divine protection. With regard to Amarnath in Kashmir, where he had also been, the young *Jogi* said that till recently it had been the custom for persons visiting the sacred ice-cave on the mountain-top to divest themselves (both men and women) of every stitch of clothing, as it was thus that lord Siva wished them to appear and dance before him; but my informant added that *now*, owing to the wishes of the father of the present Maharajah of Kashmir, the women were allowed to cover themselves, but with a single garment only. The men enter

GRAVES OF YOGI MAHANTS AT BHAIRON-KA-THAN, NEAR LAHORE.

FIG. 18.

To face page 268.

the ice-cave with *langotis* or breech-clouts on; but each man divests his neighbour of his *langoti*, so in the end they stand in the cave stark naked. Whether these details about the annual pilgrimage to Amarnath are true or not I have not been able to ascertain, but they are certainly in harmony with what we know of Indian *sadhus*, amongst whom the tendency to run to nudity is a very marked characteristic.[1] A few years ago an application was made to the High Court at Bombay to cancel an order of the District Magistrate prohibiting the *Gosavis*, a religious sect of mendicants, from walking in procession naked, and then bathing at Nasik as a religious duty during the Sinhasta festival. In support of this appeal, it was urged by the petitioners that bathing naked had always been allowed at Hardwar and Allahabad.[2]

[1] Vigne, who visited Kashmir in 1835, states that the Brahmans at Amarnath divest themselves of all clothing excepting some pieces of birch-bark which do duty for fig-leaves (*Travels in Kashmir*, etc., vol. ii. chap. i.); and Dr. Neve (*Picturesque Kashmir*, 1900, chap. vii.) says that the worshippers throw themselves naked upon the block of ice in the cave which represents Siva.

[2] *Times of India* (Bombay), 12th August 1896.

CHAPTER XII

National Ideals of Life as indications of National Character—European and American Ideals contrasted with that of India—A Life involving Renunciation regarded by the Hindus as the only possible Holy Life—Sadhuism in its Religious, Social, Political, Intellectual, and Industrial Aspects—The probable Future of Sadhuism considered.

IF in the ideal of life which claims especial regard or is the object of the supreme ambition of any people their character is discernible, it may be profitable, in connection with the subject of this volume, to pause for a moment to contrast the highest ideals of the busy practical West and of the tranquil dreamy East.

Though Mammon worship prevails largely in England, the loftiest aspirations of the vast majority of Englishmen still tend towards aristocratic ideals, the objects of highest admiration amongst them, after royalty with its old-world glamour, being the hereditary nobleman or landed gentleman who takes a leading part in public life, the strenuous statesman, and the victorious general. Royalty being excluded, the hero-type which in each case attracts the homage of the English world is still the aristocrat successful as a *man of action*. In the United States of America, which have no royal court and no hereditary nobility, which until recently had no foreign relations of magnitude, where the feeling is intensely democratic, and where the best energies of the people are untiringly devoted to industrial pursuits, the prosperous business man sprung from the ranks of the *people*, the clever accumulator of wealth, the plutocrat, the self-assertive millionaire, is the beau-ideal of the nation, and next after him the wide-awake pushing politician. Here also, it is evident, popular admiration is given to what is regarded as the embodiment of success in fields of activity congenial with the national taste and leanings.[1] For the professedly religious life there exists both in England and the United States—perhaps in all Protestant countries—a separate and distinct ideal of perfection, yet certain it is that the respect of the pious Protestants of Britain and the States is commanded by the vigorous active worker for the good of others, and not by the retiring self-contained ascetic.

Very different indeed from the business-born ideals we have been considering is the hero-type which for ages has drawn the admiring homage of India and the Far East. The covetous Westerns may have their eyes riveted with greedy appreciation upon the bejewelled Rajahs of India and their barbaric pomp, but, for reasons already indicated, it is the ascetic profession that time out of mind has been of pre-eminent dignity in the eyes of the Indian *people*. The quiet inactive recluse, the retired ascetic detached from the world and its petty rivalries, has since the earliest ages occupied the very highest place in the national esteem—a fact which speaks volumes for the condition and psychology of the Hindus, because, as Carlyle has well said, "The manner of men's Hero-worship, verily it is the innermost fact of their existence and determines all the rest."

That the only possible state of a religious (holy) life is

[1] It is interesting that, in Europe, lunatics suffering from the delusion of self-importance commonly imagine themselves to be princes and kings, and on the other side of the Atlantic the megalomaniacs are usually millionaires.

one involving asceticism and renunciation of the world, has been for ages such a deeply rooted idea in India, that Hindu apologists for the more active life have felt constrained to devise apologues which might be cited in support or justification of men of acknowledged goodness who did not withdraw themselves from the temptations and toils of mundane existence. For example, Rajah Janak, who ruled his kingdom with great ability, had the reputation also of being a very *religious* man; but the ascetics scouted this notion, and it was arranged by some *sadhus* that they should have an interview with the king in order to test his pretensions. Ten of them accordingly asked for an audience and received permission to approach the king, but only on certain prescribed conditions. Each man amongst them was to carry a large earthenware vase full of water on his head, and should suffer death if he allowed even a single drop of the contents to spill.

The stipulations were accepted, and Rajah Janak's capital made preparations for the reception of the holy *sadhus*. The shops and houses were gaily decorated, the multitudes were out in their gala attire, and troops lined the streets along which the visitors were to pass.

Slowly, and very carefully (for their lives were at stake), did the king's guests wend their way to the royal palace, where they were graciously received by the Rajah, who asked them, in an affable manner, what they thought of his capital, through the best streets of which they had just passed on their way to the presence-chamber. The indignant *sadhus*, perceiving that they were being laughed at, replied with chagrin that they were unable to express any opinion on this point, since through the king's unreasonable tyranny they had not been able to look either to the right or to the left, having to think about the brimful water-pots on their heads.

The Rajah very politely begged his visitors not to be annoyed, as what he had done was only to inculcate an important lesson.

"You most venerable *sadhus*," said the king, "have passed along the streets without any mishap; your eyes have directed you and your limbs have carried you while you wended your way through the streets of this great city, but your attention was mostly concentrated upon the water-pots on your heads. Just in the same way do I pass along the world's great highway, doing what is necessary, but with my attention fixed on things above."

After this preamble, we may profitably cast a rapid glance at the religious, social, political, intellectual, and industrial aspects of *sadhuism*, and also venture, but not too boldly, to forecast its future.

Sadhuism in its Religious Aspect.

Sadhuism, whether perpetuating the peculiar idea of the efficacy of austerities for the acquisition of far-reaching powers over natural phenomena, or bearing its testimony to the belief in the indispensableness of detachment from the world as a preparation for the ineffable joy of ecstatic communion with the Divine Being, has undoubtedly tended to keep before men's eyes, as the highest ideal, a life of purity, self-restraint, and contempt of the world and human affairs. It has also necessarily maintained amongst the laity a sense of the righteous claims of the poor upon the charity of the more affluent members of the community. Moreover, *sadhuism*, by the multiplicity of the independent sects which have arisen in India, has engendered and favoured a spirit of tolerance which cannot escape the notice of the most superficial observer.

Sadhuism in its Social Aspect.

Socially, *sadhuism* has, in its spirit and practice, always tended towards the recognition of the equality of all Hindus, and has therefore been inimical to the rigid caste-system so dear to the Brahman priesthood. The warfare between Brahmanism and Sadhuism has been carried on with varying fortune for thirty centuries; but the democratic leanings referred to have proved too strong for the opposition of the "twice-born" classes, and the inevitable result was long since grudgingly admitted, as the following prophecy, put into the mouth of the Vedic god Indra, shows clearly enough :—

"When this *krita* (or golden) age," says the god, "has come to a close, innumerable mendicants and hypocrites shall arise and the four orders become disorganised." [1]

A noteworthy statement this, the fulfilment of which is amply attested by the foregoing chapters.

That the *sadhu* as such should enjoy popular consideration has undoubtedly been at all times a very sore trial for the proud Brahman, and especially hateful to him when it was a low-caste *Sudra* who, in virtue of being an ascetic, received the respect and homage of the people. But, as already remarked, the Brahmanical opposition, however strong, has proved unavailing, and the *right* of the *Sudra* to the privileges of *sadhuism* and ascetic practices, at any rate during the present age, has been authoritatively, if reluctantly, *admitted* in the Ramayana.[2]

[1] Mahabharata—Santiparvan, sec. lxv. Muir's *Sanskrit Texts*, vol. i. p. 485.

[2] The curious legend which contains this admission is as follows :—A Brahman youth died suddenly without apparent cause. The father of the boy, bewailing his loss, came to the king's palace, and in his lamentations accused the king, the semi-divine Rama himself, of having, through some fault of his, as ruler of the land, brought about the untoward event. The imputation reached Rama's ears, and he summoned a council of sages to consider the matter. Narada being present, explained that the death of the Brahman boy was due to the presumption of a *Sudra* who was practising austerities for the attainment of certain objects. Men of his caste, explained the sage, were not entitled to this great privilege in Rama's age (the *Treta yuga*), though he admitted prophetically that in the *Kali yuga Sudras* would practise austerities freely, and righteously too. Rama, as became the guardian of his people, set off immediately in quest of the audacious offender. After searching in many regions, he discovered the ascetic near a tank by the Saivala mountains, "performing the most austere penances with his legs upwards and head downwards." In reply to Rama's inquiries, the topsy-turvy ascetic, still standing on his head, said, "O highly illustrious Rama, I am born in the race of *Sudras*, and, with a view to reach the region of the celestials with my body, I am going through these austere penances." On hearing this, the king drew his sword and forthwith cut off the ascetic's head. After this *act of justice*, the Brahman boy was restored to life.—Ramayana—Uttarakandam, sec. lxxxvi.-lxxxix., Manmatta Nath Dutt's translation.

CONCLUSION

SADHUISM IN ITS POLITICAL ASPECT.

Politically, *sadhuism*, through the perennial wanderings of the ascetics over the length and breadth of the land, has tended to preserve a certain homogeneity throughout India, and, so far, has been acting counter to that tendency to fission and disintegration which is natural in such a vast country of many languages and races. At the same time, the *detachment* from human affairs which *sadhuism* demands must have been at all times adverse to patriotism in any form, and there can be no doubt that it is largely due to the subtle effects of the spirit of *sadhuism* upon the character of the people of India that that country is so easily governed by a handful of foreign officials and a few thousand white soldiers.

THE INTELLECTUAL ASPECT OF SADHUISM.

Intellectually, the spirit of *sadhuism* has unquestionably proved most baneful, its tendency being to regard passing events — that is, history in the making — with undisguised contempt and the study of nature as useless, since true knowledge and power over phenomena could be acquired only by contemplation and austerities.

INDUSTRIAL EFFECT OF SADHUISM.

Many estimates have been made, and at different times, of the proportion which the number of religious mendicants in India bears to the entire population. Mr. Ward, the Serampore missionary, writing a century ago and with special reference to Bengal and Behar, says: "I have endeavoured to ascertain the probable number of Hindus who embrace a life of mendicity, and am informed that scarcely less that an eighth part of the whole population abandon their proper employments and live as religious mendicants by begging." Mr. Crookes, in his *North-Western Provinces of India* (1898), puts the figure for that territory at two millions out of forty millions, or one-twentieth of the population.

Naturally, everyone who believes that the chief end of man is to *produce things of various kinds* grieves over the deplorable waste of productive energy represented by the *sadhu* population of India. But, after all, is it of no importance that the country has been able to *produce* for a hundred generations whole armies of men able to practise, *with a religious purpose*, that contempt of the world and earthly riches which is, at least theoretically, one of the most important of Christian virtues? [1]

No doubt, the philosophy and art, I might say the cult, of chronic idleness is thoroughly understood and acted upon in India; still, in estimating the extent to which its *sadhu* population is a burden upon the country, several facts have to be borne in mind which the most superficial analysis of the composition of the religious mendicant class brings to light. In the first place, amongst *sadhus* are included a very considerable percentage of what in other countries are merely the destitute paupers supported by the State out of the proceeds of taxation, but in India out of the alms of the people. Again, *sadhus* are to no small extent religious teachers (*gurus*) of the masses, and this must be recognised in any estimate of their value or otherwise to the community.

In the ranks of the *sadhus*, too, there is honourable room for those men, present in every community, who, as Bishop Creighton once said, "although as good as gold and fit for heaven, are of no *earthly* use." Further, the incorrigible idlers who in Europe become intolerable and dangerous vagrants, pursue a more reputable course in India. They simply adopt the religious habit of some sect or order, and enter the ranks of the peregrinating *sadhus*.

There are other points, also, which in this connection deserve attention. For example, *sadhus* are prominently in evidence on account of their peculiar dress and appearance, while their wandering habits taking them, often in huge parties, from place to place throughout the circling year, seem to multiply them many times over. Their necessary daily appeals for a dole of simple food to

[1] John ii. 15, 16; James iv. 13, 14; Rom. xiv. 17; Luke xiv. 26; Matt. xix. 21.

sustain life also helps to keep them before the public eye, and to unpleasantly remind the world of their existence. But, whether or not *sadhus* are too numerous for the industrial well-being of the country, it should not be forgotten that, though there are undoubtedly many worthless *sadhus*, the converse is also not less true, and that to the multitude a majority of these religious mendicants are types and *exemplars* of a holy life, and, as such, help them to make for righteousness.

While, in connection with religious mendicancy, so much attention has been bestowed upon the obvious withdrawal of a host of men from contributing towards the work of production, one point, less obvious it is true, but not less interesting perhaps, has been quite overlooked, viz. the influence which *sadhuism*, by the alarm which its violent spread occasioned amongst Indian rulers and legislators, has indirectly had, and still has, in keeping up and maintaining the population of the country. This statement may seem somewhat paradoxical, but there is, I think, reasonable foundation for it.

Let me explain. Amongst the social and religious precepts observed by the Hindus, perhaps the most important in their eyes is the rule which requires that every man, rich or poor, should have a son or male descendant to perform his funeral and post-funeral rites. Obviously, therefore, every Hindu should marry, and as early as possible. Hence every Hindu father is strictly bound, under the sternest social and religious penalties, to find a wife for his son, and also a husband for his daughter, even before she attains the age of pubescence. To be without a son or a male descendant is a terrible curse, entailing upon the unhappy defaulter the severest purgatorial suffering. In the case of Hindu women, childlessness is a dishonour so unendurable that it often leads to suicide or strange immoralities.[1]

Whence came these ideas and ecclesiastical ordinances about the all-importance of male issue? They are the result, I am inclined to think, of the worldly wisdom

[1] *Hindu Manners, Customs, and Ceremonies*, by the Abbé J. A. Dubois, part iii. chap. iv.

of the prescient Hindu legislator, seeking to counteract the depopulating effects of that spirit of asceticism and renunciation of the world which at its height probably threatened to lead to national extinction. And so, if I am right, an ordinance aimed at asceticism has been powerfully instrumental in keeping up the population of India, probably far above the limit most advantageous to the country. During the period when the spirit of asceticism was most influential in the Christian world, laws were passed and every hindrance put to the spread of monachism, and for the avowed reason of its injurious effect upon population.[1] And so also in more modern times, and on the same grounds, Peter the Great prohibited the adoption of a monastic life by persons under fifty years of age. The Brahman legislator secures the same end by a very different process. Unable, and in all probability unwilling, to enforce repressive measures against *sadhuism*, he appeals to the *religious* feelings and the fears of the people, insists upon the *obligation* of every Hindu to have a son, and threatens punishment in a future life to such as fail in this duty. As a result, the numerical strength of the nation is maintained, and at the same time the ceremonies connected with marriages and births help the clever hereditary priesthood to keep their hands perpetually in the purses of their lay brethren.

The Future of Sadhuism.

If with an eye to the future of *sadhuism* we consider its present state, the conviction is forced upon us that it is not in as much favour as at many former periods in Indian history; or, perhaps, I should rather say that the thoughts of men in India are now being strongly attracted to more worldly ideals.

British rule, with its strong bias towards material improvements, its encouragement of trade, and the facilities it affords for cheap locomotion and for emigration, has opened up a variety of careers, official and other, to all castes alike, and also many new ways to the acquirement

[1] Bury's *Later Roman Empire*, vol. ii. pp. 466–468.

of riches, while its stability guarantees the safe possession of wealth by all races alike. However enamoured of *sadhuism* Hindu India may have been, there were, of course, at all times good Hindus who fully appreciated the advantages of worldly possessions and were assiduous worshippers of Kuvera, their god of wealth. Merchants, indeed, are prominent characters in some of the oldest tales that have come down to us from Buddhist times, but under despotic rulers the accumulation of riches was not an easy matter, and certainly their display would have been dangerous. The ever-present proportion of wealth-seekers in the population has its opportunity now, and is reinforced by crowds allured away from their old ideals by the special attractions of the new age. As in the West, so in India to-day, the possessors of the world's goods, however their treasures may have been acquired, are objects of popular respect, and receive marked consideration from the ruling powers, sharing with favoured officials to an appreciable extent the honours which the State has to bestow. Hence the desire for affluence and for the ostentatious parade of wealth has become very pronounced; and the more so since outside the "Native States" most of the old hereditary dignities have ceased to be of much account under the new régime. Hindu caste distinctions necessarily receive little, if any, recognition under British rule, and the pride of the "twice-born" classes no encouragement at all. *Sadhus* are not more fortunate; for, whatever their merits or their claims may be, they are looked down upon with contemptuous indifference by the ruling race, the new *twice-borns* of the Indian world, now in effect the *predominant caste*, exhibiting all the virtues and the vices of its peculiar position, privileges, and pretensions.

Moreover, while old social landmarks are thus disappearing, it cannot be denied that a new *national spirit*, naturally opposed to *sadhuism*, is beginning to awaken and to manifest itself sporadically in acts whose intention at least is unmistakable.

Another potent factor in determining the fate of *sadhuism* is English *education*, which, being indispensable for an official career, is eagerly sought for by all the ambitious youths of the country; and the alumni of the Indian schools and universities, inoculated with Western ideas, and anxious to do credit to their training, generally affect, though they may not always feel, a supercilious unconcern about *sadhus* and *sadhuism*. The *sadhus* themselves, though professing, as heretofore, a life of complete detachment from the world, feel in an unwonted degree the effects of the currents of modern activity which are circulating through the land, and, under this stimulus, are awakening to combined actions of a very unusual and noteworthy character. For example, we learn from the Press, with feelings of satisfaction not unmingled with grave concern, that at a great bathing fair at Allahabad the *sadhus*, "sinking their animosities, joined in prayers for the success of the British arms, while their leaders delivered speeches full of loyalty and devotion to the English Raj."[1]

Without doubt, then, existing circumstances are tending in many ways to discredit and undermine *sadhuism*, and the continuance of these conditions will inevitably affect its position in the future. Yet, to conclude that the desire for wealth and position so strongly stimulated by present circumstances, that the political awakening of these times, that the spread of education and the general feeling of unrest in India, will, all combined, prove the death-knell of *sadhuism*, would hardly be justifiable. Possibly, the very reverse might happen; for as long as the common standards of living in India are low, and the religious ideas of the people substantially unchanged, a large part

[1] *Saturday Review*, 3rd March 1900. The deep significance of this display of good feeling on the part of the religious ascetics towards their foreign rulers, few, I fancy, have realised. What a shattering of British prestige, once heaven-high, all this reveals. Think of it! The mendicant *sadhus* offering up prayers to such gods as they worship to come to the assistance of their defeated English masters. For years to come the story will be told, with many additions, by *Yogis*, *Sanyasis*, and *Bairagis* in every village south of the Himalayas, setting the minds of many millions of people a-thinking in unaccustomed ways. And the presence of a few thousand Boer prisoners in India will only serve as a testimony *to the efficacy of the intercessions of the Hindu saints.* Little do people know how much has been lost on the inglorious battlefields of South Africa.

of the wealth that under new political and economic conditions may be accumulated will assuredly be expended in charity, in accordance with the feeling and practice of the country, especially in the feeding of Brahmans and poor religious mendicants. Gifts and bequests to this end, which the stability of British rule render easy and permanent, may be looked for, and thus it may come to pass that a goodly portion of the newly acquired wealth will provide an unexpected fund for the further support of idle *sadhus*. Any way, admiration of the ascetic ideal is so deeply rooted in the nature of the Indian people, and their devotion to quietism so completely in harmony with the physical influences of their environment, that it will not be easily overcome; hence, notwithstanding the present state of things, a general revival of *sadhuism* at any favourable moment is by no means improbable. The leaven of imported European ideas now fermenting in the Indian mind is alien, unnatural, and disquieting, and though it produces some of the results which the Western world admires and labels "progress," yet there undoubtedly lurks beneath this progress a very real, if smothered, discontent.

Well has the poet expressed in the following lines the true sentiments of the Orient:—

> "The brooding mother of the unfilial world,
> Recumbent on her own antiquity,
> Aloof from our mutation and unrest,
> Alien to our achievements and desires,
> Too proud alike for protest or assent,
> When new thoughts thunder at her massy door;
> Another brain, dreaming another dream,
> Another heart, recalling other loves,
> Too grey and grave for our adventurous hopes,
> For our precipitate pleasures too august,
> And, in majestic taciturnity,
> Refraining her illimitable scorn."
>
> WILLIAM WATSON.

Thus would Hindu India willingly live a life of simple, easy, quiet, uneventful days, steeped in dreamy speculations and indulging in wild imaginings. But Fate has decreed otherwise; and this stirring, mechanical age finds the disillusioned descendants of the *rishis* roughly awakened out of their old dream-world. Bewildered, resentful, but unable to resist the new stimulation from without, they are galvanised into feverish unhealthy cravings for material things not always harmless, into new expensive modes and standards of living, which in their innermost hearts they do not appreciate, and into enterprises for which they have no real vocation. Some term this *progress*; but, even if it be so, the situation is not without a certain pathos, for, after all, man's highest destiny is hardly realised by his being perpetually engaged in *manufacturing things of various kinds*, however useful in themselves, nor even in helping to distribute such productions, often with the aid of quick-firing guns, over the face of the inhabited globe.

Holding as I do that happiness, virtue, dignity, *personal* freedom, and reasonable comfort are quite compatible with modes of life, political institutions, industrial systems, and religious creeds which are not those of England or the Western world, the present transition state of India seems to me a subject of much more than passing interest.

By no means enamoured of Indian *sadhuism*, I feel at the same time no particular admiration for the *industrialism* of Europe and America, with its vulgar aggressiveness, its eternal competition, and its sordid, unscrupulous, unremitting, and cruel struggle for wealth as the supreme object of human effort. But, whatever may be the merits or demerits of these two systems, they are essentially antagonistic, since the economic ideal of life, being frankly worldly and severely practical, excludes imagination, emotionalism, and dreamy sentimentalism, and consequently religion also, except of the philanthropical or pharisaical type. Hence a momentous, if unobtrusive, struggle in India is inevitable under new conditions between the forces which make for the *renunciation of the world* on the one hand, and for the *accumulation of wealth* on the other; and there is no doubt that, as a consequence, the immemorial civilisation of the Hindus will undergo change, both in its spirit and practice, under the stimulus of the potent foreign influences to which it is now exposed. Yet I cannot help hoping that the Indian people, physically and mentally disqualified for the *strenuous life* of the Western world, will long retain, in their nature, enough of the *spirit of sadhuism* to enable them to hold steadfastly to the simple, frugal, unconventional, leisured life of their forefathers, for which climatic conditions and their own past history have so well fitted them, always bearing in mind the lesson taught by their sages, that real wealth and true freedom depend not so much upon the possession of money, or a great store of goods, as upon the reasonable regulation and limitation of the desires.

INDEX

INDEX

INDEX

T

U

INDEX

Printed by
MORRISON & GIBB LIMITED
Edinburgh

27465061R00190

Printed in Great Britain
by Amazon